Mother, She Wrote

PETER LANG
New York • Washington, D.C./Baltimore • Bern
Frankfurt am Main • Berlin • Brussels • Vienna • Oxford

Yi-Lin Yu

Mother, She Wrote

Matrilineal Narratives in Contemporary Women's Writing

PETER LANG
New York • Washington, D.C./Baltimore • Bern
Frankfurt am Main • Berlin • Brussels • Vienna • Oxford

Library of Congress Cataloging-in-Publication Data
Yu, Yi-Lin.
Mother, she wrote: matrilineal narratives in
contemporary women's writing / Yi-Lin Yu.
p. cm.
Includes bibliographical references and index.
1. English prose literature—Women authors—History and criticism.
2. English prose literature—20th century—History and criticism.
3. Mothers and daughters in literature. 4. Drabble, Margaret, 1939– Peppered moth.
5. Forster, Margaret, 1938– Hidden lives. 6. Fredriksson, Marianne.
Anna, Hanna och Johanna. 7. Chang, Jung, 1952– Wild swans.
8. Feminism and literature. 9. Mothers and daughters.
10. Women and literature. I. Title.
PR808.W65Y8   828'.9108093520431—dc21   2003013707
ISBN 0-8204-6900-9

Bibliographic information published by **Die Deutsche Bibliothek**.
Die Deutsche Bibliothek lists this publication in the "Deutsche
Nationalbibliografie"; detailed bibliographic data is available
on the Internet at http://dnb.ddb.de/.

Cover photo by Tzu-Dien Yu
Cover design by Joni Holst

© 2005 Peter Lang Publishing, Inc., New York
275 Seventh Avenue, 28th Floor, New York, NY 10001
www.peterlangusa.com

All rights reserved.
Reprint or reproduction, even partially, in all forms such as microfilm,
xerography, microfiche, microcard, and offset strictly prohibited.

For my parents and
in memory of my late grandparents

CONTENTS

Tables ix

Acknowledgments xi

Introduction 1

Part 1: The Feminist Theoretical Context 13
   Chapter 1 Feminism and Matrilinealism 15
   Chapter 2 Feminism, Matrilinealism, and Psychoanalysis 31

**Part 2: New Feminist Family Romances in
Contemporary Matrilineal Narratives** 61
   Chapter 3 New Feminist Family Romances 63
   Chapter 4 Marianne Fredriksson's *Hanna's Daughters* 77
   Chapter 5 Jung Chang's *Wild Swans* 87
   Chapter 6 Margaret Forster's *Hidden Lives* 95
   Chapter 7 Margaret Drabble's *The Peppered Moth* 101
   Chapter 8 A Poetics of Matrilineal Narratives 111

**Part 3: Diasporic Matrilineal Narratives in
Contemporary North American Women's Fiction** 125
   Chapter 9 Diasporic Matrilineal Narraties 127
   Chapter 10 Toni Morrison's *Beloved* 135
   Chapter 11 Jamaica Kincaid's *Annie John* 151
   Chapter 12 Joy Kogawa's *Obasan* 163

Chapter 13 Amy Tan's *The Joy Luck Club* 179
Chapter 14 Judy Budnitz's *If I Told You Once* 193
Chapter 15 A Poetics of Diasporic Matrilineal Narratives 205

    Conclusion 213

    Bibliography 219

    Index 229

Tables

1 Freud's Family Romances 116

2 Hirsch's Feminist Family Romances 116

3 Lorde's Grandmother-Mother-Daughter Triad 117

4 The "Two Time-Frames" of Cosslett's
   Feminist Matrilinealism 117

5 Marianne Fredriksson's *Hanna's Daughters* 118

6 Jung Chang's *Wild Swans* 119

7 Margaret Forster's *Hidden Lives* 120

8 Margaret Drabble's *The Peppered Moth* 121

Acknowledgments

I am greatly indebted to my PhD supervisor, Dr. Tess Cosslett, for having "mothered" me and my work on which this book is based. Without her great encouragement, this book would not have been completed!

For their insightful comments and suggestions, I thank Dr. Alison Easton at English Department, Lancaster University, UK, and Professor Andrea O'Reilly, the President of Association for Research on Mothering (ARM) at York University, Canada, who have enabled me to see through some of the blind-spots in my book. Much credit goes to my great friend, Dr. Sharon A. Bong, who suggested book titles for my textual analysis and has generously shared her ideas and helped me see more clearly. I very much appreciate Dr. Xiaolan Fu and Soonho Ong for teaching me how to use computer software to draw diagrams.

I would also like to express my gratitude to the Department of Foreign Languages and Literatures, National I-Lan University, Taiwan, for providing me invaluable research support. In particular, I owe a great deal to my family, whose love and unwavering belief in me have sustained me throughout the completion of the book.

Last but not least, I am especially indebted to several copyright holders for permission to reprint the following copyrighted material:

Yi-Lin Yu, "Relocating Maternal Subjectivity: Storytelling and Mother-Daughter Voices in Amy Tan's *The Joy Luck Club*." This article previously appeared in *thirdspace* 1/2 (March 2002): 29 pars. <http://www.thirdspace.ca/articles/yu.htm>. Reprinted by permission of the publisher. All rights reserved.

Yi-Lin Yu, "The Grandmother/Mother/Daughter Triad: A Feminist Matrilineal Reading of Jung Chang's *Wild Swans*." First published in *The Journal of the Association for Research on Mothering* 4.2 (Fall/Winter 2002): 215-24. Reprinted by permission of the publisher. All rights reserved.

Yi-Lin Yu, "Motherline Violated and Restored: Othermothering in Toni Morrison's *Beloved* and *Sula*", Kaohsiung, Kaohsiung Normal University, 2003. Reprinted by permission of the publisher. All rights reserved.

Introduction

> Women who write fiction write stories about mothers and daughters. Often, a woman writer's first published story is about the relationship between a mother and a daughter. Nor do women writers abandon this subject as they grow in their craft and their lives. They return to the literary contemplation and portrayal of mothers and daughters again and again throughout their careers. Women of every race, ethnicity, religion, region, and historical period write stories about mothers and daughters, and the similarities among the stories are greater than the differences because what we share as women, at least in terms of this primary relationship, is more than whatever else divides us.[1]

Here Susan Koppelman suggests a close connection between women's personal experience and their creation of literary texts. The personal experience in question is the one almost all women share as their first, most intimate relationship: the mother-daughter relationship. The theoretical aspects of the mother-daughter relationship have received attention and respect, especially in women's studies, since the appearance of Adrienne Rich's book *Of Woman Born: Motherhood as Experience and Institution* in 1976. One of the chapters in Rich's book, "Motherhood and Daughterhood," which she calls, "the core of my book,"[2] is a blend of autobiography, myth, fiction, interviews, and anecdotes, covering a variety of disciplines: literature, psychology, sociology, psychoanalysis, and anthropology. Rich's chapter on mothers and daughters indicates the depth, the diversity, and the complexity of the subject and stimulates a new interest in it. This new interest has been particularly evident among feminist scholars, and it has manifested itself in various kinds of women's writing. In literature, for instance, women have written about mothers and daughters in poetry, plays, fiction, short stories, novels, and autobiographies. As Koppelman mentions, the mother-daughter relationship has long been an important preoccupation of women writers, and it seems to serve as an unfailing source of inspiration for them. In their use of the genres of memoir, autobiography, biography, and fiction, twentieth-century women writers such as Virginia Woolf, Colette, Simone de Beauvoir, Sylvia Plath, Adrienne Rich, Maya Angelou, Toni Morrison, and Maxine Hong Kingston have devoted themselves to writing about mothers and daughters. This similarity among women of different cultural, racial, ethnic, and religious backgrounds is what Koppelman envisions as a shared preoccupation of womanhood.

Realizing the important place of mother-daughter relationships in the works of several women writers, I have chosen this subject as the main concern of my book, but I will focus in particular on an exploration of texts by a host of women writers published predominantly from the 1970s to the present—Toni Morrison, Jamaica Kincaid, Joy Kogawa, Amy Tan, Jung Chang, Marianne Fredriksson, Margaret Forster, Margaret Drabble, and Judy Budnitz as well as many feminist maternal writers and thinkers. A majority of these women writers participate in the development outlined in the previous paragraph: the subject matter of their works circles around motherhood, mothering, and mother-daughter relationships. In their presentation of these topics, they are all involved in the textual practice of breaking genres: of interweaving autobiography, biography, fiction, memoir, and other literary genres. Furthermore, their common experience of being women in male-dominated societies creates similarities in their delineations of the mother-daughter relationship. However, at the same time, given their considerable differences of race, class, culture, and geographical and historical locations, we are able to comprehend how mother-daughter relationships might be nuanced according to these valences. Through the recognition of their differences, we can enrich our understanding of both mothers and daughters.

More significant, having this mother-daughter matrix as a frame of reference for my main investigation in the book, I will also look at a wider parameter, the grandmother-mother-daughter triad, which has formed a distinct mode of women's writing, matrilineal narratives. Tess Cosslett defines matrilineal narratives thus: "a 'matrilineal narrative' I define as one which either tells the stories of several generations of women at once, or which shows how the identity of a central character is crucially formed by her female ancestors."[3] Cosslett's definition rings true to Jo Malin's study of the embedded maternal narratives in twentieth-century women's autobiographies. Featuring the blurring of the boundary between autobiography and biography in women's writings about themselves and their mothers, Malin claims that the interweaving of two life stories with the mother as "a subject or rather an 'intersubject' in her daughter's autobiography" establishes a dialogic relationship between mothers and daughters.[4]

What I would like to add to Cosslett's definition of matrilineal narratives is a further expansion of matrilinealism, which I will develop at length in my book. As will be elaborated on in parts 2 and 3, there are certain important features concerning the representations of matrilinealism. First, there is a sense of strong identification between mothers and daughters, as highlighted in both Cosslett's and Malin's studies. Second, women writers' preoccupation with female family relations often leads to the relative obscurity of father figures in most matrilineal narratives. As will be shown later in my textual analysis, the theme of matrilinealism becomes differently inflected in the literary texts written by women who are nonwhite and nonmainstream. Even though it has been a global phenomenon that women of different classes, races, and cultures engage themselves in the writing of matrilineal narratives, matrilinealism is also significantly the lifeline and the family line that sustain and safeguard the continuation of marginalized, endangered cultures or subcultures. In addition, by delving in my books into the texts written by nonwhite women, the definition of matrilineal narratives will be expanded further to include both the biological and nonbiological aspects of motherhood and mothering. That is to say, the concept of matrilinealism goes beyond its essentialist and relational definitions.

Further, when addressing the issue of matrilineal narratives, one cannot eschew the sustained relation between feminism and matrilinealism. The questions worth pursuing are: What is exactly this relation between feminism and matrilinealism — What are their mutual influences? Would their alliance reflect, represent, and/or revise recent feminist development of maternal studies for the last three decades? And how will my research into matrilineal narratives fit into current feminist study of motherhood and mothering — While admitting women's writing of matrilineal narratives "as a part of the feminist movement's recovery of the mother/daughter bond," Cosslett also argues that the proliferation of mother-daughter texts, both "autobiographical and fictional," for example, Rich's *Of Woman Born* and Maxine Hong Kingston's *The Woman Warrior* published concurrently in the year of 1976, should not necessarily be seen as a causal relation between "the rise of second-wave feminism" and matrilinealism.[5] Moving into the 1980s further, as Andrea O'Reilly notes, feminist writers, "both lay and academic," have been united by their concerted efforts to uphold and "celebrate mother-daughter connection" exhibited distinctly through writing of "maternal narratives, the motherline, feminist socialization of daughters, and gynocentric mothering."[6] O'Reilly envisions this development of feminist writings about mother-daughter relationships since the 1980s as "an alternative mother-daughter narrative scripted for empowerment as opposed to estrangement," as prescribed in the works of certain 1970s influential Anglo-American feminist theorists.[7]

What both Cosslett and O'Reilly have marked respectively regarding these particular periods of feminist thought on motherhood and mother-daughter relationships signals significantly a historical tendency for both feminist and women's writers to consolidate the mother-daughter bond and connection in response to feminist advocacy of relationality. With the burgeoning development of feminist discourses on motherhood for the past three decades, the attempt to explicate the intricate relation between feminism and matrilinealism and to situate where one's study stands becomes daunting and elicits far more complicated issues than one would expect. In what follows, I will turn to a broader historical framework where feminist contentions of relationality and recuperative motherhood are questioned. But, in contrast, I will argue that alongside this feminist questioning of relationality, a revisiting of and an illuminating approach to thinking about motherhood and feminist relationality via feminist matrilinealism can also be developed.

Elaine Tuttle Hansen, for instance, sketches out three phases of feminist studies of motherhood for the last three decades beginning as early as the 1960s. To summarize this wide-ranging and prolific strand of feminist development, Hansen puts it succinctly and aptly thus:

> The story of feminists thinking about motherhood since the early 1960s is told as a drama in three acts: repudiation, recuperation, and, in the latest and most difficult stage to conceptualize, an emerging critique of recuperation that coexists with ongoing efforts to deploy recuperative strategies.[8]

Hansen's declaration of "the latest and most difficult stage" in feminist development on the subject of motherhood emanates from the focus of her study on "the most inadequately explored aspect of *mother* as concept and identity: its relational features." And as the title of her book *Mother without Child* attests, her main aim is to look at the nonrelational aspect of maternity with reference to those mothers who either voluntarily or involuntarily leave or live without their children.[9] Ellen Ross, another feminist maternal scholar, corroborates Hansen's view by indicating that "the celebratory mode of the 1980s" inadvertently bypasses and excludes the demoralizing or even agonizing aspects of motherhood and mothering, one of them being those of nonmothers.[10] What Hansen interrogates further in her pioneering study of "the figure of the mother without child" in a series of contemporary women's fiction is the double-sided maternity, as portrayed in the characterization of the mother without child. Contesting the social and cultural normalization of a mother as a relational entity, Hansen maintains that "the figure of the mother without child," despite the absence of her child, does not subscribe to the dichotomous "categories of criminal or victim, bad or good mother"; instead, her presence suggests a liberating proposition by playing out these two roles simultaneously.[11] The overall arguments both Hansen and Ross point to are that feminist recuperation of motherhood launched since the 1970s is not necessarily denounced at the most recent stage but subject to change in its present reformulation and transformation since the mid-1990s.

In an analogous fashion to Hansen's study, my purpose in this book is also to embark on an innovative critique of this recuperative stage in conjunction with rethinking and recreating feminist mothering in new lights. However, rather than examining this nonrelational aspect of motherhood, I seek to invoke a feminist revisiting of relational motherhood and mothering. While I am definitely reluctant to eschew current feminist maternal scholarship on nonrelational and nonbiological motherhood, what I would like to highlight here is that, apart from the emergence of mother without child, whose significance reformulates contemporary feminist discourse of motherhood, there is also the resurgence of mothers with children. By saying so, I suggest that matrilinealism, as unfolded and developed continuously and notably in the delineations of female genealogy in contemporary women's fiction, calls forth not only a reaffirmation of relationality within feminist and women's writing of motherhood and mothering but also its readjustment and transition. To clarify my argument concerning a feminist revisiting of relationality within motherhood, I will go back to the 1970s to rediscover what relationality in accordance with the recuperation of motherhood could mean through the perspectives of several feminist and women writers from the 1980s to the present. Alongside my illustration of this feminist revisiting of relationality, I find it useful to refer to some of Hansen's arguments in order to elucidate, if not argue, my stance in relation to several heated maternal debates and issues.

As I will explicate in greater detail later in my book, the mid-1970s feminist accentuation of relationality and woman-centeredness, as explored in the two landmark studies Rich's *Of Woman Born* and Nancy Chodorow's *The Reproduction of Mothering*, departed from the original radical feminist critique and introduced a new outlook favoring a distinct and separate womanculture in which women's experiences and virtues such as motherhood, mother-daughter relationships, pacifism, and nurturance are celebrated and esteemed as privileges over men. Although the second-wave feminist movement of celebrating womanhood (motherhood) was an influential and significant event in the history of the feminist movement, this feminist embrace of relationality also provoked confusion and dissension among later generations of feminists. The toughest critique leveled against second-wave feminist advocacy of relationality is its resorting to essential womanhood (motherhood) or what Hansen criticized as the taken-for-grantedness of the mother as a relational concept. In Hansen's opinion, as long as the notions of motherhood and mothering are still grounded in essentialist and "relational features," the "real and vexed" questions of whether motherhood and mothering should be seen as "biological" or "metaphorical" remain unresolved, and this politics of motherhood will continue to divide women and feminists.[12]

While Hansen's sharp observation pinpoints the blind spot of feminist allegiance to relationality and motherhood, her study, although innovative and worthwhile, reveals only certain truths about feminist development of motherhood and mothering for the past three decades. As noted by both Cosslett and O'Reilly, the proliferation of women's writing about mother-daughter relationships beginning as early as 1976, in the form of matrilineal narratives in particular, I would argue, suggests something else about the notion of relationality in connection with motherhood. The most crucial transformation of relationality, as I have mentioned earlier, is its expansion of the mother-child (daughter) relation from dyad to triad. Although the construction of matrilineal narratives still rests on mother-child relations per se, there are four significant aspects of matrilineal narratives that contribute to reconceptualizing and retheorizing feminist thinking on motherhood and mothering in "the latest and most difficult stage."[13]

First, the emergence of another maternal figure, the grandmother, manifests the representations of motherhood and mothering in its multiple dimensions. In a vein similar to the mother without child in Hansen's study, the figure of the grandmother is both a mother and a nonmother (or even better, an othermother, whose maternal practice and function are not bound in a strictly biological sense). This move beyond essential motherhood, coupled with the advent of the grandmother-mother-daughter triad, complicates the culturally perceived notions of motherhood and mothering. The triadic relation of grandmother-mother-daughter, as delineated in most matrilineal narratives, transforms the concept of the mother into fluid and flexible identities. In other words, through their mutual mothering of each other, the figure of the mother, whether being taken up by grandmother, mother, or daughter, is not fixed only by her relation to her child. More significant, as I will demonstrate at length in parts 2 and 3, the extension of the mother-child relation into a triadic one surpasses the "power-over"[14] mechanism of the mother-child dyad, as grounded in the theoretical tenets of psychoanalysis or psychoanalytic feminism.

Second, the triadic formation of matrilineal narratives suggests the relocation of maternal subjectivity. Feminist scholars such as Sara Ruddick, Marianne Hirsch, Susan Rubin Suleiman, Maureen Reddy, Jessica Benjamin, Tess Cosslett, and Jo Malin have all been concerned with maternal subjectivity—positioning the mother as a subject in her own right. What all these feminist scholars perceive concertedly is that the viewpoints of Anglo-American feminist theorists and writers especially in the 1970s are infused with "a mother-blaming" or child-centered "psychoanalytic emphasis."[15] As these feminist scholars contend, a mother's narrative should not necessarily be seen as "embedded," to use Malin's word, or subsumed into that of her child.[16] Further, Malin indicates the relative paucity of works written and narrated by women as mothers and expresses her concern with this area of heated feminist enquiry.[17] Suleiman, in particular, concentrates her study on mothers as writing subjects.[18]

Bearing this feminist preoccupation in mind, I discovered that my selection of texts strikes a balance between the mother's and the child's subjectivities. While in some of the texts covered in my study, it is the daughter who takes the initiative in writing stories about herself and her mother or her female ancestors, there is also the first-person narrative of the (grand)mother in conjunction with that of her descendant, her (grand)daughter in particular (for instance, in the works of Marianne Fredriksson, Margaret Forster, Toni Morrison, Amy Tan, and Judy Budnitz). As we saw earlier, Malin has noted with regard to the mother as "an 'intersubject' in her daughter's autobiography,"[19] what I would also like to point out in my presentation of the texts is precisely the distinct quality of what I term *intersubjective mothering* (re)enacted in the writing practice of matrilineal narratives. This intersubjective mothering, I would argue, registers the representation of maternal subjectivity as intersubjectivity. Using the relational psychoanalytic tenets of Benjamin's intersubjectivity, I seek to demonstrate how the concept of intersubjective attunement will be adopted by either the writing or speaking subjects, be they mothers or daughters, to implement their identifications, negotiations, and dialogues.

Third, the narrative development of most matrilineal narratives following the trajectory of misunderstanding, reconciliation, and final recognition between mothers and daughters[20] proposes a likely feminist resolution in "the latest and most difficult stage"[21] of settling the contentious feminist issue between repudiating and recuperating motherhood. Put more crucially, in an analogous fashion to feminist development of motherhood, most mothers and daughters, as represented in contemporary matrilineal narratives, go through a similar process of repudiation and recuperation in their interactions with their mothers. However, unlike the feminist story of motherhood, which recommends hardly any decisive conclusion for future development, the final, happy reunion between mothers and daughters in contemporary matrilineal narratives, as indicated by Cosslett, makes a further feminist step by suggesting the idea of reconnection for feminist rethinking of relationality and motherhood. In a similar vein, feminist thought on matrilineage exhibits the division between repudiation and recuperation and, as I will show in chapter 1, the construction of contemporary matrilineal narratives reconciles this feminist dilemma.

Finally, I would also like to point out that the nonbiological and the nonrelational aspects of motherhood and mothering are not necessarily thwarted or erased by the dominance of relational motherhood and mother-daughter relationships. In the first book-length study of the motherline, *Stories from the Motherline*, Naomi Ruth Lowinsky extends her motherline, whose parameter is initially predicated on the mother-daughter dyad within two or three generations or more, to include those in nonbiological and mother-son contexts.[22] In a fundamental way, Lowinsky's extended paradigm of the motherline corresponds, in part, to current feminist concern with nonbiological motherhood, and it also enlightens our further thinking on feminist matrilinealism. For instance, my matrilineal reading of selected literary texts enables me to discover the appearance and coexistence of different facets of motherhood and mothering such as biological motherhood, surrogate motherhood, mothers who leave their children, adoptive motherhood, and single motherhood presented in various cultures and subcultures, races and ethnicities. All the aforementioned preoccupations will contribute greatly to the formation of matrilineal narratives. These are what I will elaborate on in depth in parts 2 and 3 of this book.

The main body of this book is divided into three parts; part 1 consists of two chapters. Chapter 1, "Feminism and Matrilinealism," begins with an attempt to establish what factors contribute to the contemporary interest in motherhood and matrilineal narratives. Referring back to the feminist debates on motherhood and reproduction in the 1970s and moving into the mid-1990s and onwards, I will especially draw on the ideas of recent feminist theorists such as Hansen's charting of the three stages of feminist maternal studies to highlight the vexed and unresolved relation between feminism and motherhood with an aim to provide a possible solution to the question concerned. Elaborating on Rich's description of her own experience of motherhood that leads to her celebration of it, I will then move to my discussion of certain positive theorizations of maternal values, such as Sarah Ruddick's maternal thinking and the idea of matrilineage as advocated by Virginia Woolf, Alice Walker, Trinh T. Min-ha, and Nan Bauer Maglin. These feminist theorists have advocated a positive view of matrilineage as a feminist metaphor. While offering a feminist celebration of matrilineage, I will also bring up feminist debates on matrilineal differences pertaining to issues such as female rivalry, competition, and ambivalence as raised by Sandra Gilbert and Susan Gubar, Evelyn Fox Keller and Helen Moglen, Jane Gallop, and Linda Williams. These feminist views assume a negative attitude toward matrilineage. Setting against these two opposing feminist positions, I will then propose a third position, as inspired by Cosslett's study, arguing that the matrilineal narratives I am looking at aim at working through this ambivalence and tension toward a sense of connection.

In chapter 2, I will conduct a theoretical exploration of the intersection of feminism, matrilinealism, and psychoanalysis. Drawing from psychoanalytic feminists' extensive research, as developed from the studies of the pre-Oedipal mother-child relationship, I will bring in the complexities and intricacies of the psychoanalytic relational paradigm by presenting different feminists' interpretations of relationality, including the theoretical works of Nancy Chodorow, Jane Flax, Luce Irigaray, Julia Kristeva, and Jessica Benjamin. In response to my research concern with the subjects of motherhood and maternal subjectivity, I will suggest how a theoretical progression, moving from object-relations, which are orientated at the objectification of the (m)other, to subject-relations, whose view strives to maintain a balance between two subjects, the mother and her child, could serve as illuminating and interesting ways to theorize maternal subjectivity and matrilineal relation as intersubjectivity. On the one hand, I attempt to demonstrate how the psychoanalytic relational paradigm reflects and parallels the emergence of matrilineal narratives in literary texts. On the other hand, I will also argue that matrilineal narratives go beyond the relational premise to constitute a more complex and diverse narrative structure and framework.

Part 2, titled "New Feminist Family Romances in Contemporary Matrilineal Narratives," comprises four main chapters and focuses on a close and critical reading of four matrilineal narratives, Marianne Fredriksson's *Hanna's Daughters*, Jung Chang's *Wild Swans*, Margaret Forster's *Hidden Lives*, and Margaret Drabble's *The Peppered Moth*. Illuminated by Audre Lorde's groundbreaking statement in the prologue of her book *Zami*, in which she articulates the construction of a new triangular structure informed by three generations of women—grandmother, mother, and daughter—I seek to propose the advent of what I term *new feminist family romances* founded tentatively on a textual analysis of this intergenerational relationship among women in the aforementioned four matrilineal narratives. While devoting separate chapters to detailed readings of these different texts, I will also enumerate a series of common themes drawn from them. In addition, given the varied narrative constructions of these matrilineal texts, I will also draw diagrams to illustrate their different narrative shapes.

Part 3, "Diasporic Matrilineal Narratives in Contemporary North American Women's Fiction," explores another rich literary corpus of matrilineal narratives found especially in works written by five contemporary American women writers. The part is mainly divided into five chapters with each discussing one of the selected writers' works: "Toni Morrison's *Beloved*," "Jamaica Kincaid's *Annie John*," "Joy Kogawa's *Obasan*," "Amy Tan's *The Joy Luck Club*," and "Judy Budnitz's *If I Told You Once*." Based on their commonality as women of diaspora, I will investigate how themes of motherhood and the mother-daughter relationship in these five texts are compounded by issues of migration and dispersal and the politics of gender, racial, and cultural identities within their particular diasporic (con)texts. Although different thematics and narrative strategies will be interrogated in each individual text, several interlinking matrilineal themes will also be discovered in them. Finally, in the conclusion, I will evaluate the relation between feminist psychoanalytic theory and contemporary women writing of matrilineal narratives by highlighting their similarities and differences.

Notes

1. Susan Koppelman, *Between Mothers and Daughters: Stories Across a Generation* (New York: Feminist Press, 1985), 15.
2. Adrienne Rich, *Of Woman Born: Motherhood as Experience and Institution* (1976; reprint, London: Virago, 1992), 218. References are to the reprint edition.
3. Tess Cosslett, "Feminism, Matrilinealism, and the 'House of Women' in Contemporary Women's Fiction," *Journal of Gender Studies* 5, no. 1(1996): 7.
4. Jo Malin, *The Voice of the Mother: Embedded Maternal Narratives in Twentieth-Century Women's Autobiographies* (Carbondale and Edwardsville: Southern Illinois University Press, 2000), 1–2.
5. Cosslett, "Matrilineal Narratives Revisited," in *Feminism and Autobiography: Texts, Theories, Methods*, ed. Tess Cosslett, Celia Lury, and Penny Summerfield (London and New York: Routledge, 2000), 142–3.
6. Andrea O'Reilly, "In Black and White: Anglo-American and African-American Perspectives on Mothers and Sons," in *Mothers and Sons: Feminism, Masculinity, and the Struggle to Raise Our Sons*, ed. Andrea O'Reilly (New York and London: Routledge, 2000), 106. See also Andrea O'Reilly and Sharon Abbey, "Introduction," in *Mothers and Daughters: Connection, Empowerment and*

      Transformation, ed. Andrea O'Reilly and Sharon Abbey (New York and Oxford: Rowman & Littlefield, 2000), 2.
7. O'Reilly, "In Black and White," 107.
8. Elaine Tuttle Hansen, *Mother without Child: Contemporary Fiction and the Crisis of Motherhood* (London: University of California Press, 1997), 5.
9. Ibid., emphasis original.
10. Ellen Ross, "New Thoughts on 'the Oldest Vocation': Mothers and Motherhood in Recent Feminist Scholarship," *Signs: Journal of Women in Culture and Society* 20, no. 2 (Winter 1995): 398.
11. Hansen, *Mother without Child*, 27.
12. Ibid., 3–4.
13. Ibid., 5.
14. Janet L. Surrey, "Relationship and Empowerment," in *Women's Growth in Connection: Writings from the Stone Center*, ed. Judith V. Jordan et al. (New York and London: Guilford Press, 1991), 164–5.
15. Cosslett, "Feminism, Matrilinealism, and the 'House of Women' in Contemporary Women's Fiction," 7–8.
16. Malin, *The Voice of the Mother*, 89.
17. Ibid., 90–9.
18. Susan Rubin Suleiman, "Writing and Motherhood," in *The (M)other Tongue: Essays in Feminist Psychoanalytic Interpretation*, ed. Shirley Nelson Garner, Claire Kahane, and Madelon Sprengnether (Ithaca: Cornell University Press, 1985), 352–77.
19. Malin, *The Voice of the Mother*, 2.
20. Cosslett, "Feminism, Matrilinealism, and the 'House of Women' in Contemporary Women's Fiction," 8.
21. Hansen, *Mother without Child*, 5.
22. Naomi Ruth Lowinsky, *Stories from the Motherline: Reclaiming the Mother-Daughter Bond, Finding Our Female Souls* (Los Angeles: Jeremy P. Tarcher, 1992), 199–206.

Part 1
The Feminist Theoretical Context

Chapter 1

Feminism and Matrilinealism

Having broadly explicated my research in relation to feminist historical development of maternal discourse in the introduction, I find it crucial here to elaborate on the feminist matrilineal context, as developed from the second-wave feminist movement of recuperative motherhood. Elaine Tuttle Hansen's charting of the three stages of feminist study of motherhood, as outlined in the introduction, is illuminating in mapping my investigation of different feminist views on matrilineage and how my study of matrilineal narratives will reconcile the two opposing views—recuperation and repudiation—while at the same time creating new forms of expression. Although feminist thought on matrilineage does not follow exactly a progressive and developmental trajectory such as the one chronicled by Hansen, it basically adheres to a similar conceptual framework. With the emergence of woman-centered analysis in the 1970s, Western feminism has begun a reevaluation of motherhood, as is highlighted in Adrienne Rich's classic *Of Woman Born*. Where some feminists had advocated that motherhood should be eliminated because they believed that women's reproductive capacities—what Hester Eisenstein described as their "mammalian responsibility"— rendered motherhood contradictory to feminism and was a site of women's oppression,[1] others, such as Rich, argued that motherhood was not necessarily a stumbling block for feminism: the problem lay rather in the fact that motherhood had been institutionalized as a means of male control over women. Rich's distinction between motherhood as experience and institution elucidates how feminism could begin to look at motherhood differently; that is to say, motherhood might still be seen as a source of "creativity and joy" for women.[2]

Furthermore, in Rich's chapter "Motherhood and Daughterhood," she makes the striking point that every woman, as a matter of fact, participates in the experience and institution of motherhood: "We are, none of us, 'either' mothers or daughters; to our amazement, confusion, and greater complexity, we are both." Why Rich makes such a statement stems from her argument that "mothering and nonmothering have been such charged concepts for us, precisely because *whichever we did has* *been turned against us."*³ Rich's persuasive statements open up a problem for contemporary feminism: that is, whether or not we choose to be mothers, motherhood has been institutionalized to the extent that it involves and engulfs all women. The institution of motherhood has become not only a cause of women's oppression but also a problem between women. This, of course, needs to be recognized, and this recognition marks the beginning of a deep elaboration of those relationships between women within which we as daughters all have our most intimate, personal, and complex experiences with other women: our relationships with mothers.

What Rich's book has produced for feminism is not only a revision of motherhood as such but also an insurgent interest in studies of mothers and daughters. This new interest in mothers and daughters leads to new areas of philosophical and political thinking, new issues for cultural feminism, and new debates on concepts such as maternal thinking and matrilineage as historical and literary frameworks. All these developments contribute to the shape of contemporary feminism, and all, I would argue, have had more or less impact on contemporary women's writing.

Sara Ruddick's Maternal Thinking

The term "maternal thinking" is inaugurated by Sara Ruddick. "Maternal" for Ruddick is "a 'thought' arising out of maternal practices organized by the interests of preservation, growth, and acceptability." These interests are the concerns and demands of the maternal practice that children are reared in a sense of well-being; that is, they are well taken care of physically and emotionally, so that they will become agreeable and acceptable in society. Also, maternal thinking entails a "conception of achievement," which is produced by a "capacity of attention" and a "virtue of love." With reference to Simone Weil and Iris Murdoch, Ruddick explains that "attention is an *intellectual* capacity connected even by definition with love, a special 'knowledge of the individual.'"[4]

For Ruddick, to celebrate maternal thinking is to have a positive image of oneself, thus freeing women from the ideology of womanhood that has been created by men. Demystifying the cultural construction of images of good and bad mothers, Ruddick emphasizes the reality of the practical work involved in mothering, which, she argues, passes on good values to society in general. These womanly values are what Ruddick celebrates in another essay, "Preservative Love and Military Destruction: Some Reflections on Mothering and Peace." Judging from the peacemaking events women have been involved in, Ruddick is convinced that pacifism is a "*given*" maternal attribute arising from the maternal practices women have undertaken.[5] Accentuating these good aspects of the maternal, Ruddick elevates it as a highly valuable way of thinking. Nonetheless, Ruddick says that she does not intend to idealize mothers. What she envisions in maternal practices are "distinctive ways of conceptualizing, ordering, and valuing" and the fact that women "*think* differently about, what it *means* and what it takes to be 'wonderful,' to be a person, to be real."[6] This distinctive way of thinking is also manifest in "'peacefulness,'" which creates "reconciliation between opponents" and restores "connection and community." The maternal capacity for peacefulness comes from a distinctive kind of love Ruddick names "preservative love," which assimilates differences and maintains life and harmony.[7] But to preserve this maternal virtue, Ruddick demands "feminist politics" by which she means "the commitment to eliminate all restrictions of power, pleasure, and mastery arising from biological sex or social construction of gender."[8] The purpose of this is to protect maternal power from male control and to allow it to be used for the public good, employed by women themselves in the hope of terminating violence, hatred, and militarism.[9]

Using the idea of maternal thinking, it is possible to conceptualize a mother-daughter relationship that is not based exclusively on confusion of identity and ambivalence about being female under patriarchy. In the later part of her essay "Maternal Thinking," Ruddick points out:

> Maternal thought does, I believe, exist for all women in a radically different way than for men. It is because we are *daughters*, nurtured and trained by women, that we early receive maternal love with special attention to its implications for our bodies, our passions, and our ambitions. We are alert to the values and costs of maternal practices whether we are determined to engage in them or avoid them.[10]

What Ruddick assumes is that even those of us who are not mothers think maternally because we are daughters. I think what Ruddick's statements imply is related to the pre-Oedipal phase daughters have with their mothers. For now, suffice it to say that as a girl tends to have a longer pre-Oedipal phase, because of her strong identification with the mother, she is likely to be the object of more care and nurturance. Therefore, it is daughters who are most taken to be endowed with maternal thought. Ruddick's proposal of maternal thinking is a celebratory breakthrough for feminism, but her concept of the maternal is informed by "the fantasy of the perfect mother," a phrase mentioned by Nancy Chodorow and Susan Contratto[11] in a critique of the feminist revision of motherhood and mother-daughter relationships which I will explain in the second chapter.

Following this feminist critique of Ruddick's maternal thinking, Jean Grimshaw, working from a critique of the social demands of mothering, raises a number of points. First, the conception of childrearing needs to be questioned, because "most theories of how to bring up children, of what adequate mothering demanded, have been put forward by male 'experts.'" Second, mothering has been interpreted as "a response on the parts of mothers to the needs of children" mainly because of its inseparability from other social relations that have been institutionalized. Third, the descriptions of mothering that have been considered as the norm ignore the differences that might exist in a working class or black family unit.[12] Grimshaw's criticism invites us to rethink the concepts of motherhood and the mother-daughter relationship. This rethinking, in my view, can be centered on an elaboration of *"the fantasy of the perfect mother."* The phrase is crucial because it exposes the weaknesses to which most theories, feminist or nonfeminist, have been blind.

However, in her later study of maternal thinking, Ruddick answers these accusations by modifying and explicating further her configuration of mothering. Emphasizing mothering "as *work* rather than an 'identity' or fixed biological or legal relationship," Ruddick amplifies the core concepts of maternal thinking to be applicable to people of different ages, sexes, and "social circumstances," including different family structures.[13] Furthermore, mothering is viewed by Ruddick as a collective activity shared by couples and among communities. That is, mothering is no longer an isolated work done by women, but rather mothering persons could draw strength and resources from their groups and communities while implementing the work of mothering. It is apparent that Ruddick's attempt is to de-essentialize the concept of mother in a biological sense, as she also makes a discreet distinction between birth giving and mothering, that mothering is not necessarily seen as a corollary of birth giving.[14] Reverberating with her previous study of maternal thinking, Ruddick enumerates in birth-giving analogues "maternal practices and thinking for ideals of nonviolence": "active waiting, resistance to fantasies of perfect control or despairing passivity, and the capacity to wonder."[15] It is noteworthy that Ruddick's main purpose in her more recent study strives again to perceive the mother and mothering as a metaphor, or poetics, for both personal and political transformations.

Feminist Thought on Matrilineage

Akin to feminist thought on matrilineage, Ruddick's contention of maternal thinking refers to both biological and metaphorical usages. However, Ruddick envisions a conceptual framework of thinking maternally for the future, while feminist use of matrilineage is connected with the past. The feminist search for matrilineage was perhaps initiated by Virginia Woolf in her book *A Room of One's Own*. Comparing the social situations of men and women, Woolf exposes the inequity between the sexes. Giving the example of real and invented women such as Jane Austen, Charlotte Brontë, George Eliot, and "Shakespeare's sister," Woolf delineates how women were restricted materially and psychologically. In addition, Woolf believes that women are different from men: it is not clear whether she means socially or essentially. Using the idea of the sentence as an index of sexual difference, Woolf thinks that men and women do write differently:

> The sentence that was current at the beginning of the nineteenth century ran something like this perhaps: "The grandeur of their works was an argument with them, not to stop short, but to proceed. They could have no higher excitement or satisfaction than in the exercise of their art and endless generations of truth and beauty. Success prompts to exertion; and habit facilitates success." That is a man's sentence: behind it one can see Johnson, Gibbon and the rest. It was a sentence that was unsuited for a woman's use.[16]

As there was, metaphorically speaking, only one kind of sentence available in the literature of the past, women writers had to disguise their own identities if they wanted to write. So "it is," as Woolf asserts, "useless to go to the great men writers for help, however much one may go to them for pleasure." Commenting on the absence of women writers from the mainstream literary tradition, Woolf urges that "we think back through our mothers if we are women." Taking the exceptional example of Jane Austen, who "devised a perfectly natural, shapely sentence proper for her own use and never departed from it", Woolf argues that there is a woman's sentence. The fact that a woman's sentence failed to appear for so long was because "such a lack of tradition, such a scarcity and inadequacy of tools, must have told enormously upon the writing of women." So the act of "thinking back through our mothers" is to "think back through the absence of mothers" and to discover and reclaim a female literary tradition.[17]

Woolf's proposal of matrilineal thinking informs Alice Walker's approach to creating an understanding of African-American women's literary tradition. In her book *In Search of Our Mothers' Gardens*, Walker describes the effects of sexism and racism on black women's artistic creativity in the United States. With great social injustice to endure, the sufferings of black women have been far more severe than those of most white women, especially in the days of slavery. In every aspect of life, white women were typically privileged over black women. White women of the upper classes would have access to education; they would know how to read and write despite being restricted by other social boundaries. But under slavery, it was considered "a punishable crime for a black person to read or write," let alone to have freedom of artistic expression.[18]

Walker gives a matrilineal description of famous black women writers such as Phillis Wheatley, Nella Larsen, and Zora Neale Hurston, but she also includes those anonymous mothers, those black women who, Walker considers, had creative spirit. Taking the example of her mother's garden, Walker praises her mother's great skill at gardening as a form of artistic creativity. More important, Walker regards this maternal creativity as matrilineal: it is what black women have preserved and passed on to each other for generations, although it may never have been consciously seen as matrilineal before. The message that Walker attempts to convey in her essay is the importance of daughters' recognizing and reclaiming matrilineage:

> Only recently did I fully realize this: that through years of listening to my mother's stories of her life, I have absorbed not only the stories themselves, but something of the manner in which she spoke, something of the urgency that involves the knowledge that her stories—like her life—must be recorded.[19]

Walker's *In Search of Our Mothers' Gardens* provides a good starting point for thinking about mothers and daughters, for seeing the mother-daughter relationship as a source of strength.

While Woolf proposes a written matrilineage, Trinh T. Minh-ha evokes an oral one. Going further than what Walker has demonstrated, Minh-ha empowers African women as "keepers and transmitters" of an oral tradition by tracing a long history of non-Western women as storytellers.[20] Unlike Woolf whose attempt to build up a female literary tradition derives from her awareness of the relative absence of women writers in the West, Minh-ha presents a different matrilineage that has long existed and been passed down from mother to daughter for generations:

> Tell me and let me tell my hearers what I have heard from you who heard it from your mother and your grandmother, so that what is said may be guarded and unfailingly transmitted to the women of tomorrow, who will be our children and the children of our children. These are the opening lines she used to chant before embarking on a story. I owe that to you, her and her,

who owe it to her, her and her. I memorize, recognize, and name my source (s), not to validate my voice through the voice of an authority (for we, women, have little authority in the History of Literature, and wise women never draw their powers from authority), but to evoke her and sing.[21]

This opening speech before the actual storytelling embodies a narrative voice that represents separately but also synthesizes the double voice of a mother and a daughter. The words "tell me" indicate the narrator's identity as a daughter who implores her mother to tell stories whereas the succeeding phrase "let me tell" divulges a maternal identity which serves as one of the "keepers and transmitters" to both preserve and pass on stories from her (their) motherline. As this motherline is looped in a chain of generations ranging from grandmothers, mothers, and daughters, it reinforces an unfailing source of productivity, empowerment, and strength.

More significant, this inaugural address is consonant with a particular structure of matrilineal narratives. Adopting the Bakhtinian concept of the chronotope, Cosslett illuminates how a feminist matrilineal narrative is built on two frameworks of time: "There is a synchronic, horizontal plane, on which the generations of women are united by a common femaleness; and a diachronic, vertical axis of descent, leading back into the past and forward into the future."[22] For Minh-ha, African women are linked together synchronically by a close connection between femininity and creativity. Moreover, by identifying themselves as "keepers and transmitters" diachronically, they create a matrilineage which not only refers them back to the past but also passes them down into the future:

> In this chain and continuum, I am but one link. The story is me, neither me nor mine. It does not really belong to me, and while I feel greatly responsible for it, I also enjoy the irresponsibility of the pleasure obtained through the process of transferring. Pleasure in the copy, pleasure in the reproduction.[23]

As narrated in the passage, the woman's voice is invariably connected with the multiple voices in her female descent line. Be it a distinct form of communication, this matrilineal concatenation formulates and constitutes collectivity, plurality, and complexity. However, every woman in this matrilineal chain is not just a passive recipient of her maternal heritage. In the process of transmitting, she is also a creator; she repeats but re-creates the same story. In the African context, the root of this female creativity can be traced back to the great power of such mythical female figures as "Diseuse, Thought-Woman, Spider-Woman, griotte, storytalker, fortune-teller, witch."[24] The regenerative, healing, and protective power of these Great Mothers represents positive images for black women. Symbolically, they become an unfailing inspiration for black women writers in their literary representations of mothers and daughters.[25]

Feminist Debates on Matrilineal Differences

As can be discerned from the works of Woolf, Walker, and Minh-ha, matrilineage has been employed as a feminist metaphor for female bonding and solidarity irrespective of its varied forms and configurations. Nonetheless, other feminists perceive the matrilineal metaphor as problematic and even contradictory to feminist politics of sisterhood. The following excerpt from Sandra Gilbert and Susan Gubar's *No Man's Land* points to the existence of female rivalry in women writers' relationship with each other:

> In fact, we suspect that the love between women writers sent forward into the past is, in patriarchal culture, inexorably contaminated by mingled feelings of rivalry and anxiety. Though there is no mythic paradigm of Jocasta and Antigone which parallels Bloom's archetype of Laius and Oedipus, strong equals at the crossroads, most literary women do ask — as Sylvia Plath did about women poets — "who rivals?" partly because, as Margaret Atwood explains, "members of what feels like a minority" must compete for "a few coveted places" and partly because those coveted places signify, as Freud's model tells us, the approbation of the father who represents cultural authority.[26]

Given the Bloomian model of patrilineage, a literary adaptation of Freudian Oedipal conflict with a son who endeavors to overturn and supercede his father, what Gilbert and Gubar have been concerned with is that women writers have been placed in a vulnerable position, engaged in an unequal relationship with male predecessors.[27] Consequently, feminist writers and critics have commenced with their construction of matrilineage as a continuum of "nurture and empowerment" in contrast to a patrilineal parameter of struggle and resentment.[28] Yet Gilbert and Gubar have also unequivocally exposed the cause of female rivalry emanating from the limited resources available to women that dupe and ensnare them in a competitive relationship with one another. Thus, in order to gain such "a few coveted places," the daughterly women writers need to please and seek the approval of "the father who represents cultural authority."[29]

While Gilbert and Gubar address women's ambivalent relationship from the perspective of literary matrilineage, Evelyn Fox Keller and Helene Moglen note the similar occurrence of competition among academic women. Keller and Moglen summon up their courage to investigate the conflicts some feminists are prone to experience in their sisterhood despite their initial reluctance to attend to this disquieting confrontation happening between them and among their feminist friends and acquaintances. In their views, feminists' hesitation to acknowledge their ambivalence toward other women who are either older or younger than they are arises from their unquestionable political advocacy of the notion of identification predicated by psychoanalytic feminists as a nurturing mother-daughter relationship. Instead, they think that it is intense attachment and identification that cause conflicts, ambivalence, and competition between mothers and daughters or between women in general. Rendering it as a loss of feminist "innocence and purity," Keller and Moglen discover their awareness of women's competition as "different, deeper, and more painful" than that of their male counterparts.[30]

The women's stories concentrating on relationships between senior and junior women in the academy as assembled in Keller and Moglen's examples are illustrated as a mother-daughter relationship. These stories reverberate with analogous conflicts between unsympathetic, overwhelming mothers and resentful, rebellious daughters. Keller and Moglen argue for these telling evidences that feminisms simply lack "an account of the overtly and covertly aggressive components in the dynamics of the mother-daughter relationship" and that psychoanalytic feminist accentuation of identification as an important feature in mother-daughter relationships bypasses and marginalizes the hidden dark side of women's relationships. In short, Keller and Moglen remark that women's internalization of their roles in conformity with the patriarchal dualism of separation/connection, identification/differentiation, and good/bad mothers (daughters) weighed down also by "scarce material and emotional resources," as mentioned by Gilbert and Gubar, precipitate such an inevitable feeling of ambivalence for women in both intergenerational and intragenerational contexts. In a fundamentally critical way, Keller and Moglen are skeptical about the feasibility of feminists' celebration and perpetuation of "the romance of women's culture" premised upon feminist belief in cooperation over competition.[31]

Elaborating on her own experience in a similar vein, Jane Gallop considers herself as "the disregarded daughter 'watching her [the mother] look at herself in the mirror'" after Gallop was asked to contribute to a feminist issue of *Yale French Studies* but somehow did not receive any response from the Seven Dartmouth faculty women.[32] As the editors have described themselves as "a seven-headed monster from Dartmouth," Gallop deploys the notion of monstrosity to express her disquiet with women's "neither totally merged nor totally separate" identification with each other (48). This discomfort is extended to the psychoanalytic notions of "a 'double self'" and "mirroring" in the mother-daughter relationship (49). Tracing evidences of women's desperation to separate and "delineate their own boundaries" in certain psychoanalytic feminist writings, Gallop, on the one hand, voices in many aspects a daughterly resentment against a matrilineal impetus (50). But on the other hand, she also strives to "untangle" the intersecting knot of "good" and "bad" maternal mirroring as enacted by a few feminists' daughterly readings of women's texts (54).

In a more straightforward critique, Linda R. Williams in her essay "Happy Families? Feminist Reproduction and Matrilineal Thought" expresses her skepticism at the portrayal of a happy feminist family romance in both women's literary tradition and psychoanalysis. Williams argues that what seems to be ignored in a feminist family romance is "the notion of unmediated feminine communication" as idealized in a matrilineal (mother-daughter) metaphor and its reactivation of Oedipal family power dynamics:

> What is feminist transmission? Why do we so often employ familial metaphors to interpret our conceptual and scholarly relationships with each other? What are the power relations at stake in setting up feminist networks of thinking which rely on mother-daughter or sisterly ties? Why are we so reluctant to rid ourselves of the family? ... Thus it seems, ironically, that the very force which some writers have drawn upon to signal the breakdown of patriarchal family relations—a feminine communication which disrupts normal epistemologies—has been used to make coherent an alternative Great (female) Tradition.[33]

Williams advocates an "embrace of generational forgetting."[34] The problem she warns us of here is the outcome of an unequal power relation involved with the process of intergenerational transmission. Linking the idea of transmission with that of transference in a psychoanalytic context, Williams indicates that women would not be immune from the system of power imbalance founded on a mentor and disciple relationship. Thus, she writes:

> If we were to read women's communication or literary history as a process of transmission we would have to impose this master-slave relationship on to our idealized model of mothers and daughters, the mother being the "authorized source" and the daughter being the "passive recipient."[35]

Rather than viewing this feminist familial metaphor as a regenerating force, Williams contends that it is degenerating and reducing feminist thinking. What Williams has posited is not to combine "motherhood and pre-Oedipal communion," as maintained by literary and psychoanalytic feminists alike, with "systems of knowledge and mastery within the realm of the symbolic." She is also concerned with the adaptation of the matrilineal metaphor as "used in service of an alternative, stable, 'legitimized' (thus "dependent upon the law") tradition."[36]

However, in relation to Minh-ha's viewpoint as noted earlier, what Williams has argued is apparently a Western white middle-class model of thinking. For example, Minh-ha delivers a powerful statement quoted in parenthesis earlier: "for we, women, have little authority in the House of Literature, and wise women never draw their power from authority."[37] Minh-ha ironically refutes Williams' proposition from the perspective of a postcolonial feminist where women from the Third World have little access to authority. Additionally, as elucidated previously in my analysis of Minh-ha's matrilineal concept, Min-ha, observing from a daughterly standpoint, takes pleasure in being a creative transmitter of this matrilineal chain of communication. While I do not purport to overidealize this matrilineal metaphor of mother-daughter relationships, Minh-ha's aspiration to an oral tradition of matrilineage in a scenario of racial and cultural differences cannot be seen as contaminated and hampered by the hierarchal structure of power relations upheld in the disseminating process of knowledge in the circle of Western élites and intellectuals.

Feminist Matrilinealism: Another Feminist Solution

Judging from the previous two sections, we can see that conflicts and discrepancies do occur among feminists pertaining to their different views on matrilineage. While these feminists working from the two converse stances have not either completely realized or resolved this knotty problem, in certain women's creative experimentation with matrilineal narratives, there is the surprising emergence of a working out of a reconciliation of the issue concerned. Bearing in mind these two opposing positions, I want to propose a third position, derived from a recurring pattern in matrilineal narratives, as I shall demonstrate in greater detail shortly with reference to Cosslett's findings. This third position incorporates the two apparent divisions into a whole; that is, conflicts are involved with a necessary and inevitable process for matrilineal recognition. Women writers' celebration of the mother-daughter relationship in most of the matrilineal narratives does not circumvent the ambivalence and anxiety already existing between mothers and daughters. It is rather the working out of their conflict and dissension that reconnects mothers and daughters. This important feature of matrilineal literature can be encapsulated in Nan Bauer Maglin's formulation. According to Maglin, the characteristics of matrilineal literature are fivefold:

> 1. The recognition by the daughter that her voice is not entirely her own;
> 2. The importance of trying to really see one's mother in spite of or beyond the blindness and skewed vision that growing up together causes;
> 3. The amazement and humility about the strength of our mothers;
> 4. The need to recite one's matrilineage, to find a ritual to both get back there and preserve it;
> 5. And still, the anger and despair about the pain and the silence borne and handed on from mother and daughter.[38]

These five themes generate a number of concepts directly relevant to feminism. Points one and four recommend a sisterhood based on shared daughterhood, as the task of "think[ing] back through our mothers" needs the communal and collective effort of women. Matrilineal thinking provides a family line for feminism and consolidates female strength and solidarity. It is a feminist quest for recovering women's knowledge, history, and culture. Points two, three, and five point to the ambivalence between mothers and daughters. Although matrilineage denotes female bonds, this does not mean that it does not involve conflicts and tensions. Feelings of anger, pain, and despair are included in and are perhaps resolved by mutual understanding and respect which are based on a recognition of a common heritage.

More significant, to reinforce and elucidate how a matrilineal narrative works in certain women's texts, Cosslett in her earlier study of this topic raises an inspiring point based on her reading of Amy Tan's *The Joy Luck Club*:

> While I am interested in stories that present the matrilineage positively, the negative, matrophobic construction of it is often also present as a possibility. But a very common pattern in matrilineal narratives is one of initial fear, mistrust and misunderstanding between generations being overcome at some climactic moment of coming together or mutual recognition. For instance, the majority of the sixteen stories, told by mothers or daughters, in Amy Tan's *The Joy Luck Club* (1989) end like this. This transforming moment is almost as predictable as the marriage that concludes the romance plot: these stories could be seen as a new kind of matrilineal romance.[39]

What Cosslett has suggested here is not to impose homogeneity on matrilineal narratives. However, reflecting on feminists' different views on matrilineage that have been outlined in this chapter, I would argue, stemming from and in accordance with Cosslett's premise, that feelings of rivalry, competition, and ambivalence, as perceived by some feminists, are mainly caused by "initial fear, mistrust, and misunderstanding" between women of different generations. Further, Cosslett's Bakhtinian reading of the coexistence of two frameworks of time in feminist matrilineal narratives sheds new light on feminist debates on matrilineal differences by providing and advancing a constructive reading of matrilineal narratives. She maintains:

> This climactic moment often forces the women onto the synchronic plane—the position of holding hands. We could say that without this dimension, the matrilineage would just be a mirror-image of the patrilineage: a hierarchical descent line. But the diachronic dimension is not devalued: it is not just presented as a hierarchy to be broken and dispensed with. Instead, it can figure feminist progress, and/or a way back to a powerful female past.[40]

Emphasizing female development in "a diachronic, vertical axis of descent," to use Cosslett's words, the aforementioned feminist theorists who have shown their apprehension about matrilineage have perhaps forgotten about the joining of women or mothers and daughters "onto the synchronic plane." Besides, as Cosslett argues, "the diachronic dimension" could often lead to a "feminist progress." In her opinion, this regenerating progression from the past marching into future cannot work without our significant link with "a powerful female past."[41] Notably, this matrilineal relation is not a "power-over" model of a patrilineal development but a "power–*with*" and "power–*together*" dynamics[42] which can be considered as a breakthrough for rethinking feminist politics of sisterhood in connection with the matrilineal metaphor of mother-daughter relations. What a matrilineal narrative can afford is an illuminating way of thinking and theorizing a new feminist family romance. This new feminist family romance, in particular, reshapes feminist advocacy of relationality in relation to motherhood, mothering, and maternal subjectivity, which I will investigate in great detail in part 2.

Notes

1. Hester Eisenstein, *Contemporary Feminist Thought* (London: George Allen & Unwin, 1984), 69.
2. Adrienne Rich, *Of Woman Born: Motherhood as Experience and Institution* (1976; reprint, London: Virago, 1992), 71. References are to the reprint edition.
3. Ibid., 253, emphasis original.
4. Sara Ruddick, "Maternal Thinking," in *Mothering: Essays in Feminist Theory*, ed. Joyce Trebilcot (Maryland: Rowman & Littlefield, 1983), 223–4, emphasis original. See also her book, *Maternal Thinking: Toward a Politics of Peace* (Boston:

Beacon Press, 1989).
5. Ruddick, "Preservative Love and Military Destruction: Some Reflections on Mothering and Peace," in Trebilcot, *Mothering*, 233, emphasis original. See also her later article, "Making Connections between Parenting and Peace," *Journal of the Association for Research on Mothering* 3, no. 2 (Fall/Winter 2001): 7–20.
6. Ruddick, "Maternal Thinking," 224, emphasis original.
7. Ruddick, "Preservative Love and Military Destruction," 239.
8. Ibid., 240.
9. Ibid., 257.
10. Ruddick, "Maternal Thinking," 225, emphasis original.
11. Nancy Chodorow and Susan Contratto, "The Fantasy of the Perfect Mother," in *Feminism and Psychoanalytic Theory*, ed. Nancy Chodorow (Cambridge and Oxford: Polity Press, 1989), 79–96.
12. Jean Grimshaw, *Feminist Philosophers: Women's Perspectives on Philosophical Traditions* (Brighton: Wheatsheaf, 1986), 243–5.
13. Ruddick, "Thinking Mothers/Conceiving Birth," in *Representations of Motherhood*, ed. Donna Bassin, Margaret Honey, and Meryle Mahrer Kaplan (New Haven and London: Yale University Press, 1994), 35, emphasis original.
14. Ibid., 37–8.
15. Ibid., 44.
16. Virginia Woolf, quoted in Rachel Bowlby, *Virginia Woolf: Feminist Destinations* (Oxford and New York: Basil Blackwell, 1988), 28.
17. Ibid.
18. Alice Walker, *In Search of Our Mothers' Gardens* (1983; reprint, London: Women's Press, 1984), 23. References are to the reprint edition.
19. Ibid., 24.
20. Trinh T. Minh-ha, quoted in Mary Eagleton, *Working with Feminist Criticism* (Oxford: Blackwell, 1996), 38.
21. Ibid.
22. Tess Cosslett, "Feminism, Matrilinealism, and the 'House of Women' in Contemporary Women's Fiction," *Journal of Gender Studies* 5, no. 1 (1996): 7.
23. Trinh T. Minh-ha, quoted in Eagleton, *Working with Feminist Criticism*, 38.
24. Minh-ha, *Woman, Native, Other: Writing Postcoloniality and Feminism* (Bloomington and Indianapolis: Indiana University Press, 1989), 121.
25. See Susheila Nasta, ed. *Motherlands: Black Women's Writing from Africa, the Caribbean and South Asia* (New Jersey: Rutgers University Press, 1992).
26. Sandra Gilbert and Susan Gubar, quoted in Eagelton, *Working with Feminist Criticism*, 41.
27. Ibid., 37–8.
28. Ibid., 37.
29. Ibid., 41.
30. Evelyn Fox Keller and Helene Moglen, "Competition and Feminism: Conflicts for Academic Women," *Signs: Journal of Women in Culture and Society* 12, no. 3 (1987): 495.
31. Ibid., 509.
32. Jane Gallop, quoted in Eagleton, *Working with Feminist Criticism*, 46. Hereafter, page numbers to this volume are cited parenthetically.
33. Linda R. Williams, quoted in Eagleton, *Working with Feminist Criticism*, 44–5.
34. Williams, "Happy Families? Feminist Reproduction and Matrilineal Thought," in *New Feminist Discourses: Critical Essays on Theories and Texts*, ed. Isobel

Armstrong (London and New York: Routledge, 1992), 53.
35. Ibid., 56.
36. Ibid., 61, emphasis original.
37. Minh-ha, quoted in Eagleton, *Working with Feminist Criticism*, 38.
38. Nan Bauer Maglin, "Don't Never Forget the Bridge That You Crossed Over On: The Literature of Matrilineage," in *The Lost Tradition: Mothers and Daughters in Literature*, ed. Cathy N. Davidson and E. M. Broner (New York: Frederick Ungar, 1980), 258
39. Cosslett, "Feminism, Matrilinealism, and the 'House of Women' in Contemporary Women's Writing," 8.
40. Ibid.
41. Ibid.
42. Janet L. Surrey, "Relationship and Empowerment," in *Women's Growth in Connection: Writings from the Stone Center*, ed. Judith V. Jordan et al. (New York and London: Guilford Press, 1991), 164–5.

Chapter 2

Feminism, Matrilinealism, and Psychoanalysis

> The person is comprehensible only within the tapestry of relationships, past and present. . . . The figure is always *in* the tapestry, and the threads of the tapestry (via identifications and introjections) are always in the figure.[1]

This illustrative analogy of a person as the figure "within the tapestry of relationships" drawn by Stephen Mitchell subtly and aptly captures the essence of relational theory. What Mitchell demonstrates is that the self as "the figure" establishes an inseparable interconnection with external reality as "the tapestry" to the extent that one cannot work without the other in a spider's spinning web of connections and links as woven by "the threads." This intriguing relational concept links significantly with an interesting relational pattern with regard to the interrelation between a female auto/biographer or protagonist and her female ancestors, namely her mother and grandmother, in matrilineal narratives written mostly by women. To explicate such a matrilineal relation, Tess Cosslett affords a clear-cut definition of matrilineal narratives. She writes thus: "a 'matrilineal narrative' I define as one which either tells the stories of several generations of women at once, or which shows how the identity of a central character is crucially formed by her female ancestors."[2] Moreover, in her later study of matrilineal narratives, Cosslett also points out the identification existing between a female protagonist and her female ancestors: "the identity of the subject is assumed to be dependent on or in relation with the identities of her female ancestors."[3] Cosslett's exposition of this matrilineal key concept of relationality reverberates with Mitchell's analogy of the connection between a person and relationships surrounding her/him. That is to say, the person or the subject can become intelligible and meaningful within the context of relationships or in relation to others.

Nonetheless, in Mitchell's relational parameter, he only indicates a linkage between past and present whereas in Cosslett's matrilineal relation, there is a triadic connection among past, present, and future presented in a triangular relationship among grandmother, mother, and daughter. Further, Mitchell's relational theory as predicated on the notion of identification and introjection is gender neutral whereas the relationality as investigated in Cosslett's study of matrilineal narrative is premised on and evolved from the mother-daughter identification. This concept of relationality founded on mother-daughter identification is also a subject of heated feminist theoretical enquiry and debate undertaken by psychoanalytic feminist relational theorists, which I will explore in detail in this chapter.

Feminist Matrilinealism, Psychoanalytic Relationality, and the Search for Maternal Subjectivity

As developed in psychoanalysis, the relational-model theories are, in particular, drawn from certain psychoanalysts' extensive clinical researches on the pre-Oedipal mother-child relationship. My investigation of matrilineal narratives in this book as represented in contemporary women's writing is an intriguing area of study where different literary genres and cultural representations such as autobiography, biography, fiction, storytelling, myth, and folktales are mixed and woven together. Literature, as a type of reality construction where humans (re)present, negotiate, and (re)construct their relationships with the outside world (especially with other human beings), offers a site of possible connections, mutuality, and diversity that can develop further the relational concepts. Although my purpose in adopting psychoanalytic relational-model theory is not mainly aimed at applying a psychoanalytic reading to the literary texts I have selected, I do attempt to draw on the intricacies and complexities of this early human relationship as envisioned in the theory concerned in order to provide an insightful way of revisiting the feminist research into motherhood and maternal subjectivity. My approach to a feminist search for and positioning of maternal subjectivity does not reside only within a feminist liberal and individualistic notion of subjectivity—mothers as individuals and subjects of their own—but goes beyond this feminist individualist stance to a feminist intersubjective one.

Proposing a gradual progression from object-relations to subject-relations theory, I intend to envisage and relocate the figure of the mother as a subject of her own but also to reformulate maternal subjectivity as intersubjectivity. To a great extent, I do agree with certain feminists' concern with conceiving maternal identity as nonrelational, as already highlighted in my introduction with respect to Elaine Tuttle

Hansen's study, that we do need to take into consideration those women who are culturally viewed as mothers but without their children.[4] But arguably, we cannot deny this fundamental relational aspect of mothering; that is, every human being, regardless of their sex, goes through this early human relationship whether they are raised or brought up by their biological or nonbiological mothers or whether they are mothers without their children. If we rethink this relational model in psychoanalysis, intersubjective theory or subject-relations theory does espouse a theoretical premise of the coexistence of two subjects right at the beginning of the mother-infant relationship. This perception of a mother's identity as self in relation entails a recognized, separate individual self but also a self that is engaged in a constant interaction with the other. More significant, by drawing on human diversities and complexities brought out by different races, classes, cultures, and even sexual orientations as revealed also in recent feminist theories and women's writings, my main purpose in this book is to utilize and develop the notion of intersubjectivity into a subject-relations theory where different subjectivities embodied in a matrilineal relation, whether they belong to a mother or a daughter, are equally visible, balanced, and valued.

Before proceeding to a theoretical investigation of the relational paradigm, it is noteworthy that certain misunderstandings and misconceptions do arise even among feminists themselves with regard to using this relational model as a distinct form of self-development for women. Some fear that this relational proposition might reassign women to fulfilling their traditional role of serving and caring for others, thereby sacrificing their own needs and depriving them of an isolated and autonomous selfhood. Others worry that feminism will risk the dangers of idealizing or romanticizing women and relationships if such a relational development is accentuated as a privileged and harmonious female model. However, one of the Stone Center theorists,[5] Jean Baker Miller, argues that idealizing is, in fact, "a falsity" per se; it is at least a mental state that cannot possibly be achieved within a psychoanalytic milieu. According to Miller, an empathic relating to others entails being "with the truth of the other person's experience in all of its aspects," including the encounters that are "difficult, conflictual, and destructive."[6] In order to explicate this relational concept as "mutuality and movement in relationship," another Stone Center theorist, Judith V. Jordan, uses the term *"being in relation"* to denote its characteristics "as *mutually forming processes*" of "growth-fostering relationships."[7] And in order not to conflate this relational development with a pathologized female selfhood, Jordan invents the concept of "clarity in connection" to elucidate the "capacity to integrate individual and relational goals and to deal with conflict within relationship."[8]

With reference to the aforementioned feminist perception of the relational model as mutual, empowering, but also "conflictual," we do need to rethink the resourcefulness a relational development could possibly bring to illuminate matrilinealism and vice versa. This paradoxical characteristic of the relational paradigm as conceived by feminist psychoanalysts strikes a chord with feminist engagements with matrilineages or feminist matrilinealism. For instance, Nan Bauer Maglin's formulation of five defining characteristics of matrilineal literature, as mentioned in the first chapter, encompasses both the empowerment and conflict in a mother-daughter dynamic.[9] Further, Cosslett maintains that the narration "of several interconnected life-stories at once" also features the accentuation of "both the similarities and the differences, the interrelationship and the separateness, of their subjects."[10] Cosslett's matrilineal contour of the coexistence of resonance and differences also rings similar to the basic tenet of Jessica Benjamin's intersubjective theory; her theoretical contentions will be discussed at length in the latter part of this chapter. What is unique or liberating about feminist matrilinealism is Cosslett's discovery of the coexistence of two frameworks of time—"a synchronic, horizontal plane" and "a diachronic, vertical axis." Explaining her observation of "a new kind of matrilineal romance" in which generations of women are reunited out of their dissention and conflict at a climactic moment that brings them together "onto the synchronic plane," Cosslett specifically indicates that without the "synchronic" reunion of mothers and daughters, "the matrilineage would just be a mirror-image of the patrilineage." And without "the diachronic dimension," there will not be "feminist progress, and/or a way back to a powerful female past." In short, in Cosslett's view, without either of the two frameworks of time, both feminist solidarity and progress will not be possible.[11] The way in which Cosslett's relationality as illustrated in her study of feminist matrilinealism differs from that in psychoanalytic feminisms is that Cosslett imbues matrilinealism with a feminist political consciousness and agenda and adds more dimensions to the liberating and positive aspects of relationality, which have been actively explored in the textual practice of an ever-increasing number of women's writings about matrilineal narratives.

For the purpose of my theoretical investigation in this chapter, I particularly will take on the lens of psychoanalytic feminisms. Apart from looking at feminist object-relations theorists such as Nancy Chodorow and Jane Flax, I also focus on post-Lacanian feminist theorists such as Luce Irigaray and Julia Kristeva to provide a more complex and in-depth picture of pre-Oedipal mother-child relationships. Then emerging from them and making a move forward, I will suggest a more dynamic and interactive reading of the matrilineal relationship by adopting Benjamin's intersubjective concept. Finally, in my conclusion for this chapter, I hope to strike a link among a feminist psychoanalytic concept of intersubjectivity, feminist mothering, and matrilinealism.

Psychoanalytic Feminist Theories on Mothering and the Mother-Daughter Relationship

For the past two decades, psychoanalysis and feminism have cooperated and developed to the extent that their mutual influences are very evident today. Psychoanalytic feminism has focused in interesting and illuminating ways on the exploration of the mother-daughter relationship, and in particular on an evaluation of the mother-child relation in the pre-Oedipal phase. The pre-Oedipal phase is regarded as fundamental to the intricacies and complexities of the mother-daughter relationship because it is the root of the specificity of female development and of the way the construction of gender differences affects relationships among women and between women and men. Seeing the pre-Oedipal phase as the cornerstone of an understanding of the mother-daughter relationship, psychoanalytic feminisms such as Chodorow's and Flax's object-relations theory and Irigaray's and Kristeva's post-Lacanian theory peruse the problems most mothers and daughters confront and recommend certain strategies in order to mend these relationships. These theories, of course, have opened up a new area for contemporary women writers on mother-daughter relationships to explore and have also been used by feminist literary critics to elucidate our readings of the mother-daughter texts.

Feminist Object-Relations Theory

A host of Anglo-American feminist theorists such as Chodorow, Dorothy Dinnerstein, Flax, and Miller have drawn on object-relations theory to explore mother-daughter relationships. One of Chodorow's essays, "Family Structure and Feminine Personality," which she does not include in her book *The Reproduction of Mothering*,[12] provides a lucid account of feminine ego structure and the formation of the feminine personality as they emerge from the mother-daughter relationship. Chodorow bases her view of the pre-Oedipal period on an interpersonal relationship internalized by the infant. This interpersonal relationship is mainly established between mother and child due to the dominant practice of females being the primary caretakers of girls and boys and forms the basis of the differences between male and female personality.[13]

In the infant's earliest experience with the mother, s/he forms a "primary identification with" her; that is, the infant has no idea of two separate beings in her or his perception of a relation with the mother.[14] Citing from Margaret S. Mahler, Flax gives a clear account of this first period of the infant's life that lasts for six or seven months and is called "*symbiosis*": "the infant behaves and functions as though [s/]he and [her/]his mother were an omnipotent system—a dual unity within one common boundary."[15] Distinct from this primary identification is the secondary one, in which an awareness of individuation and separation begins to emerge. At this point, Chodorow indicates that boys and girls experience things differently. This is linked to the fact that mothers arguably treat children of either sex differently. A mother, Chodorow claims, tends to identify more strongly with her daughter because she will be likely to see her daughter's life as a reliving of her own. This may cause problems for the daughter, as she will find the process of separation and individuation difficult to carry out. By contrast, a mother identifies less with her son; she differentiates more strongly from him and even encourages him to take up the process of individuation and separation.[16] What is exciting and perhaps illuminating in Chodorow's object-relations theory is her analysis of the mother-daughter relationship. As long as a woman grows up without distinct ego boundaries or a sense of individuated self, mother and daughter are always vulnerable to confused feelings about self and others. So not only do daughters have difficulty separating from their mothers but mothers, too, have a similar problem.

In her essay "The Conflict between Nurturance and Autonomy in Mother-Daughter Relationships and within Feminism," Flax elucidates the cause of women's conflicts in this troublesome relationship. In reply to Sigmund Freud's question "What do women want?" Flax points out that "what women want is an experience of both nurturance and autonomy within an intimate relationship."[17] But within the current division of gender roles and identities, women find it difficult to attain these two experiences simultaneously. Like Chodorow, Flax thinks that as long as a mother is typically assigned the role of nurturer—a role that is not gender neutral—this will definitely influence her mothering and especially create conflict between nurturance and autonomy. Again, this conflict will not be experienced by the daughter only; the mother will also encounter it. The mother's conflicted feelings about being a woman and a mother will, more or less, inform her daughter's perception of herself as a female; hence, the daughter unconsciously acts out her mother's experiences. As we have seen, because of the asymmetrical nature of gender identity, a boy is forced to identify with his father, who is culturally portrayed as a more positive and desirable role model, because the recognition of masculinity is established by rejecting femininity and dependence on the mother. A girl, on the contrary, is not expected to take up a male identity, so she is asked to remain with the mother, who socializes her as a female. Furthermore, the mapping of the dichotomy between nurturance and autonomy onto female and male, with men's role more valued than women's, also leads to a woman seeing conflict between these two identities. As this kind of gender inequality persists, so the conflict and ambivalence women experience will be repeated and developed in a generational cycle.[18]

What object-relations theories have offered us is a chance to rethink two important issues. One is a new type of family organization (Chodorow); the other is a new model of mothering (Flax). First, we need to bear in mind that the mother-daughter relationship Chodorow and Flax describe is the product of a nuclear family. In her essay "Family Structure and Feminine Personality," Chodorow indicates that it is mainly Western women who experience this kind of mother-daughter relationship. In the same essay, Chodorow also includes other kinds of households, which to some extent have in common the presence of a strong mother figure. To name these households, Chodorow gives the examples of the working-class family in East London, nuclear families in Java, and the Atjehnese extended families in Indonesia. In these female-dominated households, the mother-daughter relationship is not necessarily so conflictual. On the contrary, these mothers and daughters seem to create a firmer sense of self out of their mutual support and companionship. In their daily life, the mother-daughter relationship is valued because of the strength that ties them together.[19] So within different family structures, there are different patterns of the mother-daughter relationship. Chodorow's essay "Family Structure and Feminine Personality" points to the possibility of differences, although she does not explicitly state that these other models entail class and race issues. But the examples she gives provide a useful guideline for reassessing mother-daughter relationships.

Second, referring back to the conflict between nurturance and autonomy as proposed by Flax, Chodorow suggests shared parenting, with men as nurturers as well as women. But it remains doubtful as to how effective Chodorow's recommendation would be, since the involvement of men in mothering does not necessarily guarantee that the problem will be solved. In her attempt to eliminate this conflict, Flax, speculating from her therapeutic experiments with female patients, argues that women do desire the twin experiences of nurturance and autonomy, so she recommends a strategy to draw on the strength of the mother-daughter bond. That is, women need mutual support from each other, offering each other not only nurturance but also encouragement toward autonomy. But all these steps, in Flax's view, cannot proceed without the elimination of social boundaries and restrictions such as homophobia.[20] What is illuminating in Flax's essay is that she not only envisions, like Chodorow, the mother-daughter relationship as perpetuating a system in which women are oppressed, she goes beyond Chodorow's point to see it as an issue between women and within feminism. But where Chodorow views this complexity as a problem, Flax is more in favor of seeing it as strength. Whether it is a problem or strength, however, both theorists present to us the richness and sophistication of the mother-daughter relationship as a valuable female cultural resource for feminism and as rich material for contemporary women's writing. In what follows, I will take another look at mothers and daughters from the position of French feminist psychoanalysis, mainly because their different mode of feminism provides another analytic tool and directs us toward different political and cultural strategies.

A Dialogue between a Daughter and a Mother: Irigaray's and Kristeva's Post-Lacanian Psychoanalytic Feminist Theory

Two well-known contemporary feminist theorists who talk about the mother-daughter relationship are Irigaray and Kristeva. Reading Irigaray's and Kristeva's works on mothers and daughters, Jane Gallop discovers an interesting relationship between them. That is to say, in their separate arguments, Irigaray and Kristeva effectively produce a dialogue between daughter and mother. Gallop argues that Irigaray speaks from a daughter's position whereas Kristeva adopts a mother's point of view.[21] Gallop's idea offers a fascinating way to approach these two theorists and coincidentally corresponds to my preoccupation in this book. My main purpose in employing Gallop's view is to attempt to present the two voices of mothers and daughters. The attempt is significant because most psychoanalytic feminist theories developed so far, such as Chodorow's, have been child centered. For instance, as the name *object relations* suggests, the (m)other is generally positioned as an "object" that is perceived in a child's eyes.[22] So what I hope to do is to strike a balance in this mother-child dyad.

In Irigaray's essay "And the One Doesn't Stir without the Other,"[23] we have, Gallop posits, a daughter's plea to her mother. Irigaray, speaking as an infant daughter, reexperiences a pre-Oedipal relation with the mother. From the title, we can infer a paradoxical aspect of the mother-daughter relationship. The title tells us that there are two separate beings, "the one" and "the other," but that their relationship implies an impossibility of separation as "the one doesn't stir without the other."[24] Being satiated with the mother's nurturing, the daughter resents the paralysis her mother has caused for her. The daughter's anxiety about her inability to separate from the mother is exemplified in a paragraph about being fed by the mother:

> You've prepared something to eat. You bring it to me. You feed me/yourself. But you feed me/yourself too much, as if you wanted to fill me up completely with your offering. You put yourself in my mouth, and I suffocate. Put yourself less in me, and let me look at you. . . . Keep yourself/me outside, too. Don't engulf yourself or me in what flows from you into me. I would like both of us to be present. So that one does not disappear in the other, or the other in the one. (61)

In this process of feeding, a sense of consuming and being absorbed prevails in the text. The self and the (m)other seem to be enmeshed, combined, and integrated into each other. Seeing through the daughter's eyes, we can sense her fear and worry at being deluged by the mother, thus losing or failing to achieve her own identity. But what the daughter wants is not only her own subjectivity but also her mother's autonomy. She is desperate for a separate existence for both of them. However, this does not seem an easy task to accomplish. The daughter feels that she is still connected with her mother as she says, "I look like you, you look like me. I look at myself in you, you look at yourself in me" (61). Being two biologically alike bodies, there is hardly any distinction between the mother and the daughter. As a consequence, ambivalence exists between mothers and daughters, as is revealed in another of Irigaray's sentences: "I would like us to play together at being the same and different" (61).

As the daughter finally cannot endure the paralysis the mother inflicts on her, she leaves the mother and turns to the father, who represents the symbolic order. The daughter's embrace of the father enables her to be freed from this state of immobility, as she will have access to autonomy and independence. But what becomes of the mother? The daughter's rejection of the mother leaves her only emptiness and stillness. As the mother is suddenly devoid of any function and meaning, she becomes "faceless" and "nameless" (63). Then, the daughter starts to reason the mother out of her circumstances, but she speaks in a reproachful tone as if the mother is to be blamed. At this moment, the loss of a daughter to a mother means for the mother a sense of self-loss:

> You move toward a future that is lacking. There is no one in whom to remember the dream of yourself. The house, the garden, everywhere is empty of you. You search for yourself everywhere in vain. Nothing before your eyes, in your hands, against your skin to remind you of yourself. To allow you to see yourself in another self. And this makes you empty yourself even more into my body—to maintain the memory of yourself, to nourish the appearance of yourself. No, Mother, I've gone away. (65)

The passage reminds us of the loss of Persephone to Demeter. After knowing that her daughter has disappeared, the mother searches everywhere for her. Realizing eventually that she can no longer keep her daughter at her side all the time, Demeter mourns Persephone's absence during the period she is not with her. Typically, the story of Demeter and Persephone is told from a mother's point of view. The daughter's is therefore silenced. But in this passage from Irigaray, she reverses it by taking the daughter's angle. With the daughter's assertive, "No, Mother, I've gone away," the mother is recalled again to accept her loss (65). For Irigaray, this void between mother and daughter is unlikely to be refilled; it only ends up with two of them wondering, "Where are you? Where am I? Where to find the traces of our passage? From the one to the other? From the one into the other?" (65).

What comes to an end is the daughter's grief over the impossibility of an authentic relationship between mother and daughter. What the daughter is afraid of is the imposition of the role of mothering on her even after she has rejected her mother. The daughter will remain a captive and is symbolically trapped in the mirage that she is eager to escape. The inability of the daughter or the mother to control their situation lies in the fact that they have "never, never spoken to each other" (67). This is mainly because women do not have their own language to speak, that they only speak for others. Thus, Irigaray claims finally, "And what I wanted from you, Mother, was this: that in giving me life, you still remain alive" (67).

What Irigaray has written in "And the One Doesn't Stir without the Other" has some similarities to Chodorow's object-relations theory. But unlike Chodorow, Irigaray regards the mother-daughter relationship as a result of women's position in the symbolic order; that is, women are perceived as the lack in the family drama of psychoanalysis. So, according to Margaret Whitford, Irigaray's main aim in describing the mother-daughter relationship is to unravel the inadequacy of the symbolic order. Whitford points out that Irigaray uses the word "*dereliction*" to depict women's relationship to patriarchy, which refers to "women's failure to individuate and differentiate themselves from their mothers."[25] Irigaray believes that as long as women are situated in this state of "dereliction," they will not be able to "recognize" each other, and there will not be any love between them. So Irigaray argues that this should be dealt with between or among women. In other words, women need to learn how to love each other in order to speak to each other as two subjects. As women's undifferentiated relationship with each other keeps them in conflict, they are in need of a female language:[26]

> But there is no possibility whatsoever, within the current logic of sociocultural operations, for a daughter to situate herself with respect to her mother: because, strictly speaking, they make neither one nor two, neither has a name, meaning, sex of her own, neither can be "identified" with respect to the other. ... How can the relationship between these two women be articulated? Here "for example" is one place where the need for another "syntax," another "grammar" of culture is crucial.[27]

This need for "another 'syntax', another 'grammar' of culture" is essentially the need for a new language for women to speak. This kind of female language is created and spoken in another of Irigaray's essays, "When Our Lips Speak Together."

In "When Our Lips Speak Together," Irigaray addresses the "You" about the love between them. Although Irigaray emphasizes that she is imagining a woman rather than a mother saying, "I love you who are neither mother (forgive me, mother, I prefer a woman) nor sister," the messages that underlie her statement echo with the love for one's mother:

> One is never separable from the other. You/I: we are always several at once. And how could one dominate the other? impose her voice, her tone, her meaning? One cannot be distinguished from the other; which does not mean that they are indistinct.[28]

With reference to the mother-daughter relationship, Irigaray thinks that it "makes neither one nor two," which means mother and daughter are neither the same nor different; they are the same and different.[29] This concept, as suggested by Whitford, relates to the term "multiplicity," which is celebrated by Irigaray as a kind of body language emerging from an autonomous feminine sexuality based on the pleasure women can have by touching rather than seeing.[30] More important, this multiplicity, as explained by Domna C. Stanton, represents "women's capacity for an (over)flowing diffusiveness that is 'alien to unity'" and challenges the metaphysics of sameness of phallocentrism.[31] Irigaray believes that this new language of love will create a new relation to the other, by which the relationship between subject and object, man and woman, and mother and daughter might be refigured. So only through this new free love between women, embodied in a language with which women can challenge the law of the father and establish new forms, can change take place.

In "And the One Doesn't Stir without the Other," it is evident that Irigaray is using a daughter's voice to persuade her mother to change things. But the fact that she is spoken from a daughter's point of view still imprisons the mother in the position of the other. As Gallop hints, what Irigaray presents is only a monologue, a plea to the mother whose subjectivity is subsumed in the daughter's narrative.[32] Thus, it is necessary to create a dialogue between mother and daughter, which enables the two women as two individuated and yet mergent selves to speak to each other. Now I will add Kristeva's theory to the conversation to hear what the mother might want to say and how she responds to and interacts with the daughter.

The clearest example of Kristeva's position as a mother is her famous essay on motherhood called "Stabat Mater." In "Stabat Mater," Kristeva speaks with two voices: one is theoretical and intellectual whereas the other is personal and subversive. The one with a personal tone is Kristeva's writing of the maternal. Modeling her discourse on the cult of the Virgin Mary, Kristeva speaks as a mother her bodily pre-Oedipal connection with the child. In this piece of writing, the mother conjures up various kinds of feelings such as pain, pleasure, guilt, blame, and fear through the sensuality of her body. The writing is interpreted by Kristeva as a representative of "'a return of the repressed.'"[33]

This "return of the repressed" is referred to one crucial point, the semiotic, which Kristeva links with the maternal. In Kristeva's view, the semiotic represents the pre-Oedipal period characterized by drive energies, which are manifested in the child's babblings, gestures, tones, and body movement. The state of the semiotic is a necessary phase the child must go through before s/he can acquire an independent selfhood and language. However, once the child steps into the symbolic, all the elements that go with the semiotic have to be repressed. Although Kristeva's semiotic is developed from Freud's and Jacques Lacan's models, she employs it against patriarchal law. She advocates that the repression of the semiotic does not mean that the semiotic will thus be minimized, silenced, and excluded. On the contrary, the semiotic has, in fact, the potential to disrupt the symbolic.[34]

As the semiotic is linked to the pre-Oedipal relation with the mother or, to be more precise, the maternal body, Kristeva sees it as a site of disruption. That is, women need not separate themselves from others; they as mothers have already integrated self and other into one body. Based on this notion of the maternal, Kristeva describes in her essay "Motherhood According to Giovanni Bellini" how "Cells fuse, split and proliferate; volumes grow, tissues stretch, and body fluids change rhythms, speeding up or slowing down. Within the body, growing as a graft, indomitable, there is an other."[35] For Kristeva, the mother is no longer regarded as the other. Inside the maternal body, which embodies the self and the other, the mother becomes her own subject while the child is seen as the other. Kristeva's celebration of women's bodily experience of motherhood offers a different relation to the other, not the one prescribed by patriarchal law. Therefore, although the mother forms a distinct connection with others, she also signifies "a continuous separation, a division of the very flesh" and "a division of language." In Kristeva's opinion, the mother is situated on the threshold of separation/connection, preverbal/language, and the semiotic/the symbolic. Aware of the unsettled position of the mother, Kristeva asks: "What connection is there between myself, or even more unassumingly between my body and this internal graft and fold, which, once the umbilical cord has been severed, is an inaccessible other?"[36] Explicitly or implicitly, the mother resents the possibility of a connection with her child as this relation is established at the expense of silencing the maternal voice and of a love that is built on her ability to nurture the other.

Apart from Kristeva's exploration of the mother's relation with the child, who is male in this context, she also comments on the mother-daughter relationship. What Kristeva points out here is an unsymbolized mother-daughter relationship similar to that highlighted by Irigaray. The mother-daughter relationship is unsymbolized because women have always been outside the symbolic:[37]

> Women doubtless reproduce among themselves the strange gamut of forgotten body relationships with their mothers. . . . We are in it, set free of our identification papers and names, on an ocean of preciseness, a computerization of the unnamable. No communication between individuals but connections between atoms, molecules, wisps of words, droplets of sentences.[38]

In an attempt to restore an identity for women, Kristeva, like Irigaray, is concerned with creating a new language. Kristeva thinks women need the language of the symbolic order in order to let the repressed, the maternal, burst out. In "About Chinese Women," she says:

> A woman has nothing to laugh about when the symbolic order collapses. She can take pleasure in it if, by identifying with the mother, the vaginal body, she imagines she is the sublime, repressed forces which return through the fissures of that order.[39]

The language Kristeva refers to is the language of motherhood. It is, as she argues, "the ultimate language of a jouissance at the far limits of repression, whence bodies, identities, and signs are begotten."[40] But in Kristeva's view, women should neither reject the symbolic order nor accept the roles imposed by patriarchy. She assures us that by deploying the symbolic order, women will be capable of claiming their own truth: "*Jouissance*, pregnancy, marginal discourse: this is the way in which this 'truth,' hidden and cloaked [*dérobent et enrobent*] by the truth of the symbolic order and its time, functions through women."[41] So in order to let this truth come out, women need to identify with the mother in order to create a maternal discourse.

Moreover, this language of motherhood is viewed by Kristeva as a common language for women. She applies it to the relationship between women, celebrating maternity as a privileged aspect of femininity. Stemming from her belief that, as mother and daughter are both women, it is difficult for them to have separate identities. This is bound up with their ability to "reproduce among themselves the strange gamut of forgotten body relationships with their mothers." This common experience of women, Kristeva believes, will link women together and help them rediscover their own subjectivity.[42]

Drawing from these discussions of the works of Irigaray and Kristeva, I would like to highlight two crucial points. First, what Irigaray and Kristeva have in common is their preoccupation with a new mode of language. Elaborating on Kristeva's idea, Susan Rubin Suleiman confirms that motherhood or the maternal actually offers an alternative, new kind of language. Yet, diverging from Kristeva's concept, Suleiman also says that the language of the symbolic "is especially difficult for women to accede to, whether for historical or other reasons." Taking into consideration the reality of motherhood, which connects women with the social world, Suleiman believes then that motherhood "provides a privileged means of entry into the order of culture and language."[43] What Suleiman aims at is woman centeredness. She centers on the mother not to imprison the mother as signifier of the other but to relate her to feminine creation as presented in women's writings. As soon as the maternal voice is found and heard, there will be the possibility of a female language.

Second, French feminism's concern with a new language is bound up with "an Ethic of Nurturance," especially mentioned in Irigaray's estimation of the mother-daughter relationship. Eleanor H. Kuykendall sees the nurturance manifest in Irigaray's story of the mother and daughter as a power because it is "healing, creative, and transformative."[44] Besides, nurturance has mutuality and reciprocity as its characteristics, which are understood by Kuykendall in terms of the mother-daughter bond.

Emphasizing these two concepts as strength serves to disprove the rule that the mother-infant relationship is necessarily a process of separation. So, as Kuykendall states, the mother's and daughter's need to identify with each other is actually the bottom line of the relationship. Quoting from Irigaray, Kuykendall claims that "our irreparable wound is the cutting of the umbilical cord, and not, as Freud had fantasized, castration."[45] In other words, nurturance, in fact, is a heritage, which is passed on from mother to daughter. It is a "matriarchal ethic" that assures identification, mutuality, and reciprocity.[46]

Working Toward Connection: Representation and the Mother-Daughter Relationship

Looking back over this account of psychoanalytic feminisms, I would like to conclude for the time being in this part of the chapter by raising a number of points. First, in their concentration on the pre-Oedipal phase, which has the mother-child relation as its center, psychoanalytic feminisms have participated in minimizing the dominance of the father. For Chodorow, Flax, and Irigaray, although the father is the one who can save the daughter from being locked in a symbiotic paralysis with the mother, he can also serve as the enforcer of the mother-daughter separation. For Kristeva, the father is scarcely visible in her writing of the semiotic/the maternal. The only function the father has is that he who possesses the language within the symbolic order can bring the unsymbolized mother-daughter relationship onto the surface. As we shall see, this diminution of the father also occurs in the texts I will discuss in detail in parts 2 and 3. Suffice it to say for the moment, when the mother-daughter relationship is prioritized, the role of the father seems to be automatically attenuated.

Second, although feminists' revisions of psychoanalysis add the female elements to the male paradigm in explicating difference in the construction of gender identity, their approaches and perspectives, except Kristeva's employment of a maternal voice, are still based on those of psychoanalysis. The feminist theorist Marianne Hirsch points out that as long as psychoanalysis is written from a child's point of view, the mother can only be seen as "object of desire and fantasy" by which "she may be idealized or disparaged."[47] Similarly, Chodorow and Susan Contratto also criticize the predominance of "the fantasy of the perfect mother" in feminists' and nonfeminists' writings. In their opinion, the "belief in the all-powerful mother" directs our attitude toward mother blaming on the one hand and "a fantasy of maternal perfectibility on the other."[48] Taking Flax as one of their examples, Chodorow and Contratto argue that Flax's explanation of women's unmeetable need for nurturance and autonomy is built on this fantasy of the perfect mother.[49] As with Hirsch, this split in two different directions shapes our perceptions of the mother as both powerful and powerless. Nonetheless, what Chodorow has accused Flax of is also what she and Irigaray are both engaged in, because the conflict and the ambivalence mothers and daughters experience about separation are created by this fantasy. In Kristeva's writing of the semiotic, however, she is able to adopt a mother's voice. This articulation of the maternal voice is also adumbrated in the mother-daughter texts I will look at in parts 2 and 3. Rather than speaking with a single voice, that of the mother or the daughter, the maternal voice in these literary texts embodies the mother-daughter voices. As a new mode of expression, these mother-daughter voices become a unique source of feminine literary creativity.

Finally, one of the points that Chodorow's object-relations theory may illuminate our thinking about the mother-daughter relationship is her discovery of the prolongation of the pre-Oedipal identification with the mother. Chodorow thinks that the daughter does not actually abandon the mother when she enters into the Oedipal period but that she only adds her love for the father to that for the mother. And at an unconscious level, this kind of strong identification with the mother still persists in her adult life.[50] Chodorow's new insight into the mother-daughter relationship matches the strategies Flax and Irigaray propose to mend and rescue the bond between women. What they all advocate is the need to establish the connection and the recognition of mutual understanding through women's identification with each other.

Although connection and separation, as two contrasting motions, trouble and even damage the mother-daughter relationship, it is precisely the relatedness between mothers and daughters that connects them together and causes separation to be a problem for them. As a result, psychoanalytic feminisms' revision of this relationship calls forth a rethinking of opposing concepts such as identification/differentiation, nurturance/autonomy, connection/separation, and male/female. What psychoanalytic feminisms have retrieved for us is the plenitude and richness of female cultural virtues rather than the lack and emptiness as prescribed by Freudian and Lacanian psychoanalysis. As we shall see, this complex identification between mothers and daughters will emerge in the literary texts I have chosen.

Feminist Psychoanalysis (Subject-Relations Theory)

As noted in the previous sections, what Chodorow, Flax, and Irigaray have all arrived at is a strong identification with the mother or the mother-daughter bond even though their theoretical propositions are developed from the Freudian and Lacanian psychoanalytic models, which are mainly masculine oriented. The theoretical stance of Chodorow, Flax, and Irigaray, no matter it is presented in the form of either object-relations or post-Lacanian analysis, is rather one-dimensional, catering only to that of a child's (in this case, a daughterly) subjectivity. It is this weakness for which the object-relations theory has been strongly criticized. Nonetheless, with an aim to fill this gap as already existing between motherly and daughterly subjectivities, an attempt has been made in this chapter to strike a balance between the two by bringing in Kristeva's maternal voice to establish a dialogue between mother and daughter. This dialogue between mother and daughter, although it is crucial, is not yet sufficient to accommodate both or more subjectivities. The result is such because a subject-object divide or formula still operates within this mother-daughter scheme. Therefore, it would have been more a breakthrough if a subject-subject position had been postulated right at the beginning of this dialogue.

Developing from this stream of thinking, I now attempt to embark on *subject-relations theory*, a term that Barbara Ann Schapiro has used in her discussion of the work of the Stone Center theorists:

> Stone Center theorists also prefer Stern's notion of intersubjectivity, or what they term "subject relations theory," as opposed to an "object relations theory" where the object "may not be experienced fully as a subject with his or her own comprehensive personal construction of continuous reality."[51]

What I want to pursue further is an intersubjectivity from which human diversities and complexities, deepened by the versatility of different races, cultures, classes, and even sexual preferences, are evolved and developed. In relation to matrilineal narratives where a wide spectrum of maternal practices or mothering and matrilineal relations are included and explored, I seek to present this subject in a more dynamic and interactive way, encompassing mothering in a variety of contexts in which the power of mothering lies in its capacity to nurture and preserve another subject(s) like or unlike her own. This intersubjective stance that subject-relations theory has taken up can also be accredited and named as feminist psychoanalysis because it considers women or humans in general as their own subjects. In what follows, I will go into detail with regard to this subject-relations theory.

Jessica Benjamin's Intersubjective Theory and the Mother-Child Relationship

Benjamin's perception of intersubjective theory is a breakthrough in psychoanalytic research into the pre-Oedipal mother-child relationship. Working from the theoretical paradigms of well-known psychoanalytic theorists, Benjamin adds social interactions and interpersonal dimensions to the existing classical psychoanalytic model of intrapsychic theory, in which each individual person is considered as "a discrete unit with a complex internal structure."[52] One of the basic assumptions of intersubjective theory, according to Benjamin, is that an infant has the ability and the intention to differentiate from and relate to the outside world from birth, and there is always an active, responsive interaction going on between the infant and her/his parents or other adults. Unlike Freud's "oral drives," where the relationship between a baby and a caregiver is only founded on the satisfaction of basic needs such as food and comfort and the caregiver is usually objectified as the breast to cater to the baby's desires, the intersubjective theory focuses more on the social element of this early human relationship, such as "the curiosity and responsiveness to sight and sound, face and voice" between the two parties (16). Moreover, diverging from Margaret Mahler's separation-individuation theory, where an individual self's development into an autonomous and independent being relies on a separation from a symbiotic relation with the (m)other, the intersubjective theory reinforces the growth of the self in relation with the (m)other (18).

Based on extensive research into this earliest development of human relationship where "infants do not begin life as part of an undifferentiated unity," Benjamin emphasizes that the critical issues involved are "not only how we separate from oneness, but also how we connect to and recognize others; the issue is not how we become free of the other, but how we actively engage and make ourselves known in relationship to the other" (18). Benjamin does not attempt to negate and undermine this classical psychological model of separation and individuation but instead proposes and advocates the existence of other processes of human relationship. To elucidate this relational paradigm further, Benjamin summarizes the intersubjective theory in the following passage:

> The intersubjective view maintains that the individual grows in and through the relationship to other subjects. Most important, this perspective observes that the other whom the self meets is also a self, a subject in his or her own right. It assumes that we are able and need to recognize that other subject as

different and yet alike, as an other who is capable of sharing similar mental experience. Thus the idea of intersubjectivity reorients the conception of the psychic world from a subject's relations to its object toward a subject meeting another subject. (19–20)

What Benjamin has illuminated from this intersubjective view is the recognition of the other as being "also a self, a subject in his or her own right" that counteracts and even balances the objectification of the (m)other in the object-relations theory (19). One key concept, which activates this operation of self in relation, is what Benjamin has named "*mutual* recognition, the necessity of recognizing as well as being recognized by the other" (23, emphasis original). In Benjamin's opinion, this has been largely unexplored in major psychological theories. In contrast to the notion of self-development as defined by a linear and gradual progression from one phase to another, recognition is required throughout all stages and events. More significant, this concept of mutual recognition entails the recognition of resonance and difference between self and the other (21–3).

With further engagements and interactions with recent feminist critical and literary theories over the years, Benjamin began to modify, reformulate, and develop further her concept of intersubjective theory. In her subsequent book on intersubjectivity, *Like Subjects, Love Objects*, Benjamin proposes "the nonexclusivity of the intrapsychic and intersubjective psychoanalytic models of the mind" and also reinforces "the necessity of sustaining a kind of paradoxical tension in theory."[53] What Benjamin has envisioned is "the double-sidedness of intersubjectivity and the intrapsychic, as well as the tension between sameness and difference in gender relations" (7). Acknowledging, on the one hand, the importance of a self's internal identification with and projection onto the other in fantasy as perceived in intrapsychic theory, Benjamin, on the other hand, introduces and adds this intersubjectivity to the psychoanalytic scheme by stressing the self's recognition of the outside other in reality. In Benjamin's opinion, the other is not only "the object of the ego's need/drive or cognition/perception but has a separate and equivalent center of self" (30). By pinpointing the child-centered premise of the intrapsychic, Benjamin argues that the failure to recognize the mother's subjectivity in an early mother-child relationship can result in our inability "to see the world as inhabited by equal subjects" (31).

Certain key notions, which interlink Benjamin's overall argument in *Like Subjects, Love Objects*, include her conception of tension, conflict, and paradox in relation to this intersubjective drama. Benjamin asserts that the state of mutual recognition should not be seen as "a normative ideal" (20) or be idealized as a "should-be harmony" to which one should return (23). As has been pointed out in Benjamin's *The Bonds of Love*, the achievement of such an intersubjective state that she terms *"mutuality"* is full of tension in a culture that values individualism, as manifested in G. W. F. Hegel's master-slave dialectic and classical psychological premises such as Freud's theory of narcissism. This cultural praise for "our subjective feeling of being 'the center of our own universe'" naturally leads to a social system of domination and submission on which a master-slave relationship is based (25). Instead, Benjamin accentuates the unavoidable and undeniable existence of tension and conflict in a relationship built on intersubjectivity. Her idea of tension is evolved first from her interpretations of Hegel's perception of the problem involved with a self's need for recognition. For Hegel, a self encounters a problem or a conflict because in seeking her/his absolute independence, s/he also relies on a need to be recognized by the other. In accordance with Hegel's view, Benjamin elucidates further this problem of recognition as a "fundamental paradox" where human beings all need to recognize our own constraints and limitations (36–7). In order to resolve "the paradox of recognition," Benjamin suggests a continuum of "a *constant tension* between recognizing the other and asserting the self" (38, emphasis original).

In *The Bonds of Love*, Benjamin introduces attunement, the "pleasure in being with the other" in order to maintain an equal, dynamic, and interactive balance of two oppositions such as omnipotence/recognition or recognition/assertion (31). This feeling of being affected is not associated with the process of destroying the other in fantasy, as perceived in D. W. Winnicott's concept of "transitional objects" (36–42). Neither is it analogous to the state of "one subject regulating another" and its subsequent internalization as indicated in internalization theory (45). As Benjamin asserts, this key insight of combining resonance and difference culminating in "being with" one another "breaks down the oppositions between powerful and helpless, active and passive; it counteracts the tendency to objectify and deny recognition to those weaker or different—to the other" (48). By linking the idea of attunement with the subversion of a binary schemata— master/slave, subject/object, and man/woman—Benjamin goes on to explain, using Milan Kundera's term *"co-feeling,"* that it is "the ability to share feelings and intentions without demanding control, to experience sameness without obliterating difference" (48, emphasis added).

Adhering to her observation of the tension in *Like Subjects, Love Objects*, Benjamin takes on Mahler's notion of rapprochement to demonstrate a crisis in recognizing the (m)other where an infant develops her/his capacity to realize the simultaneity of independence/ dependence and separation/connection. Referring again to Winnicott's notion of destroying the object, Benjamin claims that destruction establishes a contact and a connection with the objectively perceived other; that is, in destroying the other in fantasy, we also discover "whether the real other survives" (39). If the other does survive "without retaliating or withdrawing under the attack, then we know her to exist outside ourselves, not just as our mental product" (39). Therefore, Benjamin emphasizes that the process of mutual recognition entails a disruption and its subsequent restoration of the tension. According to Benjamin, the ideal state of mutual recognition can only be achieved when it is also a site of "struggle and negotiation of conflict" and where different conditions with regard to "its impossibility and the striving to attain it" are equally contained (23). The intersubjective theory constitutes tension not contradiction.

When applying this notion of mutual recognition to the context of a pre-Oedipal mother-child relationship, Benjamin asserts, "the child has a need to see the mother, too, as an independent subject, not simply as the 'external world' or an adjunct of his[/her] ego" (*The Bonds of Love* 23). This concept of the mother as a person in her own right corresponds to the feminist quest for maternal subjectivity, a recovery of the maternal voice that allows mothers to speak as persons with their own needs and rights. To make explicit her statement about maternal subjectivity, Benjamin continues to argue that the mother not only functions as "a mirror" that "reflect[s] back what the child" sees in himself or herself but also as "something of the not-me" (24). Indeed, Benjamin's concept of "maternal mirroring" is linked to the aforementioned idea of the coexistence of likeness and difference in this earliest human relationship. There is, as Benjamin contends, "the need for a theory that understands how the capacity for mutuality evolves, a theory based on the premise that from the beginning there are always (at least) two subjects" (24).

In addition, the "double-sided" view of intersubjectivity is incorporated into the pre-Oedipal mother-child relationship: "the fantasy of maternal omnipotence and the capacity to recognize the mother as another subject" coexist to form a "duality of psychic life" (*Like Subjects, Love Objects* 85). Using Elsa First's interpretation of play as a child's identification with the leaving mother and Winnicott's concept of the "transitional space," Benjamin regards this "symbolic play" as facilitating the development of intersubjectivity (44). In Benjamin's view, First's discovery of the child's game with the leaving mother articulates an interaction, which is involved with mutual recognition between the mother and the child. On realizing that the mother is leaving, the child retaliates by viewing the mother as a fantasy object. Then, by taking up the leaving mother's role in reversing a relationship between mother and child, the child also comes to understand finally that her/his mother is a subject outside her/his own control (92–5). As for Winnicott's "transitional space," it also refers to a game between mother and child developing from "the earliest play of mutual gaze" (44).

In this type of "symbolic play" as envisioned by both First and Winnicott, an interplay of destruction and recognition constitutes an ongoing tension and negotiation between internalized fantasy and external reality. "This intersubjective space," as Benjamin renames it, enables the child to distinguish "between the real mother and the symbolic mother" (*Like Subjects, Love Objects* 95). However, this recognition of the maternal difference, as Benjamin goes on to emphasize, does not necessarily require "the intervention of a 'third term'"; that is, the intrusion of the father figure in this Oedipal triangular family drama (95). Rather, it is "the evolving capacity of communicative interaction to digest and transform affect and create self-other awareness" that enhances the progression of intersubjectivity (95). Later, to explicate further her notion of symbolic play, Benjamin differentiates her idea from a restoration of "a lost maternal or feminine order," as illustrated in recent feminist writing such as Irigaray's and Kristeva's works (107). This recuperation of "preoedipal play, creativity and erotic life, the nonverbal representations of mutuality" is viewed by Benjamin as "counteridealization" in which "old paternal orders" are replaced by maternal ones (107–8). What is essential about the intersubjectivity in this early mother-child relationship is not a "continuous harmony" but a "continuous disruption and repair" (47).

Pursuing her line of intersubjective thinking, Benjamin elaborates further on the interdependence between self and the other in her recently published book, *Shadow of the Other*.[54] Reviewing, analyzing, comparing, and contrasting between critical theory and poststructuralism and object-relations and Lacanian theory in light of their perceptions of the self and subject identification, Benjamin demonstrates how the intersubjective view in psychoanalysis can assimilate and negotiate the oppositions and disparities existing among these dominant theories in order to build a more other-inclusive and hence holistic model of subjectivity. Stressing the importance of the other, Benjamin postulates that a psychoanalytic view of the self is the one who reacts in relation to or in confrontation with an other whether internally or externally. This is a self who "always includes what 'comes to me,' even if felt to be alien" (87). Drawing on the concept of splitting, Benjamin makes an illuminating distinction between a subject that "*is* split" as perceived in Lacanian theory and a subject that "*splits*" (88, emphasis original). She argues that splitting should be regarded "as an active, ongoing process of psychic defense performed by the self" rather than that "of a split subject or identity constituted by discourse, language, normative practices, or any other structures that render the subject an 'effect'" (88). Benjamin intends to delineate splitting as a site of interactions, negotiations, and even transformations between subjects where even "the negativity that the other sets up for the self has its own possibilities, a productive irritation" (85).

This notion of the negation as embodied in the other is linked to a creation of "the tension between negation and recognition dependent on the recognition of the negation, of the other's impact or intent" (*Shadow of the Other* 96). In Benjamin's opinion, the other plays a crucial role in facilitating an intersubjective relationship between self and the other accomplished through a process of mutual recognition. As Benjamin states, it is only "when the Other intervenes" that "the barbarism of incorporating the Other into the same" can be dismantled (99). As a consequence, "*any subject's primary responsibility to the other subject is to be her intervening or surviving other*" (99, emphasis original). What Benjamin has called forth is a subject's recognition of the other subject as an external "concrete other" and not only as the one who is assimilated and internalized within by the subject (82). Benjamin uses the concept of "inclusion," which does not imply "assimilating or reducing" the other, to propose an intersubjective paradigm of "multiplicity" that works "beyond the binary alternatives of self-enclosed identity" as prescribed in the classic model of selfhood and "fragmented dispersal" as formulated by deconstruction and Lacanian theory (104). Benjamin's notion of multiplicity includes "tolerating ambivalence," which incorporates both love and hate (105). In other words, the subject's capacity to split means an embodiment of "difference, hate, failure of love" in its relationship with the other (105).

Further, quoting Margo Rivera's concept of dissociation and multiple personality, Benjamin emphasizes that a combination of difference and sameness as premised in an intersubjective "consciousness" is the one "that can handle the contradictions of the different voices and different desires within one person. . . . [N]ot the silencing of different voices with different points of view—but the growing ability to call all those voices 'I'."[55] For Benjamin, the significance of "the surviving other" lies in its integration of "double identification, recognizing the position of the subject without wholly abandoning her own position" (107). Reformulating Freud's usage of "the shadow of the other," Benjamin concludes her concept of the other in an intersubjective theory as follows: "owning the other within diminishes the threat of the other without so that the stranger outside is no longer identical with the strange within us—not our shadow, not a shadow over us, but a separate other whose own shadow is distinguishable in the light" (108).

Although not the first or only theorist to explore the concept of intersubjectivity, what Benjamin has shed light on are two crucial issues, which afford a more advanced version of the mutual influences between feminism and psychoanalysis. One is to rethink the relational paradigm from a subject-relations position. The other is to resurrect the (m)other from an object-relations position. First, Benjamin relocates human subjects in relationships and contexts where two or more people are engaged in a more dynamic and interactive connection. Within this relational context, Benjamin aims to build a holistic picture of intersubjectivity as the hallmark of humans' self-development. Basing her intersubjectivity on a subject-subject premise, Benjamin is able to accommodate two or more subjectivities provided that mutual recognition is made between these same but different subjects. Benjamin's proposition is illuminating for both feminism and psychoanalysis because her reformulation of the (m)other as a subject of her own meets feminism's concern and interest, on the one hand, and fills the gap of child centeredness in psychoanalysis, on the other hand. As a result, Benjamin's intersubjective theory has created a more mutual and meaningful dialogue between feminism and psychoanalysis. The intersubjectivity has indeed expanded the relational paradigm to encompass more othernesses and more diversities.

Second, for Benjamin, rescuing the (m)other from being objectified requires a process of recognizing tensions and negations. The "intersubjective space" is, as Benjamin perceives it, the meeting point where different subjects come to face and negotiate with their similarities and differences. What Benjamin's intersubjectivity has also contributed to current critical theory is to reassess and reevaluate all the negations and negativities that are associated with the (m)other. That is, to reread them in a positive and growth-enhancing sense. By so doing, Benjamin has resurrected and restored the (m)other from the margin to the center to facilitate intersubjectivity. More important, what Benjamin's intersubjectivity has enhanced is to think through the (m)other and other possibilities. To a certain extent, Benjamin's intersubjectivity serves as a benchmark for rethinking the relational paradigm.

Intersubjectivity, Feminist Mothering, and Matrilinealism

Referring back to this whole presentation of the relational paradigm, I would like to conclude by highlighting a few points for feminist rethinking. First, the main research concern, which underlies feminist maternal scholarship and the feminist discussions as outlined in this chapter, is a preoccupation with theorizing maternal subjectivity. Developing from the notion of "matriarchal ethic," as suggested earlier, where mutuality and intersubjectivity are its building blocks and driving forces, the maternal subjectivity, if theorized from the perspective of (mutual) intersubjectivity, belongs not only to that of the mother as a woman in her own right but also becomes part of the relationships she has established with others in her relational history or herstory. Put another way, matrilineal (inter)subjectivity, as conceived now, is like a spider's web or what Naomi Ruth Lowinsky terms "motherline web,"[56] linking feminist matrilinealism with relationality, whose threads are spinning around and across a complex network of relationships where self and the other are mutually included but retain their own separateness and individuality.

Second, if what all these theorists have supported is the desire to build the connection and the recognition of mutual understanding through women's identification with each other, given this preoccupation of relational theory with the great capacity of matrilineal intersubjectivity encompassing a complex web of relationships, as argued earlier, in which different subjectivities and significant others are tolerated, understood, recognized, and integrated into a whole, there is no doubt that the mother-daughter connection, as perceived by these feminist theorists, is the pillar of this relational development. Observing from the standpoint of matrilineal intersubjectivity, my attempt in the rest of this book is to propose to investigate connections and interdependences between mothers and daughters in literature and to proceed with an ongoing theorization and textual practice of the relational paradigm.

Third, what has been discerned so far is that if approached from the viewpoint of intersubjectivity, the feminist attempt to locate a maternal voice within language and representation needs not necessarily be regarded as "unsymbolized" as it is by both Irigaray and Kristeva. The rationale behind this relational theoretical hypothesis is that maternal or matrilineal (inter)subjectivity has always existed and our loss of it is by virture of patriarchal disregard and denigration. Therefore, post-Lacanian feminists' recourse to a mediation of the language of the symbolic order in order to resurrect and restore a maternal voice becomes somehow redundant and futile. If a maternal voice begins with an intersubjectivity, whereby the self-identification with and construction of we-ness are an essential part of a self-narrative and life writing, a maternal voice is then viewed as a site with which dialogues, negotiations, and interactions between or among different subjects are involved to form a poetics of matrilineal narratives. This poetics of matrilineal narratives, as represented and defined in the concept of intersubjectivity, can be illustrated as follows:

> Intersubjectivity, then, implies that the narration of a life or a self can never be confined to a single, isolated subjecthood. Others are an integral part of consciousness, events and the production of a narrative. Or, put more abstractly, the narration of a self cannot be understood in isolation from an other it acknowledges, implicitly or explicitly, and with which it is in a constitutive relationship. Moreover, this other may be either a concrete individual or a generalized subject.[57]

This illuminating definition of intersubjectivity, as quoted here, echoes Benjamin's recovery and accentuation of the other in her intersubjective theory. This poetics or syntax of matrilineal narratives has been pursued and enriched, on the one hand, by certain feminisms—particularly psychoanalytic feminisms—in the generation of new theories, and investigated and experimented with in women's autobiographical and fictional writings, on the other hand. In the selected literary texts, which are written predominantly by women and will be discussed in detail in parts 2 and 3, the matrilineal narratives are bound up with a literary investigation and experimentation, either implicitly or explicitly, of intersubjectivity and mutual empathy. These matrilineal narratives, either written or narrated by mothers or daughters, matrilineal in either a biological or nonbiological sense, also re-present and rework the psychological relational paradigm in different lights, from which other possible relational matrixes and developments are likely to be generated.

Notes

1. Stephen Mitchell, quoted in Barbara Ann Schapiro, *Literature and the Relational Self* (New York and London: New York University Press, 1994), 2, emphasis original.
2. Tess Cosslett, "Feminism, Matrilinealism, and the 'House of Women' in Contemporary Women's Fiction," *Journal of Gender Studies* 5, no. 1 (1996): 7.
3. Cosslett, "Matrilineal Narratives Revisited," in *Feminism and Autobiography: Texts, Theories, Methods*, ed. Tess Cosslett, Celia Lury, and Penny Summerfield (London and New York: Routledge, 2000), 142.
4. Elaine Tuttle Hansen, *Mother without Child: Contemporary Fiction and the Crisis of*

Motherhood (London: University of California Press, 1997), 5. See also the discussion in the introduction, 4–7.

5. In tandem with Jessica Benjamin's intersubjective theory, the Stone Center theorists make a similar theoretical proposition by employing and explicating the concept of relationality as a valuable way of perceiving human relationships. Instead of being heavily embedded in crucial theoretical concepts and jargons from psychoanalysis as is Benjamin's approach, the Stone Center theorists draw on their specific experiences as therapists and their experiments with clients to express their relational paradigm and framework. Diverging slightly from Benjamin's study, which is mainly founded on the mother-infant relationship, the Stone Center theorists' is orientated toward the later stage of human development, mostly grown adults with a main focus on women. With their common preoccupation with women's development, from which their theoretical premises are developed, the Stone Center theorists not only validate and appraise relationality as a woman-specific way of existence and perception but also advocate it as a value-added, growth-enhancing, and dynamic presentation of human relationship in general. See their works, *Women's Growth in Connection: Writings from the Stone Center* and *Women's Growth in Diversity: More Writing from the Stone Center*, ed. Judith V. Jordan et al. (New York and London: Guilford Press, 1991; 1997).
6. Jean Baker Miller et al., "Some Misconceptions and Reconceptions of a Relational Approach," in *Women's Growth in Diversity*, 27.
7. Ibid., 31–2, emphasis original.
8. Ibid., 30.
9. Nan Bauer Maglin, "Don't Never Forget the Bridge That You Crossed Over On: The Literature of Matrilineage," in *The Lost Tradition: Mothers and Daughters in Literature*, ed. Cathy N. Davidson and E. M. Broner (New York: Frederick Ungar, 1980), 258.
10. Cosslett, "Matrilineal Narratives Revisited," 142.
11. Cosslett, "Feminism, Matrilinealism, and the 'House of Women' in Contemporary Women's Fiction," 8. For a fuller discussion of Cosslett's study, see chapter 1, 26–7.
12. Nancy Chodorow, *The Reproduction of Mothering: Psychoanalysis and the Sociology of Gender* (California: University of California, 1978).
13. Chodorow, *Feminism and Psychoanalytic Theory* (Oxford: Basil Blackwell, 1989), 45–56.
14. Ibid., 47.
15. Margaret S. Mahler, quoted in Jane Flax, "The Conflict between Nurturance and Autonomy in Mother-Daughter Relationships and within Feminism," *Feminist Studies* 4, no. 2 (June 1978): 173, emphasis original.
16. Chodorow, *Feminism and Psychoanalytic Theory*, 48–50.
17. Flax, "The Conflict between Nurturance and Autonomy," 171.
18. Ibid., 172–9.
19. Chodorow, *Feminism and Psychoanalytic Theory*, 60–3.
20. Flax, "The Conflict between Nurturance and Autonomy," 182–3.
21. Jane Gallop, *Feminism and Psychoanalysis: The Daughter's Seduction* (1982; reprint, London: Macmillan, 1983), 115–6.
22. Janice Doane and Devon Hodges, *From Klein to Kristeva: Psychoanalytic Feminism and the Search for the 'Good Enough' Mother* (Michigan University Press, 1992), 46–50. See also Marianne Hirsch, "Maternal Voice," in *Feminism and*

Psychoanalysis: A Critical Dictionary, ed. Elizabeth Wright et al. (Oxford and Massachusetts: Basil Blackwell, 1992), 252.
23. Luce Irigaray, "And the One Doesn't Stir without the Other," trans. Helene Vivienne Wenzel, *Signs: Journal of Women in Culture and Society* 7, no. 1(Autumn 1981): 60–7. Hereafter, page numbers to this essay are cited parenthetically.
24. Gallop, *Feminism and Psychoanalysis*, 114–5.
25. Margaret Whitford, "Rereading Irigaray," in *Between Feminism and Psychoanalysis*, ed. Teresa Brennan (London and New York: Routledge, 1989), 110.
26. Ibid., 108–13.
27. Irigaray, *This Sex Which Is Not One*, trans. Catherine Porter with Carolyn Burke (New York: Cornell University Press, 1985), 143.
28. Ibid., 209.
29. Whitford, "Rereading Irigaray," 112.
30. Ibid., 113.
31. Domna C. Stanton, "Difference on Trial: A Critique of the Maternal Metaphor in Cixous, Irigaray, and Kristeva," in *The Poetics of Gender*, ed. Nancy K. Miller (New York: Columbia University Press, 1986), 169.
32. Gallop, *Feminism and Psychoanalysis*, 114–5.
33. Julia Kristeva, "Stabat Mater," in *The Kristeva Reader*, ed. Toril Moi (1986; reprint, Oxford: Basil Blackwell, 1990), 174.
34. Susan Sellers, *Language and Sexual Difference: Feminist Writing in France* (London: Macmillan, 1991), 98–9.
35. Kristeva, *Desire in Language: A Semiotic Approach to Literature and Art*, trans. Thomas Gora, Alice Jardine, and Leon S. Roudiez, ed. Leon S. Roudiez (Oxford: Basil Blackwell, 1980), 237.
36. Kristeva, "Stabat Mater," 178.
37. Whitford, *Luce Irigaray: Philosophy in the Feminine* (London and New York: Routledge, 1991), 77–8.
38. Kristeva, "Stabat Mater," 180–1.
39. Kristeva, "About Chinese Women," in Moi, *The Kristeva Reader*, 150.
40. Kristeva, *Desire in Language*, 247.
41. Kristeva, "About Chinese Women," 154, emphasis original.
42. Sellers, *Language and Sexual Difference*, 108.
43. Susan Rubin Suleiman, "Writing and Motherhood," in *The (M)other Tongue: Essays in Feminist Psychoanalytic Interpretation*, ed. Shirley Nelson Garner, Claire Kahane, and Madelon Sprengnether (Ithaca and London: Cornell University Press, 1985), 367.
44. Eleanor H. Kuykendall, "Toward an Ethic of Nurturance: Luce Irigaray on Mothering and Power," in *Mothering: Essays in Feminist Theory*, ed. Joyce Treilcot (Maryland: Rowman & Littlefield, 1983), 264–9.
45. Ibid., 265.
46. Ibid., 266–9.
47. Marianne Hirsch, "Maternal Voice," in *Feminism and Psychoanalysis: A Critical Dictionary*, ed. Elizabeth Wright et al. (Oxford: Basil Blackwell, 1992), 252.
48. Chodorow and Susan Contratto, "The Fantasy of the Perfect Mother," in *Feminism and Psychoanalytic Theory*, 80.
49. Ibid., 82–3.
50. Chodorow, *The Reproduction of Mothering*, 167–8.
51. Schapiro, *Literature and the Relational Self*, 19. See also Jordan et al., *Women's Growth in Connection*, 61.

52. Jessica Benjamin, *The Bonds of Love: Psychoanalysis, Feminism and the Problem of Domination* (New York: Pantheon Books, 1988), 20. In the first chapter of her book *The Bonds of Love*, Benjamin expounds her conception of intersubjectivity based on a detailed analysis of the theoretical arguments found in several prominent psychoanalytic theorists. On the one hand, Benjamin refers her discovery of intersubjective theory to certain important concepts raised by other psychoanalysts such as Daniel Stern's "intersubjective relatedness," John Bowlby's "attachment theory," and Heinz Kohut's "self psychology." On the other hand, she makes a great leap in revising and reformulating the theoretical premises of classical psychology including Sigmund Freud's "oral drives," Jean Piaget's "developmental psychology," Margaret S. Mahler's "ego psychology," and D. W. Winnicott's "transitional objects" (11–50). Hereafter, page numbers to this volume are cited parenthetically.
53. Benjamin, *Like Subjects, Love Objects: Essays on Recognition and Sexual Difference* (New Haven and London: Yale University Press, 1995), 6. Hereafter, page numbers to this volume are cited parenthetically.
54. Benjamin, *Shadow of the Other: Intersubjectivity and Gender in Psychoanalysis* (New York and London: Routledge, 1998). Hereafter, page numbers to this volume are cited parenthetically.
55. Margo Rivera, quoted in Benjamin, *Shadow of the Other*, 106.
56. Naomi Ruth Lowinsky, *Stories from the Motherline: Reclaiming the Mother-Daughter Bond, Finding Our Feminine Souls* (Los Angeles: Jeremy P. Tarcher, 1992), 12.
57. Cosslett, Celia Lury, and Penny Summerfield, "An Introduction," in *Feminism and Autobiography*, 4.

Part Two
New Feminist Family Romances in Contemporary Matrilineal Narratives

Chapter 3

New Feminist Family Romances

> There is a genealogy of women within our family: on our mothers' side we have mothers, grandmothers and great-grandmothers, and daughters. Given our exile in the family of the father-husband, we tend to forget this genealogy of women, and we are often persuaded to deny it. Let us try to situate ourselves within this female genealogy so as to conquer and keep our identity. Nor let us forget that we already have a history, that certain women have, even if it was culturally difficult, left their mark on history and that all too often we do not know them.
>
> Luce Irigaray[1]

> What I call the "feminist family romance" appears in psychoanalytic re-visions of Freudian paradigms, which highlight mother-daughter bonding as a basis for a vision of gender difference and female specificity. This family romance pattern takes on different, less idealized shapes and valences in fictional texts which are more specifically contextualized and historical situations.
>
> Marianne Hirsch[2]

This part will explore some literary representations of motherhood and mother-daughter relationships with particular reference to the life narratives of three generations of women. Dipping into different accounts of family romances, both Freudian and feminist adaptations, I seek to propose the emergence of new feminist family romances as envisioned by Audre Lorde in her depiction of the grandmother-mother-daughter triad in the prologue of her book *Zami*[3] but also constructed by a host of contemporary women writers in their literary and creative experimentations with matrilineal narratives published between 1991 and 2000. Contemporary women's writing of matrilineal narratives in either a two- or three-generational context can be viewed "as a part of" the second-wave feminist movement of recuperating the mother since the publication of Adrienne Rich's *Of Woman Born: Motherhood as Experience and Institution* in 1976[4] and also consonant with the later feminist maternal scholars' preoccupation with consolidating the mother-daughter bond in a proliferation of women's writings on "maternal narratives, the motherline, feminist socialization of daughters, and gynocentric mothering" in the 1980s.[5] The new feminist family romances as unfolded in contemporary women's writing of matrilineal narratives exhibit different rewritings of both Freudian and feminist family romances. They also go beyond the triangular relationship of family romances in displaying variations of the triadic narrative shape as described by Lorde.

The Emergence of New Feminist Family Romances

The term *family romances* was introduced by Freud in his analysis of an individual's, usually a male's, psychological development. According to this theory, the male child will sense that the love he receives from his parents is both inadequate and dissatisfying, thus making himself feel like a stepchild or an adopted one. The child will then, at an early stage in his development, imagine that he could replace his parents with superior ones. In Freud's account, the child's fantasy of repudiating his real father, "that 'pater semper incertus est' (the father is always uncertain)," indicates his unfulfilled wish for a return to this lost happy family. Freud's familial structure is built on a nuclear family model with a father, a mother, and a son; in terms of differences between male and female, we cannot hear a daughter's voice in this familial plot because "the imagination of girls" is perceived by Freud as "much weaker." As for the mother, although the child will have no doubts about his maternal origins and the mother is seen as "'certissima' (very certain)," she only serves as a medium through whom the male child projects his fantasies and desires.[6]

Freud's notion of family romances has resonance and revision in various social, cultural, and literary studies. Steph Lawler's sociological study based on a feminist appropriation of Freudian family romances offers a female version of family romances in which a majority of working-class women, especially those who have moved their class status from a working class to a middle class, exhibit their desire or ambivalence toward replacing their working-class mothers with superior and privileged ones. According to Lawler's analysis, the working-class daughters' anxiety about their mothers has something to do with what Rich has named "matrophobia" — "the fear of becoming one's mother" or as Lawler interprets it as the fear of "inhabiting" the world of one's working-class mother.[7] Later in her study, Lawler makes a notable remark in light of "both the celebration and the denigration of the mother-daughter relationship" in most of the feminist researches on the subject. She argues that "the denigration of mothering" can deprive a mother of her agency and authority whereas "its celebration" conceals mother-daughter ambivalence, thus resulting in a daughter's longing or fantasy for a better mother.[8] These two alarming consequences are, as Lawler continues to explicate, the end products of our "fantasy of the perfect mother." The figure of the mother, as a result, is being split into two opposing images of "good" and "bad" by which the mother's subjectivity is circumvented.[9]

In tandem with the recuperation of motherhood in a series of feminist writings since the 1970s, particularly the revisionary psychoanalytic paradigms of object-relations theory, Marianne Hirsch in her book *The Mother/Daughter Plot*[10] recognizes a shift from the centrality of the paternal, as formulated in the classic Freudian model, to that of the maternal in her vigorous study of selected women's texts published in the nineteenth and twentieth centuries. This modification from patrilineage to matrilineage, as Hirsch envisions it, serves as an alternative to reformulate traditional Freudian family romances whose androcentric and ethnocentric framework has failed to account for the dynamics of other discourses. Thus, Hirsch proposes the emergence of the mother-daughter plot in postmodernist women's texts to counter the paternal plot as previously constructed in a number of women's texts in the nineteenth century. In contrast to female family romances whose narratives are centered on fictional heroines' denigration of mother figures and their subsequent embrace of male (father) figures, feminist family romances render the male position as secondary, mainly because of psychoanalytic feminists' preoccupation with a pre-Oedipal mother-child bond. According to this psychoanalytic feminist revision, the relative obscurity of male figures becomes the corollary of feminist family romances. In an attempt to make clear her notion of the feminist family romance as deviating from the Freudian paradigm, Hirsch continues to reinforce that "the feminist family romance of the 1970s is based on the separation not from parents or the past, but from patriarchy and from men in favor of female alliances."[11]

In several matrilineal narratives published between 1991 and 2000, a new triangular structure of the so-called feminist family romances emerges. The new pattern is manifest in women's textual construction of grandmother, mother, and daughter in their exploration of femininity (maternity) and creativity. The idea of this new triangular structure is initiated by Lorde. In the prologue of her book *Zami: A New Spelling of My Name*, Lorde remarks:

> I have felt the age-old triangle of mother father and child, with the "I" at its eternal core, elongate and flatten out into the elegantly strong triad of grandmother mother daughter, with the "I" moving back and forth flowing in either or both directions as needed.[12]

Lorde's statement testifies to the transformation of family romances from the perspective of feminist matrilinealism. The "triangle of mother father child" has become outdated because its narrative has inadequately accounted for women's existence. The "triad of grandmother mother daughter" is depicted as "elegantly strong" because a number of women writers, including Lorde herself in her book, have participated in constructing a new narrative pattern and devising a new literary voice of their own. Yet, with regard to the narrative shape as disclosed in Lorde's cited passage, she does not suggest a tense and conflicted triangular relationship as that in a Freudian family romance. Rather, she replaces a triangle with an "elongate[d] and flatten[ed]" line, which elicits the threading of different narrative lines and shapes moving beyond the simple triangular structure. Notably, the "I" as delivered by Lorde hints at a maternal identity with the "I" at the center "moving back and forth" between grandmother and daughter, but this "'I' at its eternal core" can also be applied to any one of them in the grandmother-mother-daughter triad.

Connecting Lorde's grandmother-mother-daughter triad with Hirsch's feminist family romances, I seek to term matrilineal narratives *new feminist family romances* based on the following rationale. First, they are new because the figure of the father is not only diminished in the plot of family romances; it is also viewed as a third term to be replaced by a matrilineal family figure—the grandmother. Although certain male figures are still present in the narratives, they do not occupy mainstream positions. Moreover, Hirsch's feminist family romances are only focused on two generations of women whereas the matrilineal narratives I am concentrating on are expanded into a broader arena—mainly three generations of women. Second, the new feminist family romances are not only preoccupied with a female line of descent; that is, they share a commonality of plot, which is structured as matrilineal. They also represent multiple female voices and identities; one important feature of this being that some female protagonists embody either a double identity of being both a mother and a daughter or a triple identity of grandmother, mother, and daughter. New feminist family romances, in other words, build a female-dominated world founded on women's mothering activities and experiences. Third, even though the new feminist family romances resonate with Western feminists' recuperation of female experiences, motherhood in particular, in the 1970s, they also call forth a rethinking and even revision of the definition of motherhood in light of women's writing from different cultures, ethnicities, and backgrounds. Finally, this is called "a new kind of matrilineal romance" because most matrilineal narratives I am looking at are aimed at going back to preserve a lost matrilineal tradition with an inevitable, ongoing process shifting from misunderstanding to reconciliations or reunions among female protagonists.[13]

Therefore, in this part I intend to propose a new feminist family romance, a new triangular structure that not only revises Freud's model but also pursues further Hirsch's feminist family romances. Yet, by mapping this paradigmatic shift from Freudian family romances as a triangle to Lorde's grandmother-mother-daughter triad as a synchronic line, I do not intend to suggest that both of their narrative structures are mutually exclusive. The different versions of family romances, described by Freud, Hirsch, and Lorde, respectively, all unfold and highlight the tension and ambivalence as defining constituents of the family dramas concerned. This appearance of tension and ambivalence also recurs in matrilineal romances as shown in contemporary matrilineal narratives. Although not all of the contemporary matrilineal narratives examined in my book converge on a similar pattern of matrilineal romances moving from misunderstanding to reconciliation to final recognition between generations of women,[14] it is precisely the eventual or climactic resolution of the ambivalence between mothers and daughters that sets matrilineal romances apart from their Freudian and feminist counterparts. This differentiation from Freudian family romances indicates, in particular, a converse trajectory explored in contemporary textual practice of matrilineal narratives in which connection instead of separation is what constitutes family romances. I shall return to this crucial point in my conclusion for this part.

Before embarking on a detailed textual analysis of the new feminist family romances in matrilineal narratives, I will further elaborate on what the motherline, the grandmother-mother-daughter triad, and the mother-daughter writing are and how they have significant impacts on generations of women in forming their sense of female selfhood and personality, by bringing out some useful ideas in popular psychology and psychiatry with reference to Naomi Ruth Lowinsky's *Stories from the Motherline: Reclaiming the Mother-Daughter Bond, Finding Our Feminine Souls*,[15] Hope Edelman's *Mother of My Mother: The Intricate Bond between Generations*,[16] and Karen G. Howe's "Daughters Discover Their Mothers through Biographies and Genograms: Educational and Clinical Parallels."[17]

The Motherline, the Grandmother-Mother-Daughter Triad, and the Genogram

Lowinsky, a Jungian psychologist and clinical therapist, launches on a psychological, physical, artistic, and spiritual quest for her motherline in her book-length study *Stories from the Motherline*. When elaborating on the structure of the motherline, Lowinsky refers to the weaving of a tapestry whose threads are tied to different generations and as the spinning goes on, a more complicated network of relationships is thus developed:

> The Motherline is not a straight line, for it is not about abstract genealogical diagrams; it is about bodies being born out of bodies. Envision the word *line* as a cord, a thread, as the yarn emerging from the fingers of a woman at the spinning wheel. Imagine cords of connection tied over generations. Like weaving or knitting, each thread is tied to others to create a complex, richly textured cloth connecting the past to the future.[18]

Lowinsky's notion of the motherline, in which it is seen "as a cord, a thread, as the yarn emerging from the fingers of a woman at the spinning wheel" (12), resonates with Lorde's description of the narrative structure of the grandmother-mother-daughter triad with "the 'I' moving back and forth flowing in either or both directions as needed."[19] This motherline is not a linear progression; it is, according to Lowinsky, a cyclic life process circling around "bodies being born out of bodies" (12). Therefore, the line as generated from the mother is the lifeline that is continuously evolving and "connecting" one generation to the other and "the past to the future" (12).

To consolidate this notion of motherline in conjunction with storytelling, Lowinsky uses the term "looping" to describe women's pattern of telling stories from their motherline as they refer to themselves as mothers and daughters and traverse this journey to different times and locations:

> Looping ties together life stages, roles, and generations. It disregards linear time. It involves a cyclical view of life, it finds meaning in patterns that repeat. We measure our lives in our mother's terms, and in our daughter's terms.... You re-experience your past in your children and anticipate your future in your parents, while at the same time your children constellate the future and your parents the past. (22)

According to Lowinsky, an interesting interconnection between generations is established in this mother-daughter looping. That is to say, in our daughters and mothers, we see our past and future while simultaneously in ourselves as mothers and daughters, we revise and reincarnate our mothers' past but also envision and shed light on our daughters' future. In short, Lowinsky defines "looping" thus: "Looping is an associative process by which we pass through our own experience to understand that of another" (21–2). This looping concept links significantly with Jessica Benjamin's rendition of intersubjectivity. This intergenerational looping between mothers and daughters substantiates and materializes the authenticity and reliability of Benjamin's intersubjective theory, but it also expands, in a similar vein to Cosslett's study of feminist matrilinealism, Benjamin's theoretical trajectory in a three generational framework.

Developing her notion of the mother-daughter looping further, Lowinsky addresses a new transformation in the mother-daughter relationship happening in the middle of women's lives when they are both mothers and daughters. Serving as a bridge that connects mothers and daughters, past and present, women in their middle lives embody a Janusan thinking that enables them to look backward and forward in the times of their mothers, themselves, and their daughters. The female respondents in Lowinsky's interviews especially take their birth experiences as examples to articulate their looping between generations. Viewing their mothers in themselves and themselves in their daughters, women in the middle of their lives stand in a privileged position for connecting with their motherlines (73–95). Apart from this mother in her middle age, Lowinsky invokes later a more mature and insightful mother in this matrilineal chain of women, the figure of the grandmother referred to as a "return to origins" (115). Being empathic with her maternal grandmother's maternal thinking, Lowinsky also stretches her motherline both vertically and horizontally to include her aunts, thereby linking generations of mothers, daughters, and siblings together. What is also noteworthy and inspiring is Lowinsky's reflection on her paternal grandmother: "that the neglected ghost of a paternal grandmother haunted my life" (130). After reading a letter from her paternal grandmother written before Lowinsky's birth, Lowinsky is in a better position to understand her paternal grandmother whom she has long misunderstood and wronged. Additionally, by writing this book on the motherline, Lowinsky has reclaimed her paternal grandmother (130).

In chapter 4 of her book, "Wrestling with the Mother: Of Love, Rebellion, and Our Personal Shadows," Lowinsky explores and clarifies the most deeply felt and turbulent aspect of the mother-daughter relationship—wrestling with the mother. Redeeming the disturbing cultural messages conveyed in the rather negative feelings of ambivalence, rivalry, and resentment shared between generations of women at both biological and nonbiological levels, Lowinsky states that our "wrestling with the mother" should be integrated into the psychological makeup of our relationships with mothers and daughters and with women in general. Developing her thinking further, Lowinsky continues:

> Far from creating separation, this kind of wrestling is the beginning of an authentic relationship. Bonding and differentiation are not separate human endeavors, achieved at different developmental levels. They occur simultaneously and throughout development. (56)
>
> This is the central paradox of human relationship: although connection begins with the umbilical cord, with the looping of identification, the resonance of similarities, only the recognition and working through of difference, of otherness, secures a bond and makes it personal. (57)

In Lowinsky's view, in negotiating their resonance and difference, both mothers and daughters have to go through their wrestling with each other, trying to find their own individual identities while at the same time recognizing a connection with their motherlines. It is, as Lowinsky points out, only through working out the difficult feelings and anxieties that mothers and daughters can begin to feel connected again (53–72). Lowinsky's contention here rings true to Cosslett's observation of the matrilineal relation, which figures "both the similarities and the differences, the interrelationship and the separateness, of their subjects."[20] Linking Lowinsky's notion with feminist psychoanalytic thinking and feminist matrilinealism as discussed in my second chapter, Benjamin, Lowinsky, and Cosslett have reached a consensus in articulating and theorizing (in the case of Benjamin) an intersubjective state and relationship that has long existed between generations of women.

Lowinsky's configuration of the motherline is rooted in her allusion to essential motherhood and is foregrounded in the notion of a biological family, a highly contentious viewpoint that would be subjected to close scrutiny and critique within feminisms. In her third chapter, nonetheless, Lowinsky mentions briefly and tentatively nonbiological aspects of her motherhood and motherline. In particular, her adopted Indian daughter's double affiliation with her two motherlines—one with her birth mother in India and the other with Lowinsky as her adoptive mother—reshapes and redefines her concepts of the motherline. Lowinsky comments thus:

> My adopted child does not have to choose between her birth mother and her adoptive mother. In order to be fully herself she must claim her relationship to both Motherlines. Both her biological and her adoptive parents are essential parts of her psychological makeup. To say that biology is a potent part of the

> Motherline does not exclude the power of the nonbiological connection. She and I made our bond conscious through the recognition of its nonbiological nature. (45)

Lowinsky's realization of her adopted daughter's link with both her biological and nonbiological motherlines derives partly from the bond she establishes with her adopted daughter and partly from collective motherhood she shares with the woman on the other side of the world. More significant, Lowinsky's multiple maternal identities as a birth mother, an adoptive mother, and a stepmother of sons and daughters align her with different maternal roles and stances in relation to her different children. Reflecting on her personal experience as a mother or mothers, Lowinsky makes an interesting comparison between the fatherline and the motherline:

> Unlike the lists of "begets" in the Bible, where son is begotten by father in a clear, linear descent, the Motherline web is raggedly creative, tying in the severed connections of divorces and remarriages, creating new family fabric and inspiring our children to ask endless questions about who is related to whom and how. (46)

What Lowinsky has suggested and elicited is the flexibility, diversity, and creativity of the motherline as opposed to the fatherline that has been restricted and hampered by the rigidity of a monolithic, linear line. Like Cosslett's study of feminist matrilinealism, what Lowinsky's formulation of the motherline has contributed to extant feminist study of mother-daughter relationships and the motherline is the heterogeneity, the tolerance, and the adaptability to incorporate similarities and differences into an embodied wholeness of "the Motherline web" that does not necessarily subsume and displace otherness.

Working from the position of a psychotherapist and a psychoanalyst as is Lowinsky, Edelman provides one of the few studies on the triangular relationship among generations of women. Accentuating the figure of the grandmother and the grandmother-granddaughter relationship, Edelman also brings new insights to feminist configurations of the mother-daughter relationship by explicating the differences in the relationships between mother and daughter and between grandmother and granddaughter. As revealed in Edelman's findings gleaned from women's real-life experiences, the relationship between mother and daughter usually consists of ambivalence and conflict whereas the relationship between grandmother and granddaughter is often exempt from these agitated feelings unless the grandmother-granddaughter relationship is developed from a mother-daughter dynamic. This difference, as Edelman goes on to explain, is probably related to the fact that the identification between mother and daughter is predicated on the notion "You are me" while the relationship between grandmother and granddaughter has to do with "You are of me." As a granddaughter does not come straight out of her grandmother's body, she will be unlikely to make direct critical comments on her grandmother because their relationship is not so intimately tied together as is a mother-daughter relationship. Nor will a grandmother do so to her granddaughter unless their relationship is founded on a mother-daughter mechanism.[21]

Drawing on this liberating aspect of the grandmother-granddaughter relationship, Edelman claims that the mother-daughter relation often needs a third perspective to mend or enhance the relationship. In a mother-daughter conflict, it is often the grandmother who helps reconcile mother-daughter dissension and restore their disruption. Inversely, if a conflict occurs between mother and grandmother, it is often difficult for a granddaughter to be a conciliator. Despite this, the ambivalence existing between a mother and her daughter is invariably bound up with the mother's relation with her mother, namely the grandmother (97–122). One such example given by Edelman in her study is that the inauthentic or deficient mothering one generation receives from another is likely to be reproduced in another generational round. However, in Edelman's opinion, some granddaughters are able to regain the loss by being mothered by their grandmothers who might not sufficiently and efficiently mother their daughters either by choice or circumstance. Even though some granddaughters find themselves unlike their mothers or resent and deliberately denounce the lives their mothers have led, most granddaughters discover to their astonishment that they resemble their grandmothers in so many fundamental ways (207–9). As a result, Edelman poses a difficult and ambivalent question: "Can anyone tell me, definitively, where does one woman end and the next begin?" (214).

Edelman favors a democratic and regenerative aspect of the grandmother-granddaughter relationship in her clarification of the different dynamics of identification between mother and daughter and between grandmother and granddaughter. Although the grandmother-granddaughter relationship cannot be said to be devoid of feelings of angst and anxiety between them, the grandmother-granddaughter mechanism, by and large, bespeaks a woman's relationship between generations that is less embedded with ambivalence and strife. Yet, what I want to emphasize and make clear here is not to undermine the mother-daughter relationship in praise of the grandmother-granddaughter relationship as Edelman's study can easily lead one to think so. As Edelman indicated, "the three-generational triangles" cannot work without the mother in the middle (97). It is also the initiation of the third person, the grandmother, to paraphrase Lowinsky, that the mother-daughter relationship can be envisaged in a new light and hence be advanced into a transforming phase or level (116–8).

Thinking about the grandmother-mother-daughter triad in relation to the writing of matrilineal narratives, one important aspect that is worth noting is women writers' engagement with the use of what Karen G. Howe terms a "genogram." A genogram, according to Howe, is the clinical parallel of "the mother biography assignment" she adopts for her course Psychology of Women.[22] The genogram is widely used in family systems therapy, whose approach is targeted at a multigenerational level and provides a participant with "more objective views of one's parents and grandparents" and thus enables her or him "to know the personal history and stories of the older generations" (34). In particular, this use of the genogram is applied to healing the mother-daughter relationship in therapy (35). Lowinsky's and Edelman's studies as discussed previously could also be seen as the writings of a genogram in which they both write stories about their female genealogy. In terms of literary representations of a genogram, contemporary women's writers of matrilineal narratives have concurrently either written "one story about matrilineage that situates individual mothers in wider contexts and understands them as having other lives, beyond the maternal function"[23] or allocated in their fictional and autobiographical writings one writing figure as a (grand)daughter biographer who writes about the stories of her grandmother and mother.

Drawing a parallel between "mother biography assignment" and "genogram," Howe describes and analyzes how she utilizes the two methods to mend the mother-daughter relationship. In an excerpt quoted by Howe from one of her students' mother biography assignments, Howe highlights the multigenerational context her student is able to see through:

> I never knew my maternal grandparents and am ashamed of my former lack of interest in them. As a result, it was difficult imagining my mother as a daughter. I also recognize the importance of my mother's role as grandmother in helping my children see me as a daughter. She often tells them what I was like as a little girl and the funny things that happened to me. (36–7)

The significance of writing a mother biography assignment or genogram is that it allows daughters to see their mothers in a social context: "[N]ot only knowing the mother's story, but seeing it in the context of the family and the patriarchal society is the key to the power of the mother biographies and the genogram"(37). Viewing the mother's life in context inevitably creates a feeling of empathy in the daughter as one of the participants said: "I felt as if I knew my Mom but didn't really know her. She would tell me how she felt at a certain point in her life and I would try to remember that time and place my self back there and relate to how she was feeling all over again" (36). Indisputably, the most important technique involved with writing a genogram reverberates with Lowinsky's description of women's distinct narrative pattern as the mother-daughter looping when they are telling stories from their motherlines (21–2).

Nonetheless, a mother biography or genogram seems to be written only by a daughter. Although a lot of mothers' stories have been discovered by means of the genogram, none of them is actually narrated by a mother. In the last paragraph of Howe's article, she concludes:

> Asking questions, at the heart of both the genogram and the mother biographies, is a way of giving women a greater voice. As a number of feminist writers have pointed out in recent years, much of the recent explosion of material on mothers is presented from the daughter's perspective, not that of the mother herself. When we ask our mothers about themselves and their lives, we give them a voice. When we listen to them and see the commonalities, as well as the differences, in our experiences, we learn more about them and ourselves. As my student Ginger wrote at the end of her mother's biography, "I see this interview as the first of many explorations leading me into deeper understandings of not only women and my mother, but also myself." (39)

The idea conveyed in the above passage perhaps sounds problematic to a feminist understanding of maternal subjectivity. Howe might be accused of simplifying the concept of maternal subjectivity, which is a more diversified and complicated issue especially in recent feminist enquiry into the representation of motherhood. Therefore, can a genogram serve as an authentic means of (re)presenting maternal subjectivity? Is there any genogram written by a mother? Suffice it to say, however, if the mother dies or does not have the same privileges as the daughter such as being better educated or belonging to a higher class, the responsibility of tracing a matrilineage will usually be shouldered by the daughter. Yet, as explicated by Howe, one important feature of the genogram, which is analogous to that of matrilineal narratives in contemporary women's writing and that contributes to current feminist concern with maternal subjectivity, is its aim of retrieving the mother's subjectivity. More significant, placing the genogram in a multigenerational context initiates and instigates intersubjective empathy or attunement with the mother by which more understanding and recognition can be achieved between mother and daughter.

In what follows, I will move on to what I mean by *new feminist family romances* by investigating how a new triangular relationship—grandmother, mother, and daughter—operates in four literary texts, Marianne Fredriksson's *Hanna's Daughters*, Jung Chang's *Wild Swans*, Margaret Forster's *Hidden Lives*, and Margaret Drabble's *The Peppered Moth*. Although these texts share a commonality of scripting a grandmother-mother-daughter triad, their ways of approaching and constructing matrilineal narratives vary. Thus, in order to conduct a close and critical reading of these texts, I will divide my analysis of them into the four succeeding chapters. Fredriksson's novel was created in the form of fiction although it is structured in both autobiographical and biographical frameworks. Chang's and Forster's texts cannot be purely classified as autobiography because their books represent a mixture of fiction, autobiography, biography, and social and political history. Yet, their references and allusions to certain autobiographical facts enlighten their textual creativity. Integrating the characteristics of the aforementioned three matrilineal narratives into a substantial piece of work, Drabble's text, a semi-autobiographical novel, suggests another ingenious form of writing practice. Indeed, the creative diversities of these four matrilineal narratives explore further the ideas afforded in Lowinsky's and Edelman's work but also complicate and pluralize the homogenous writing of a genogram as described in Howe's article.

Notes

1. Luce Irigaray, "The Bodily Encounter with the Mother," trans. David Macey, *The Irigaray Reader*, ed. Margaret Whitford (Oxford: Basil Blackwell, 1991), 44.
2. Marianne Hirsch, *The Mother/Daughter Plot: Narrative, Psychoanalysis, Feminism* (Bloomington: Indiana University Press, 1989), 15.
3. Audre Lorde, *Zami: A New Spelling of My Name* (1982; reprint, London: Sheba, 1990), 7. References are to the reprint edition. See also Tess Cosslett, "Matrilineal Narratives Revisited," in *Feminism and Autobiography: Texts, Theories, Methods*, ed. Tess Cosslett, Celia Lury, and Penny Summerfield (London and New York: Routeldge, 2000), 143.
4. Cosslett, "Matrilineal Narratives Revisited," 142–3.
5. Andrea O'Reilly, "In Black and White: Anglo-American and African-American Perspectives on Mothers and Sons," in *Mothers and Sons: Feminism, Masculinity, and the Struggle to Raise Our Sons*, ed. Andrea O'Reilly (New York and London: Routledge, 2001), 106–7. See also Andrea O'Reilly and Sharon Abbey, "Introduction," in *Mothers and Daughters: Connection, Empowerment and Transformation*, ed. Andrea O'Reilly and Sharon Abbey (New York: Rowman & Littlefield, 2000), 2.
6. Sigmund Freud, quoted in Steph Lawler, "'I never felt as though I fitted': Family

Romances and the Mother-Daughter Relationship," in *Romances Revisited*, ed. Lynne Pearce and Jackie Stacey (London: Lawrence & Wishart, 1995), 266.
7. Lawler, "'I never felt as though I fitted,'" 270–1.
8. Ibid., 273.
9. Ibid., 268, 273.
10. See endnote 2.
11. Hirsch, *The Mother/Daughter Plot*, 135.
12. Lorde, *Zami*, 7. See endnote 3.
13. Cosslett, "Feminism, Matrilinealism, and the 'House of Women' in Contemporary Women's Fiction," *Journal of Gender Studies* 5, no. 1 (1996): 8. See also my elaboration of Cosslett's findings in chapter 1, 26–7.
14. Ibid.
15. Naomi Ruth Lowinsky, *Stories from the Motherline: Reclaiming the Mother-Daughter Bond, Finding Our Feminine Souls* (Los Angeles: Jeremy P. Tarcher, 1992). See also her recent article on the topic, "Mother of Mothers, Daughter of Daughters: Reflections on the Motherline," in *Mothers and Daughters: Connection, Empowerment, and Transformation*, ed. Andrea O'Reilly and Sharon Abbey (New York and Oxford: Rowman & Littlefield, 2000), 227–35.
16. Hope Edelman, *Mother of My Mother: The Intricate Bond between Generations* (New York: Dial Press, 1999).
17. Karen G. Howe, "Daughters Discover Their Mothers through Biographies and Genograms: Educational and Clinical Parallels," in *Motherhood: A Feminist Perspective*, ed. Jane Rice Knowles and Ellen Cole (New York: Haworth Press, 1990), 31–40. See also Shelley Phillips, "Bibliotherapy for Mothers and Daughters," in *Beyond the Myth: Mother-Daughter Relationships in Psychology, History, Literature, and Everyday Life* (London: Penguin, 1996), 164–88.
18. Lowinsky, *Stories from the Motherline*, 12, emphasis original. Hereafter, page numbers to this volume are cited parenthetically.
19. Lorde, *Zami*, 7.
20. Cosslett, "Matrilineal Narratives Revisited," 142.
21. Edelman, *Mother of My Mother*, 97–122. Hereafter, page numbers to this volume are cited parenthetically.
22. Howe, "Daughters Discover Their Mothers through Biographies and Genograms," 34. Hereafter, page numbers to this essay are cited parenthetically.
23. Elaine Tuttle Hansen, *Mother without Child: Contemporary Fiction and the Crisis of Motherhood* (California and London: University of California Press, 1997), 124.

Chapter 4

Marianne Fredriksson's *Hanna's Daughters*

Like most matrilineal narratives, Marianne Fredriksson's intent in writing *Hanna's Daughters*[1] is inclined to reflect a feminist political agenda—women's collective endeavor to recuperate the mother, as the following quotation from Fredriksson illustrates:

> There are no biblical words for the actions of mothers, although they are probably of greater importance than those of fathers. Ancient patterns are passed on from mothers to daughters, who have daughters, who then . . . Perhaps this is an explanation for why women have found it so difficult to stick up for themselves and make use of the rights an equal society has to offer. (1)

What Fredriksson tries to convey in the above passage, quoted from the foreword of her book *Hanna's Daughters*, reminds us of the silencing of the mother and "the great unwritten story" as Adrienne Rich phrases it in her pioneering book *Of Woman Born: Motherhood as Experience and Institution*.[2] Indeed, Fredriksson's concern echoes a constant feminist preoccupation with the voice of the mother and female heritages. She even hints that women's failure to achieve their equal rights in a society could also result from the loss of this tradition. This could perhaps explain the reason why Fredriksson intends to set her text in a matrilineal framework. Toward the end of the foreword, she also mentions:

> There are no autobiographical elements in this book. Anna, Johanna and Hanna bear no resemblance to me, my mother or my grandmother. They are imaginary characters and bear no relation to what is called reality. That is just what makes them real to me—I hope also to you, the reader, and that you will begin to wonder who your grandmother was and in what way your inherited patterns have shaped your life. (2)

Although written in both autobiographical and biographical forms, Fredriksson's text is, as she declares, a fiction conceived through her imagination and creativity. Significantly, Fredriksson's thought-provoking statement "that [fiction] is just what makes them real to me" (2) and her later encouragement of the reader to "think through our mothers if we are women"³ render this project of recovering our matrilineages as women's collective and concerted efforts.

Hanna's Daughters is mainly about stories among three generations of Swedish women. Its chapter headings are actually named after these three women, with Hanna (the grandmother), Johanna (the mother), and Anna (the daughter). The structure of the text reads like a matrilineal epic whose line of development is centered on two maternal figures, Hanna and Johanna, with occasional interruptions and divisions by Anna in the introduction, interlude, and epilogue. Compared with the two narrations on Hanna and Johanna, our knowledge of Anna is relatively scarce; Anna is a middle-aged woman who has a broken marriage and does not consider herself as a "good enough" mother. In short, the book contains autobiographical and biographical accounts of Hanna and Johanna with Anna taking the role of a (grand)daughter biographer.

The narrations on Hanna and Johanna in the novel, at first glance, follow a linear, progressive line. However, the insertion of the introduction, interlude, and epilogue on Anna into the overall narrative interrupts and intrudes into this linear progression. It suggests a narrative shape of looking back and forth in flux. Interestingly, the three women's names Fredriksson has chosen in the text can be seen as similar and even identical. She seems to imply that they could actually be one person splitting into three different identities as shown in her original title for the text, *Anna, Hanna och Johanna*. Anna, Hanna, and Johanna are three different identities, but their life stories are invariably linked with each other because of their matrilineal relations. The sequence in accordance with the sizes of their names as shown in the original book title resembles a matrushka doll with Anna the smallest and the most intricate layer incorporated into Hanna and then Hanna the middle into Johanna as the biggest of them all. More striking, Johanna as the mother in the middle of this three generational triad has a name that contains and embodies those of generations younger and older than she is, those of daughter and grandmother. Whether the obvious similarity as exhibited in these three names is deliberately constructed by Fredriksson, it bespeaks the accentuation of the maternal. My discussion of the text does not intend to include a critique of Joan Tate's translation, but I do think that the original title best captures the full spirit of the matrilineal framework Fredriksson has set up while the English title, *Hanna's Daughters*, might easily disguise the multiple female voices as produced by Hanna, Johanna, and Anna in this matrilineal narrative.

In *Hanna's Daughters*, the connection to the (grand)mother is initiated and established by Anna's, the (grand)daughter's, quest for matrilineage. The introduction opens with Johanna, the mother, in her bed in a hospital. Because of the old age that perhaps causes her consequent sickness, Johanna is presented as a helpless and infant-like patient who has already lost her memory and then her ability to speak. She is, in fact, on the brink of dying. Then comes Anna, the daughter, who keeps a vigil by the sick woman's bedside (5–24). Their present condition at the beginning of the text situates Johanna and Anna in a role reversal. Anna appears to take up the role of a mother who takes care of her infant-like daughter, Johanna. Yet, this opening episode of a mother in her sickbed and her daughter nursing her foreshadows and contextualizes the imminent matrilineal quest taken up by the daughter in the novel.

Moreover, in chapter 3 of this introduction sequence, we have a third-person narrative of Johanna's childhood memory of hiding with her family near the border between Sweden and Norway, succeeded in the next chapter by Anna's recollection of an outing she goes on with her mother to the waterfall on the border. These narrations, as a re-creation of a matrilineal past, are cast in the forms of dreams and memories. The significance of dreams and memories in these episodes lies in their function to retrieve the mother's subjectivity through resurfacing and representing her sub-conscious as the mother can neither remember nor speak now. And the truth about the mother's past is then retold by the daughter whose share of their collective memory serves as an affirmation of the mother's subjectivity and agency. Amazingly, when Anna recounts to Johanna, who is sick lying on her bed in the hospital, about this family outing to the waterfall on the border and Johanna's narration of her childhood memory there, Anna is delighted to trace the miraculous signs of "surprise," "joy," and "amusement" in Johanna's already old, numb, and dull face. At first, this is only Anna's "wishful thinking" of regaining her mother's subjectivity, but it is proved later that the mother does retain her consciousness at least momentarily (8–16).

Hanna's Daughters, like most matrilineal narratives, entails also the granddaughter's initial misapprehension of the grandmother. Interestingly, the only misunderstanding between generations is conveyed in the granddaughter's attitude toward her grandmother rather than toward her mother. It is, however, through the process of retrieving her matrilineage that Anna reaches an understanding of her grandmother, Hanna. Such an episode of searching for her matrilineal past happens when Anna goes back to her mother's house and accidentally finds a photograph of her grandmother. The grandmother's photo has been taken down from its original location of hanging on the wall to be slipped "under the floral paper with which for years her

[Anna's] mother had lined the drawers" (17). Strikingly, this sudden appearance of her grandmother's photo prompts Anna to conduct a series of family enquiries including her grandmother's relationship with her parents and the significance of knowing her family past:

> Why was it so important? Why does it seem a loss not to remember, not to have understood? In me, it's like a hole that has to be filled. As if I hadn't had a childhood, only a story about it, about what happened, or perhaps didn't happen.
> They were good story-tellers, Mother most of all with her talent for making pictures of everything. (17)

A vital source for Anna to retrieve her matrilineage derives mainly from her mother's storytelling. But to dig out more truth about her matrilineage requires Anna's physical launching into researches and writings on which she will soon embark. This retrieval of matrilineage begins first with the grandmother as already foreshadowed in the inadvertent discovery of the grandmother's photograph.

As a consequence, the grandmother's photograph reappears when Anna deliberately takes it out and studies it for a long time in an attempt to seek their resemblances:

> Then she took out the photograph of her grandmother and gazed at it for a long time. Hanna Broman. Who were you? I knew you, oddly enough, almost entirely from hearsay. You were a legend, magnificent and questionable. So amazingly strong, Mother said.
> I must have memories of my own. You lived until I was an adult, had married and produced children. But the photograph bears no resemblance to how I remember you. That's understandable. The photo was taken when you were young, a woman in her prime. I saw you only as old, a stranger, tremendously large, enveloped in huge pleated black dresses. (21)

Lacking frequent physical contact with her grandmother, Anna's impression of Hanna originates mostly from "hearsay" or from her mother's account (21). Yet, looking at a photograph of the grandmother in her youth enables Anna to perceive Hanna beyond her maternal function. Rather than seeing her grandmother as an "old," strange, and giant crone, Anna is now viewing Hanna in a different time and context (21). While observing her grandmother's photograph, Anna also recalls the talks happening several times between her grandmother and mother when the grandmother comes to visit them in the mornings while Anna is still young and the usual Sunday dinner they have with the grandmother (22). The Sunday dinner she remembers the most is when her grandmother comments on the fall of a common woman's fate on "gifted" and brilliant Anna (23). Feeling repulsed by her grandmother's discouraging remark, Anna thinks in a resentful way that "You were wrong, you old witch, . . . I went on at school, I took exams, I was successful and moved in worlds you couldn't even dream of" (24).

Despite Anna's emphasis on the education she has received and the privileges she has, as a result, gained from it as a proof of her superiority to her immediate female ancestor, she still ironically comes to recognize her grandmother on the basis of their fate as women:

> Superior I became, too, just as you said, as everyone said. And as far as you're concerned, you became a fossil, a primitive leftover from a vanished time. I excluded you from my life. You were a painful reminder of origins I was ashamed of. That's why I never got to know you and have no memory of you. But it's also why your photograph speaks so strongly to me. For it says quite clearly that you were a gifted girl, too. Your prejudices were different from mine, that's true. But you were right sometimes, especially when you said that I wouldn't get away, either. For me, too, a woman's life awaited me. (24)

Anna's resentment against her shameful grandmother who represents the past and their family history reminds us of what Steph Lawler has depicted as the female family romance as revealed in several middle-class daughters' ambivalence toward their working-class mothers.[4] Yet, Anna realizes that her sense of hostility inhibits her full understanding of her grandmother. It is through recognition of her ambivalence toward her grandmother that she acknowledges the commonality between grandmother and granddaughter. Athough Anna does not express a similar feeling of displeasure with her mother, the grandmother-granddaughter ambivalence resonates with the one often occurring between mother and daughter. This ambivalence shown by Anna also reflects what Nan Bauer Maglin has said about matrilineal literature. On the one hand, Anna senses her humiliation and contempt for her grandmother's inferiority. On the other hand, she eventually realizes her need to assert "that her voice is not entirely her own."[5]

The real investigation into her matrilineage and the writing of her genogram begins when Anna actually assigns two separate books with different colors to Johanna and Hanna. Apart from "a few scattered, disconnected notes" on the first page, the remaining parts of Johanna's blue book are filled with "unwritten whiteness" while Hanna's gray book is "stuffed with loose notes, letters, newspaper cuttings" (133). Later, Anna launches into a search for her matrilineage when she is looking for her grandmother's existence in "parish" records, "libraries and second-hand bookshops" (133). To some extent, Anna's quest for matrilineage is also her writing journey to the motherland that has not been inscribed in any form of social and political narratives. While reading her grandmother's stories from these secondary sources, Anna starts weeping for her grandmother, especially when it comes to the rape of Hanna. By making a comparison between their different situations in life, Anna is displaying her intersubjective attunement with her grandmother, an important feature involved in the practice of writing a genogram as demonstrated already in Howe's use of this clinical tool.[6] Further, while reading through their family correspondences, Anna starts speculating on other family mysteries such as the father of Hanna's illegitimate child, Anna's uncle Ragnar, who is conceived through the rape of Hanna (134–6). Notably, Anna's pondering over the truth about her family history and past is set after the whole narration on Hanna by which the reader already knows the answers to Anna's enquiries. Instead of initiating the granddaughter's doubts and enquiries prior to unraveling the naked truth about her female genealogy, Fredriksson reverses the common process of retrieving the (grand)mother's subjectivity and hence produces an effect of prioritizing maternal subjectivity.

In the interlude, Anna's writing intention becomes more apparent when she discusses her gray book on Hanna with her husband, Rickard. Significantly, the appearance of her third book in red on Anna constructs a trichotomy of grandmother, mother, and daughter. Yet, the words written on the fly-leaf by Anna "on guilt and gratitude, and on having daughters" indicates Anna's double and even triple identity as being grandmother, mother, and daughter herself (161). Her three books on matrilineal narratives are meant to be, as we realize later, passed on to her daughters and granddaughters. In the last chapter of the interlude before the next section on a life narrative about Johanna, Anna delves into her mother's subjectivity again as the mother is lying in her sickbed in a hospital. Echoing the process of beginning to understand her grandmother, Anna also discovers that her mother has become, somehow, unknown to her:

> It's more difficult to get a picture of you and your life. That's because you're so close to me and I can't see you. It's probably true that we least understand those we love most.
> I've realized you were a secretive person. So I thought you ought to be allowed to speak for yourself. You're a good story-teller, Mother. (166–7)

For Anna, the unknowability of the mother is not by virtue of the mother's death or absence; it is, ironically, their closeness that blinds Anna to seeing her mother in her different roles. Elevating her mother as "a good story-teller," Anna aims at retrieving her mother's subjectivity by giving her mother a voice of her own (167). Yet, in an attempt to relocate her mother's voice, she needs patience to "find the right key" (167).

Anna's way to find her mother's voice is to tune in her maternal voice with that of her mother. In addressing a letter to her mother who is incapable of reading it at the moment because of her illness, Anna refers to the generational differences between her and her mother compounded by the education from which Anna has gained a privileged position. Yet, telling stories from her motherline, especially the stories concerning mothering and child rearing, Anna finds an inevitable interconnection with her mother and the strength her motherline has given her in forming and sustaining her sense of self-worth and self-reliance. For instance, the following two excerpts exemplify the identification between mother (Johanna) and daughter (Anna):

> For a while, I thought I had taken away your power with my education. But when I became a mother, you recaptured your place. Do you remember when Maria was crying with hunger in her cradle? It was awful, but I had learned, from a book, of course, that infants should be fed at definite times. And you said, "But Anna dear . . . ." (272)
>
> I don't hesitate for one moment to say you're a better person than me, much better. But I am stronger. I have none the less not been bowed into total dependence. Of course, that's due to the spirit of the day, education, and I can support myself and the children. But also because I acquired my strength from a mother, not a father. (273)

After the death of Anna's father, Anna moves back to her parents' house, finishing writing her book and reviving her mother's garden until Anna and her husband manage to sell the house after her mother's death. After clearing and cleaning the whole house and passing on the keys to their good family friends Ingeborg and Rune, who are the purchasers of the house, Anna has literally finished her journey home and will embark on another journey back to her new home with her husband whose ambivalent relationship with Anna is resolved at the end. After having dinner with her husband and two daughters, Anna takes the initiative in narrating a story to entertain everyone. It is a fairy tale based on stories from her motherline, those from her mother and grandmother. In passing on this story to her female descendants, Anna also discloses her family tradition of passing on the jewelry from mother to daughter. To her daughters' astonishment, Anna instructs them to unearth the jewelry hidden inside the stone wall in the basement of Anna's parents' house. While distributing the remaining two keys to the safe in the basement to her two daughters, Anna completes her course of retrieving her matrilineage and then passing it on to her daughters. As if to move forward, Anna's final word is to thank Ingeborg for her invitation for their visit home again in the future, but deep inside Anna has made up her mind not to come back again as her grandmother, Hanna, has already done when she left the house years earlier (295–9).

As is common to most matrilineal narratives, Fredriksson's *Hanna's Daughters* demonstrates various important characteristics of the construction of a matrilineal narrative. These defining features are usually set in a framework of either first- or third-person narratives of female ancestors' lives, juxtaposed by a (grand)daughter's endeavor to search for her matrilineage and then write it down. For a (grand)daughterly researcher and writer, accomplishing her matrilineal task is often by means of discovering her female ancestors' photographs, thus enabling her to see them in a different time and context. This intersubjective attunement with her female ancestors is exactly what writing a genogram requires. In the process of recovering her matrilineal past, Anna also goes through recognition of her ambivalence toward her matrilineage, in this case, her grandmother. In other words, although enacting her female family romance by resenting her female ancestor who is seen initially as inferior to her, Anna fulfils her matrilineal romance by identifying with her female predecessors through reconciling her matrilineal conflicts and differences. As is typical of most matrilineal narratives with a (grand)daughter as a writing figure and her preoccupation with retrieving maternal subjectivity, *Hanna's Daughters* illustrates the (grand)daughter's efforts to situate the subjectivity of her mother and grandmother, respectively, through dreams, memories, photographs, and writing. In particular, Fredriksson's technique creates the effect of placing maternal subjectivity at the forefront by locating the narration of matrilineal stories prior to the granddaughter's enquiries about her matrilineal past. And the daughter's double and even triple identities as grandmother, mother, and daughter equip her with the best link in her matrilineal chain; as a result, she can pass on her matrilineage to her female descendants.

Notes

1. Marianne Fredriksson, *Hanna's Daughters* (1994), trans. Joan Tate (London: Orion, 1998). Hereafter, page numbers to this volume are cited parenthetically.
2. Adrienne Rich, *Of Woman Born: Motherhood as Experience and Institution* (1976; reprint, London: Virago, 1992), 225. References are to the reprint edition.
3. Virginia Woolf, *A Room of One's Own* (London: Granada, 1929), 73.

4. Steph Lawler, "'I never felt as though I fitted'": Family Romances and the Mother-Daughter Relationship," in *Romances Revisited*, ed. Lynne Pearce and Jackie Stacey (London: Lawrence & Wishart, 1995), 269–74.
5. Nan Bauer Maglin, "Don't Never Forget the Bridge That You Crossed Over On: the Literature of Matrilineage," in *The Lost Tradition: Mothers and Daughters in Literature*, ed. Cathy N. Davidson and E. M. Broner (New York: Frederick Ungar, 1980), 258.
6. Karen G. Howe, "Daughters Discover Their Mothers through Biographies and Genograms: Educational and Clinical Parallels," in *Motherhood: A Feminist Perspective*, ed. Jane Rice Knowles and Ellen Cole (New York: Haworth Press, 1990), 31–40.

Chapter 5

Jung Chang's *Wild Swans*

As the subtitle of *Wild Swans, Three Daughters of China*,[1] suggests, Jung Chang sets the stories of three generations of women, those of her grandmother, mother, and herself, against the background of a political maelstrom—the warlord period, Japanese occupation, nationalist corruption, fanatical communism, and the Cultural Revolution—in recent Chinese history. Spanning the period from 1909 (the year Chang's grandmother was born) to 1978 (when Chang left for England), Chang weaves her *Wild Swans* into a saga of both family and national history. In addition, the name *wild swans* implies their female identities as Chang's grandmother, mother, her older sister, and herself all have, as part of their names, the character *hong*, which carries the connotation of *swan* in Chinese. Thus, the title and the outline of the book demonstrate Chang's purpose in constructing her own matrilineal narrative.

Nonetheless, the thought of remembering her family stories and her motherland, China, especially during the aftermath of the horrifying devastation of Mao's Cultural Revolution, has always been a pain to Chang; it is a memory of a trauma she has long wanted to repress and forget. But the situation began to change when Chang's mother visited her in London in 1988, which prompted her to write the book:

> For ten years, I avoided thinking about the China I had left behind. Then in 1988, my mother came to England to visit me. For the first time, she told me the story of her life and that of my grandmother. When she returned to Chengdu, I sat down and let my own memory surge out and the unshed tears flood my mind. I decided to write *Wild Swans*. (506)

The idea of constructing *Wild Swans* with a matrilineal framework is, as Chang states, inspired by her mother's account of their life back in China. Her mother has played a pivotal role in facilitating Chang's writing from the motherline. It is the mother-daughter reunion that provides Chang with a link to her past. By writing *Wild Swans*, she not only recovers her matrilineal story but also retrieves her motherland, China. Even though both stories from patrilineage and matrilineage are narrated in the text, Chang's deliberate casting of her book as matrilineal contributes to a feminist concern with female networking and connections.

The manner in which Chang presents her *Wild Swans*, in particular, resembles the writing of a genogram as used in a therapeutic context, noted previously by Howe. At the time Chang launches the writing of her book, her grandmother has already died. As an intellectual herself and being better educated than her mother and grandmother, Chang definitely has the privilege to write. Although the idea of writing the book is initiated by her mother, Chang has apparently conducted in-depth research into her book, as she indicates in the epilogue that she made a research journey back to China in spring 1989 (507). Yet, her elaborate description of many sequences in great detail concerning the life stories of her grandmother and mother leads one to wonder whether the book also contains her fictionalizing. Although it is rather intriguing to ponder the question of whether *Wild Swans* is purely based on truth or fiction or an amalgam of several contributing factors such as oral history, social and political history, and her own research and fiction, Chang's elaboration on her family's life narratives in both extensive and intensive detail appears to re-present, to a certain degree, the truthfulness of each individual life she is narrating.

One effective means she uses to achieve this effect is by juxtaposing and contextualizing their personal life within the political and historical milieu or upheaval. Casting her matrilineal narrative in both historical and social contexts, she is able to go back to the past when her grandmother and mother are located in different times and places. The lively or near-to-life narration of the incidents happening in the lives of both her grandmother and mother engenders a truthful re-presentation of the subjectivities of her female ancestors. That is, a reader is presented with the most approximate closeness to or encounter with Chang's grandmother and mother back in their times. Although their life stories are written in an objective and third-person narrative, it is Chang's detailed descriptions of them that equip the reader with the subjective experiences of her female ancestors. Fundamentally, Chang's elaborate way of narrating life stories assists in recovering the subjectivities of her female predecessors. One such instance can be found in Chang's riveting but excruciating portrayal of how her grandmother's feet were bound at the age of two:

> My grandmother's feet had been bound when she was two years old. Her mother, who herself had bound feet, first wound a piece of white cloth about twenty feet long around her feet, bending all the toes except the big toe inward and under the sole. Then she placed a large stone on top to crush the arch. My grandmother screamed in agony and begged her to stop. Her mother

had to stick a cloth into her mouth to gag her. My grandmother passed out repeatedly from the pain. (24)

When first reading Chang's uncensored and revealing disclosure of the whole process of binding her grandmother's feet, one can be overwhelmed by a sense of uncanny terror. As is common to women either predating or contemporaneous to the generation of Chang's grandmother, Chang's grandmother's experience of bound feet can be said to be truthful or representative at least in certain significant ways. More notably, the divulgence of her grandmother's extreme agony and helpless pleading with her own mother to stop the binding reveals and brings the grandmother's subjectivity to the surface. Even though the whole episode is not articulated in the first-person narrative of the grandmother, the dramatic effect of the narration exudes the writer's and the reader's intersubjective attunement with the grandmother.

Indeed, a number of things emerge as Chang refers back to her matrilineage. What Chang learns from her grandmother and mother is the perseverance, capacity, and strength they have earned from their enduring suffering throughout their lives. Although constantly succumbing to her fate and circumstance, Chang's grandmother takes a major leap by arranging to flee with Chang's mother from the imprisonment of her concubinage and from the prospect of being manipulated as a slave to General Xue's wife upon the death of General Xue. It is by this outrageous and courageous escape from her demeaning life that Chang's grandmother brings a new life to her daughter and also the generations to come. In an analogous fashion, Chang strives to "take wing" at the end of the book by winning a scholarship to study in the West, commencing her new life after the inhuman ravages of Mao's Cultural Revolution. In retrospect, what Chang has in common with her mother and grandmother are their talent and incredible determination that make them outshine their counterparts. Chang's mother is subject to numerous trials that serve as testament to her unshakeable faith in communism. Chang, apparently following her mother's footsteps, also endures various ordeals of being a Red Guard and then working as a peasant, a barefoot doctor, a steelworker, and an electrician during the Cultural Revolution in China. These three generations of women, or the *wild swans* as named by Chang, outlive their male counterparts because their perseverance and strength allow them to be the ultimate survivors.

Inspired by the notion of progress in Tess Cosslett's reading of Margaret Forster's *Hidden Lives*.[2] I would also like to spotlight that Chang's *Wild Swans* can be interpreted in this respect. Despite the recurrence of a similar pattern and trajectory in the formation of life among these three generations of women, there are also simultaneously a moving forward or a progress in Chang's matrilineal narrative. Being located in their different times and contexts, the life of a daughter repeatedly departs from and revises the life her mother is leading. Chang's grandmother, having her feet bound, being a concubine of a general, and later a proper wife of a doctor yet under insurmountable obstacles and circumstances, cannot possibly lead the life her daughter, Chang's mother, is privileged to own by her own choice and knowledge as an educated and devout communist officer. Chang's mother, however, is trapped in her firm belief in and stout loyalty to Chinese communism and its party so that she, unlike her daughter, Jung Chang, who "take[s] wing" to fly to the West, cannot triumphantly escape from her later wasted and betrayed life under Red China. This means, as the time advances along with the blooming of new generations, a mother's footsteps are followed by her daughter but performed with a deeper and different imprint each time.

Contemplating this narrative of progress in relation to the matrilineal ambivalence as exhibited often in a three-generational triad, there is hardly any overt or explicit display of either resentment or ambivalence between mothers and daughters in Chang's *Wild Swans*. One discernible instance of dissension and conflict between mother and daughter occurs only when Chang's mother deviates from her mother's path of life, when Chang's grandmother wants to subsume her daughter to an arranged marriage, as symptomatic of a woman's life during Chang's grandmother's time. Partly due to Chang's mother's rebellious but independent character and partly because of the introduction of communism and women's equal rights into China during Chang's mother's time, Chang's mother reacts unexpectedly by running away from home and opting into being enrolled in a teacher's college with a guarantee of a prospective teaching profession that can sustain a self-reliant life for Chang's mother but also a wasted and downgrading position with regard to her talent. Although Chang's mother eventually consents to go home more often in response to Chang's grandmother's incessant pleading (83–4), Chang's mother's self-awakening is already indicative of the likely progression of this matrilineal narrative. Yet, the paucity of ambivalence existing between mother and daughter in *Wild Swans*, with the exception of this episode of conflict discussed here, could be mainly the result of the overriding importance of identification and strength between mother and daughter in order to be an ally to each other in their lifelong struggle against the overpowering impact of patriarchal dictates and political and social turmoil and chaos.

In comparison with the delineation of the mother-daughter

relationship—the strong mother-daughter identification in *Wild Swans*—the daughter's ambivalence toward her father becomes more conspicuous. For instance, Chang's father is portrayed, on the one hand, as a man of complete integrity who sticks to his communist belief and principle even at the risk of his life. He is perceived, on the other hand, as a husband and father who will sacrifice his family's needs for the benefit of his communist party. In the early years of her parents' marriage, Chang expresses several times her empathy with her mother's suffering, including her mother's miscarriage, caused by her father's indifference to her mother's needs. During Chang's mother's several unfair trials by the Chinese communist party, Chang's father does not evince any of his sympathy for his wife but instructs her to remain loyal and honest to their party. Once, Chang's father even sends her grandmother back to Jinzhou from where her grandmother is later forced to take a long march across China in order to take good care of Chang's mother who is giving birth to a child. Chang's father's incorruptibility is shown later when Chang's last hope of entering the university relies heavily on her father's assistance but is dashed by her father's unwillingness to help:

> On the hospital grounds we sat on the edge of a low stone bridge to rest. My father looked in torment. Eventually he said, "Would you forgive me? I really find it very difficult to do this." ... For a second I felt a surge of resentment, and wanted to cry out at him that there was no fairer alternative. I wanted to tell him how much I had dreamed of going to the university, and that I deserved it—for my hard work, for my exam results, and because I had been elected. But I knew my father knew all this. And it was he who had given me my thirst for knowledge. Still, he had his principles, and because I loved him I had to accept him as he was, and understand his dilemma of being a moral man living in a land which was a moral void. I held back my tears and said, "Of course." We trudged back home in silence. (456–7)

This passage typifies how Chang's attitude toward her father is mixed together with a feeling of resentment and a sense of filial piety. Chang's ambivalence toward her father is able to be understood and even reconciled by her love for him even though Chang tries hard to appease and surpass her anger and despair. Yet, it is also notable that Chang, who shows less sympathy with her father, is inclined to describe her father as a tragic hero in her book and as a figure whose character inexorably leads to his downfall in the end. Despite her father's inadequacy in fulfilling his daughter's need, Chang still enters the university thanks to her mother's resourcefulness (457).

Chang's ambivalence and resentment toward her father, as divulged in the process of writing her father's relationship with her mother and grandmother, heighten and give prominence to the importance of the mother-daughter bond in their three-generational triad of grandmother, mother, and daughter. The persistence of a sense of strong female networking and cohesion between mother and daughter or between female relations can be found in several instances in the text. One such remarkable example happens in the incident of Chang's grandmother's death. After her grandmother dies, Chang shoulders a major responsibility by blaming herself for not taking good care of her grandmother while she is terribly ill. As a kind of self-punishment, she even takes her vow of not establishing any relationship with boys in the future:

> I blamed myself for not looking after my grandmother as well as I might have. She was in the hospital at the time when I had come to know Bing and Wen. My friendships with them had cushioned and insulated me, and had blunted my awareness of her suffering. I told myself it was despicable to have had any happy feelings at all, by the side of what I now realized was my grandmother's deathbed. I resolved never to have a boyfriend again. Only by self-denial, I thought, could I expiate some of my guilt. (409)

Chang perceives her ultimate separation from her grandmother as though it were an enactment of the Demeter-Persephone separation by male intrusion. For Chang, compensating for the loss of her grandmother means a separation from men. This strong grandmother-granddaughter bond between Chang and her grandmother can be seen in their interactions with each other. Chang's grandmother has always been both physically and emotionally present in their family. While Chang's mother is forced to separate from her children because of the infliction of several political trials on her, Chang's grandmother is there to function as a substitute or surrogate mother. In addition, Chang's filial piety to her grandmother reflects what Hope Edelman has said about the reliving and reproducing of the mother-daughter relation in a grandmother-granddaughter relationship if there is a close and connected relationship between grandmother and granddaughter.[3] Chang's remorse in reaction to her grandmother's death is a result of what she has cultivated from her mother's loving and devoted relationship with her grandmother. Thus, by implementing the act of repenting and writing in response to her grandmother's death, Chang is able to reestablish her maternal connection in her mother's absence.

Another episode that delineates the mother-daughter struggle between separation and connection, although it is enacted by the outside force of social and political disruption, happens when Chang goes to visit her mother in the camp after their long separation. After staying with her mother for ten days and heading for her next destination to her father's camp, Chang and her mother experience an anguished separation. While both of them are waiting for the truck to pick Chang up to take her to her father's camp, Chang's mother, who wants to give her daughter a taste of the New Year's breakfast, runs back to her camp to fetch a bowl of round dumplings, *tang-yuan*. Unfortunately, her mother does not manage to arrive earlier than the truck. When Chang is anxiously waiting for her mother's arrival, she is astonished to see her mother carrying the bowl, striving to maintain her balance in fear of spilling the soup out of the bowl while approaching Chang at a steady speed from a distance. As Chang knows the truck will not wait any longer, she gets on the truck without waiting for her mother to arrive. The bowl Chang's mother is holding then falls to the ground when she sees that the truck will soon be taking her daughter away. Yet, Chang's mother continues walking to the spot where they previously have been waiting for the truck in order to make sure Chang has left safely. Chang rehearses hearing her mother narrate the story thus:

> Years later, she told me the bowl had fallen from her hand when she saw me climbing onto the truck. But she still ran to the spot where we had been sitting, just to make sure I had really gone, although it could not have been anyone else getting onto the truck. There was not a single person around in that vast yellowness. For the next few days she walked around the camp as though in a trance, feeling blank and lost. (434–5)

Although the physical separation between mother and daughter is inevitable, their emotional connection cannot be severed by outside forces. As round dumplings symbolize family reunion in terms of Chinese culture and tradition, the mother's insistence on running to the spot where she and her daughter have been sitting together even after the bowl of round dumplings she is carrying is gone indicates the mother's longing for the mother-daughter reconnection.

In *Wild Swans*, Chang describes vividly the torments and sufferings her family has all been through until she "take[s] wing" to fly away from her motherland, China, and separates from her family. Nonetheless, as mentioned early in this chapter, her mother's visit, which materializes the mother-daughter reunion in London, enables Chang to see through her past in a new light. Instead of suppressing this painful memory of her family history under the incessant destruction of Mao's sovereignty, Chang begins to recognize that "the past was no longer too painful to recall because I had found love and fulfillment and therefore tranquility" (506). More significant, what Chang has gained from looking back at her matrilineage is the scripting of the mother-daughter connection in resistance to the totalizing estrangement and devastation of family enforced by Chinese patriarchal doctrines and apparatus.

Notes

1. Jung Chang, *Wild Swans: Three Daughters of China* (1991; reprint, New York: Anchor, 1992). Hereafter, page numbers to this volume are cited parenthetically. References are to the reprint edition.
2. Tess Cosslett, "Matrilineal Narratives Revisited," in *Feminism and Autobiography: Texts, Theories, Methods,* ed. Tess Cosslett, Celia Lury, and Penny Summerfield (London and New York: Routledge, 2000), 149–50.
3. Hope Edelman, *Mother of My Mother: The Intricate Bond between Generations* (New York: Dial Press, 1999), 202–15.

Chapter 6
Margaret Forster's *Hidden Lives*

In Margaret Forster's *Hidden Lives*,[1] the main focus of the book is, like other matrilineal narratives discussed in this part, narrating the life stories of the female descent line and connections, including Forster's grandmother, mother, and even her little-known Aunt Alice, her grandmother's illegitimate daughter, whose unrecognized and mysterious existence puzzles and arouses Forster's enormous curiosity to trace her life. In an analogous fashion to *Wild Swans*, Forster positions and politicizes the personal and individual aspect of her family history in association with the social and political milieu and its transformation in Carlisle, UK. Forster's personal account of mainly her female family members gives credit to her choice of the title *Hidden Lives*, as it testifies to the fact that many of these women's lives are hidden and unheard of but unearthed by Forster in her book. Part of Forster's aim is, therefore, to make visible the hidden agenda of gender and class in her family history.

Forster's mode of connecting with her motherline is by means of her use of a maternal voice. Forster's identity as both a daughter and later a mother enables her to speak with a maternal voice. This maternal voice is traced historically and is articulated first through a (grand)daughter's writing of her grandmother's and mother's stories, namely her genogram. However, what I want to make clear here is that Forster's articulation of a maternal voice is more adequate and appropriate only when she becomes a mother. I shall turn to this aspect later when I come to a discussion of Forster's relation to her mother in her later adult life. Apart from reiterating or interpreting what she has gleaned from her family members and friends, as Forster does in her account of her life before the age of five, she deliberately takes the role as a (grand)daughter biographer to fill in the gaps of her grandmother's early life story and the void left by her Aunt Alice's obscurity and to narrate her mother's life story, albeit the first two stories remain unresolved at the end. Early on, Forster's inquiring mind as a historian and biographer is discernible in her preoccupation with uncovering her grandmother's early life from ages two to twenty-six:

> Mothers spent half their time referring to their own childhoods as a point of comparison when bringing up their children, but apparently not a wisp of a memory ever escaped my grandmother's lips. Nothing. A blank. She was a mother who had had no childhood, or a childhood so unhappy that she wiped it out, leaving only an impression that whatever she had suffered was too awful to remember. Her daughters were afraid of what she suppressed without knowing what it was. They were nervous, agitated, even after she was dead, at the thought of what might be uncovered if their mother's past was exhumed.
>
> But I am not. I want to know. I have even come to believe I need to know. (23–4)

As suggested in this passage, the main obstacle facing Forster in writing stories from her motherline is the irrecoverable and inaccessible aspect in terms of giving a full account of her grandmother's and Aunt Alice's lives. This void left unfilled in Forster's matrilineage disrupts and hampers what Lowinsky has conceptualized as the mother-daughter looping: "an associative process by which we pass through our own experience to understand that of another."[2] Yet, as Forster asserts, it is she as the "I" who desires to recuperate the loss of her matrilineage. The recovery of the mother-daughter looping, as it appears in the second half of Forster's autobiography, is activated and effectuated when Forster reaches her later adult life as a mother.

Forster's official affirmation and declaration of her own "I" voice comes only near the middle of the book. She proclaims her individual identity thus:

> So I can stop now, writing in the third person, stop retelling stories I was told about the years before I was born, about when I was under five, stop splicing oral history with local history and start instead letting my own version of family lore come into play. I am there, at the centre. What a difference it makes, how dangerous it is. (133)

As Cosslett notes, the revelation of the "I" voice as a (grand)daughter biographer when Forster states clearly the beginning of her conscious memory at the age of five calls forth an insightful way of representing and relocating the mother's subjectivity, as opposed to Forster's perception of her divulging of the "I" voice as a dangerous proposition. Strikingly, as Cosslett continues to elucidate, it is only with "the appearance of the 'I'" that the mother's "other" and "different" voice and subjectivity begin to emerge.[3] According to Cosslett's interpretation, Forster, on the one hand, deliberately desires "her mother to fit into her narrative of progress," while on the other hand, as Forster's mother advances in age, Forster presents her as one who "refuses to fit the story Forster is composing for her." *Hidden Lives* is predominantly written from a daughter's perspective, but it also deals with the daughter's attempt to articulate a maternal voice. "Looking back from the end," as Cosslett reminds us, the mother-daughter stories in this three-generational triad are so closely connected that the triple voices of grandmother, mother, and daughter are integrated by the (grand)daughter into one, in light of Forster's later discovery of her linkage with "the grandmother's story of unwanted, illegitimate birth" and the mother's story of "education and career" in her adult life.[4] What I would also like to add to Cosslett's explanation is that it is Forster's repositioning of the daughterly "I" voice at the center that entitles her to locate the maternal at the center, in particular when she takes up a motherly position in her older age.

Noticeably, in various sequences of the book, Forster acts out, in part, what feminist psychoanalytic theorist Jane Flax has elucidated as the cause of women's conflicts in this troublesome relationship in her essay "The Conflicts between Nurturance and Autonomy in Mother-Daughter Relationships and within Feminism."[5] In resenting her mother's delight in taking the role as a carer for the others, Forster rebukes her:

> It was another unmistakable sign to me that I wasn't going to be able to emulate my mother. I wasn't fit to do women's work. My mother blossomed in these situations—she was so calm, so gentle, so capable and kind and cheering. But I panicked, I felt faint, I was useless. The tradition of being a carer, with what it implied, would not be carried on by me. I was hardly my mother's daughter at all, although I still prayed to become like her. (186)

Forster's attempted divergence from her mother's life arises because in trying to come to identify with her mother, she cannot resolve to collude with her mother in her submissive and selfless role. Forster's "conflict between nurturance and autonomy," which leads to her final separation from her mother in terms of the transformation of their different roles and social positions, replays Freud's family romances. Employing Freud's concept of family romances in a feminist adoption and appropriation in her sociological studies of the mother-daughter relationship in the working-class context, Lawler envisions "female family romances" as denoting the accounts of the women "who defined themselves as having been brought up in working-class families and as having moved, by dint of education or marriage to a middle-class man, into the middle classes." This female family romance, as Lawler continues to elaborate, occurs in these women's "sense of not 'fitting' with their birth families, and a wish to replace their mothers, either now or in the past, with other women who displayed characteristics which they valued highly."[6] To this end, Forster paves the way by working hard to enter the university where she is able to separate from her mother's working-class life by gaining her autonomy through receiving higher education. However, rather than replacing her mother with a superior one, Forster enacts her female family romance by having her own family and accomplishing a number of tasks that her mother is not able to do: "I was determined to show my mother that marriage was not the end of ambition, that it in no way need impede my progress, that I still intended to have a very different life from hers and her mother's" (253).

Indeed, the daughter's sense of separation from the mother, which as Cosslett points out is related to class,[7] leads to a more complicated and perplexed tackling of the so-called matrilineal ambivalence, noted extensively elsewhere in this book in relation to my reading of other matrilineal narratives. The paradoxical aspect of the articulation of a maternal voice in Forster's *Hidden Lives* is, in my opinion, linked with an unavoidable occurrence of matrilineal ambivalence in most matrilineal narratives. The daughter's sense of separation from the mother in *Hidden Lives* is intensified by Forster's constant resentment against her mother's compromising life as a wife and a mother, a recurring expression of matrilineal ambivalence a reader is invited to revisit throughout Forster's narrative. This matrilineal ambivalence is revealed in one of the sentences quoted earlier from Forster: "I was hardly my mother's daughter at all, although I still prayed to become like her" (186). Despite feeling delighted at spending time with her Aunt Nan (Forster's mother's sister) in her glamorous and much envied life compared to that her mother has had, Forster displays to Nan's bewilderment her preference for going home and enjoying being nurtured by her mother who has shown herself to be more motherly than has her Aunt Nan. Thus, Forster's ambivalence toward her mother corresponds to what Flax has termed, as we have seen, "the conflict between nurturance and autonomy" in a mother-daughter relationship.

Significantly, Forster reconnects herself to her mother when she has her second child and attempts again to make a balance between her life as a mother and a writer:

> When my mother returned to Carlisle after Jake's birth she said, "You'll have your hands full now, you won't be able to keep up that writing." Almost true. Family first, writing a very poor second. This time, when winter came, there was little respite from sleepless nights and the old trick of sitting down to write exhausted and getting up refreshed didn't work. How could I be as tired as my mother had been when she had young children, yet my life was so easy? . . . It was ridiculous to feel so drained and I reminded myself over and over of my mother's much harder life at the stage I was now until it became like a horror show. (267)

Being an adult daughter and a mother herself enables Forster to exercise what Lowinsky has said about the mother-daughter looping in her reconception of her mother's story.[8] Although Forster fights hard to prove that her life outshines and supersedes that of her mother, she still comes to a recognition of herself fitting into a life that belongs to almost every woman like her mother: "I enjoyed the routine housework everyone else seemed to find tedious" (268). Strikingly, this reconciling moment of recognition and identification between mother and daughter occurs when Forster confesses this after her mother's death:

> After the funeral I began the attempt to inquire into my grandmother's past which began this book, wanting not just to satisfy my own curiosity but believing that what I said was true—I can't understand my own history unless I understand my grandmother's, my mother's, and that of the women like them, the ordinary working-class women from whom I come. The mission is only half accomplished. (304)

Irrespective of all the gaps and differences between generations of women, the sense of a motherline cannot be disrupted and discontinued. Because without it, women will have no sense of themselves, their history and their past. By connecting her motherline vertically, Forster also builds a sisterline, expanding horizontally into other women and other female connections. Forster situates her story or herstory in relation to her matrilineage whose significance also lies in an inevitable connection with others who are also "the ordinary working-class women" like her female ancestors in Carlisle.

Chang in *Wild Swans* and Forster in *Hidden Lives* share certain commonalities of adhering to auto/biographical truth in writing and politicizing their own personal matrilineal narratives. In the case of Forster, she even chooses not to fictionalize the parts of hidden lives that she as a historian and biographer cannot uncover regarding her grandmother's early life and her Aunt Alice's mysterious existence. While both Chang and Forster construct their matrilineal narratives in a conventional chronological order, or as Cosslett describes that there is "a diachronic, vertical axis of descent, leading back into the past and forward into the future," a sense of connection among three generations of women in their texts is filtered through their share of "a common femaleness" which unite them "onto a synchronic, horizontal plane."[9] Their share of "a common femaleness" is what ties them together in spite of their differences widened by their different ages, classes, and experiences. There is also both recovery and progress in the two texts. One of the discernable differences between them is that there are elaborations of female family romances in Forster's novel, whereas in Chang's they are hardly visible. This difference could be the result of the different social, cultural, and racial backgrounds against which the two texts are set. And these variables in terms of social class, culture, and race can also lead one to think whether the discourse of female family romances belongs to a white, Western context. Although the two writers aim at speaking for their female ancestors in their writing of genograms, the daughter's attempt to retrieve the mother's subjectivity is artistically experimented on in Forster's text in which the disclosure of her "I" voice allows her mother's "other" and "different" voice to exist and not to fit into the life she wants her mother's to be in the later part of *Hidden Lives*.[10]

Notes

1. Margaret Forster, *Hidden Lives: A Family Memoir* (1995; reprint, London: Penguin, 1996). Hereafter, page numbers to this volume are cited parenthetically. References are to the reprint edition.
2. Noami Ruth Lowinsky, *Stories from the Motherline: Reclaiming the Mother-Daughter Bond, Finding Our Feminine Souls* (Los Angeles: Jeremy P. Tarcher, 1992), 21–2.
3. Tess Cosslett, "Matrilineal Narratives Revisited," in *Feminism and Autobiography: Texts, Theories, Methods*, ed. Tess Cosslett, Celia Lury, and Penny Summerfield (London and New York: Routledge, 2000), 149.
4. Ibid., 150.
5. Jane Flax, "The Conflict between Nurturance and Autonomy in Mother-Daughter Relationships and within Feminism," *Feminist Studies* 4, no. 2 (June 1978): 171–89. See also my analysis of Flax's argument in chapter 2.
6. Steph Lawler, "'I never felt as though I fitted': Family Romances and the Mother-Daughter Relationship," in *Romances Revisited*, ed. Lynne Pearce and Jackie Stacey (London: Lawrence & Wishart, 1995), 269.
7. Cosslett, "Matrilineal Narratives Revisited," 148.
8. Lowinsky, *Stories from the Motherline*, 21–2.
9. Cosslett, "Feminism, Matrilinealism, and the 'House of the Women' in Contemporary Women's Writing," *Journal of Gender Studies* 5, no. 1 (1996): 8.
10. Cosslett, "Matrilineal Narratives Revisited," 149–50.

Chapter 7
Margaret Drabble's *The Peppered Moth*

Margaret Drabble's *The Peppered Moth*,[1] one of the recently published novels with matrilineal narratives, is imbued with a more pervasively scientific enquiry into the matrilineal descent line than the other works discussed in this part. Early in the prologue of her book, Drabble sets the scene for this scientific investigation. Sixty people assemble "in the hall of a Wesleyan Methodist chapel in South Yorkshire" to listen to an innovative lecture on the subject of "mitochondrial DNA and matrilineal descent" given by a prominent microbiologist named Dr. Robert Hawthorn (2). Dr. Hawthorn's speech is supposed to be cutting-edge because the time is situated in our present electronic, digital age at the turn of the century, the millennium. The importance of Dr. Hawthorn's scientific research is closely tied to the discovery of the Cotterhall Man, also named after its discoverer, Steve Nieman, as Steve the Skeleton, who is accidentally found by Steve in a cave hidden in Cotterhall. The local people who are permanent residents in Cotterhall are the Cutworths, the Bawtrys, and the Barrons. Among their descendents who lend their inquisitive ears to Dr. Hawthorn's presentation are a "stout old woman" and "a beautiful young woman" who accompanies the old lady (1–3). These two women are later known as Dora Bawtry, who has remained single and lived in Breaseborough all her life, and her great-niece Faro Gaulden, who lives in London and works as a journalist for a scientific magazine. Gaulden comes to attend Dr. Hawthorn's talk in the hope of finding her ancestors and agrees like many others to let Dr. Hawthorn take a swab from her body in order to obtain an accurate scientific proof of whether the Cotterhall Man is indeed her ancestor from millennia earlier.

In an interview published by *The Guardian* on December 16, 2000, one month before the publisher's release of her latest novel, *The Peppered Moth*, Drabble told the interviewer, Suzie Mackenzie, about her real-life experience of meeting Professor Sykes of Oxford University, who has devoted himself to searching for the last Neanderthal link and has taken Drabble's DNA to be examined to see whether its result would yield any biological connection. As Mackenzie explains in her article, "mitochondrial DNA," a woman-specific genetic substance, "stands for the transmission of female behavioral patterns from one generation to the next." Although Drabble herself dismisses the importance of this scientific and medical terminology as "only a metaphor" in her book, what Mackenzie has conveyed in her explanation links significantly this rather ponderous and jargon-laden "scientific entity" with matrilineage.[2] With this accentuation of matrilineage in its undeniable connection with biological and scientific evidence, the "mitochondrial DNA," the fatherline in the novel is, as a consequence, sidelined.

The Peppered Moth, as admitted by Drabble in the afterword, is a semi-auto/biographical novel based on her mother's life. Drabble's evocation of her mother in this novel suggests, however, a difficult mother-daughter relationship. Urged by her friends to write about her mother's life after her mother's death, Drabble is confronted with immense difficulties in locating her mother: "*She was a highly intelligent, angry, deeply disappointed and manipulative woman. I am not sure if I have been able to find a tone in which to create or describe her*" (390, emphasis original). For Drabble, to write about her mother becomes, in the first place, inaccessible and impossible. Therefore, contrary to the way Forster has composed her matrilineal narrative *Hidden Lives*, Drabble chooses to fictionalize rather than writing "*a factual memoir of*" her mother's life (390, emphasis original). Although constructing a happy ending for her heroine, Faro, in retrieving her matrilineage, Drabble still exhibits in varying degrees her unremitting anxiety about her mother and their relationship. It is only by fictionalizing that a happy matrilineal romance can be created is the connection forged and the heroine, Faro, can sing her happy song. As Drabble convincingly professes in the interview with Mackenzie, she strives to "reclaim her mother" by revisiting her mother's past and writing a genogram so "that some emotional blockage would be released" and more love between mother and daughter found.[3]

In the opening paragraphs of her article about interviewing Drabble, Mackenzie recollects graphically her repulsion at the age of fourteen, when, in 1968, her school invited Drabble to lecture them on the writer's life as a successful woman, whom Drabble back then represented: "the Newnham scholarship girl with her starred first in English Lit, her husband, her three babies and her books."[4] Extending her unpalatable feeling for Drabble to that for her schoolteachers, Mackenzie evinces the sense of resentment and fear exhibited in a metaphorical mother-daughter relationship between women of older and younger generations, namely between mentors and disciples.[5] In retrospect, Mackenzie is also amazed by their disdain and disrespect back then for the ridiculous resentment and fear their mentors displayed toward them as young girls of promising future and unlimited opportunity who reminded their senior counterparts of what they could not possibly achieve in their lives. Yet, twenty-seven years after the first encounter with Drabble, in 1995 when Mackenzie conducted her interview, Drabble's disclosure to Mackenzie of her failed suicide attempt, a coincidence occurring in both their lives, propels Mackenzie to see Drabble in a different light.[6] Mackenzie's accounts of these anecdotes open an avenue for delving into Drabble's latest novel, *The Peppered Moth*, and the agonized and unresolved mother-daughter relationship the novel is intended to unfold.

In Drabble's *The Peppered Moth*, intermeshing with the modern scientific mania for molecular biology and archeological excavations of prehistory and the ancient are the intertwining lives of three generations of women: Bessie, Chrissie, and Faro. The inextricably interconnected lives of Bessie, Chrissie, and Faro can be observed in their link with the scientific intervention that is set against their life stories. In terms of the narrative structure of *The Peppered Moth*, one important feature of this matrilineal narrative is a sustained relation between women moving back and forth through different times and spaces. This shuttling or traversing between different narrations mirrors a recurring pattern in most matrilineal narratives. Significantly, the relation between the scientific background of archeological retrieval and modern technological progression sets the perfect scene for creating an intricate tension between recovery and progress in *The Peppered Moth*. This tension has its manifestation in the life pattern of the three-generational triad of Bessie, Chrissie, and Faro. That is to say, both Bessie and Chrissie desire to escape from their mothers' lives as a kind of progress, yet paradoxically they cannot find themselves totally detached from their matrilineage; Faro, as the (grand)daughter who represents "an unknown potentiality,"[7] accomplishes recovery by undertaking a root-seeking journey back to the site of her matrilineage and helps resolve the matrilineal ambivalence happening between her grandmother and mother. The tension between recovery and progress heightens, to its full extent, some daughters' matrophobia in their attempts to break away from their matrilineages: "Do we become our mothers? And, if not, how do we break the pattern and escape?"[8] In what follows, I will demonstrate how the triad of grandmother (Bessie), mother (Chrissie), and daughter (Faro) is employed by Drabble to illustrate the tension between recovery and progress in her book.

After contextualizing an up-to-date scientific quest for retrieving matrilineage in the prologue, the novel then traces back to the late 1910s when Faro's grandmother, Bessie, lives in Breaseborough,

Hammervale, South Yorkshire. Already, the advent of progress permeates the narrative:

> The Bawtrys had stuck in Hammervale for millennia, mother and daughter, through the long mitochondrial matriarchy. Already Bessie sensed this, and already she feared it. She sensed inertia in the Bawtry marrowbone. Others had shouldered their packs, taken to the road, fled with dark strangers, enlisted, crossed the seas, crossed their bloodlines, died foreign deaths, spawned foreign broods. The Bawtrys had stuck here through the ages. Cautious and slow, they had not even crossed the grimy brook. And how should she, a puny sickly child, find the strength to loosen the grip of this hard land, these programmed cells? Yet already she knew that, whatever the cost, she must escape or die. (6)

The age-old habitation of the Bawtrys in Hammervale apparently turns static for Bessie. Instead of a progressive evolution, Bessie is apprehensive about the imminence of stasis. Although Bessie is wary of her feeble and unhealthy state, which could precipitate her inescapable fate just as her ancestors were grounded in Breaseborough forever, she still strives to escape and to progress from her little dull mining town.

For Bessie, there are two ways to accomplish such a progress. One is through education. The other is by means of migration. Bessie is recognized as an extraordinarily gifted child during her schooling by her outstanding teacher, Miss Head, her parents, peers, and local people. She is aware of her superiority and her likely progression from her ancestors and counterparts in Breaseborough, from which she does move on to study in Cambridge eventually. Bessie later marries her school friend Joe Barron, although she thinks to her surprise that she should have married someone outside her hometown. As both Bessie and Joe Barron wish to leave their hometown, Breaseborough, they migrate from there to Northam, Pennington, Holderfield, and Surrey, symbolizing the mobility and complexity of a progress narrative. Despite this narrative of ongoing journey, migration, and progress, a reversed usage of mutation by Drabble exerts its impact on Bessie. In others words, although being highly regarded as one of the "chosen few" who is meant for progressive evolution, Bessie is ironically vulnerable to occasional attacks by illness both physically and mentally: influenza, fever, endogenous depression, and agoraphobia. Her thriving and progressive state begins to decline in the middle of her second year in Cambridge. She no longer "thrive[s] and prosper[s]" as she used to (115–22), and her mutation, although it should be seen as progressive in evolutionary terms, paradoxically leads her to a downfall when her serious mental illness in her later adult life brings disastrous effects on her husband and children (170–3, 193–4). In short, the effect of mutation on Bessie should have made her progress further from her life rather than letting her degenerate. Conversely, the deterioration of her health condition later deprives her of her maternal function and agency and also causes difficulty in her relation to her daughter.

Growing up in the 1950s, Chrissie endeavors, in an analogous fashion to Bessie, to escape from her mother's life by first acting as a rebellious teenager, befriending and hanging out with "frightful frivolous lads"(213) without letting her parents know. When following her mother's footsteps to study archaeology in Cambridge, which gives Chrissie the prospect of a promising future, Chrissie, on the contrary, has her own plan:

> Chrissie thought she was breaking the pattern by refusing to study matrilineal English Literature or patrilineal Law. She knew that there must be some more decisive, some more dramatic way of expressing herself, but she couldn't yet work out what it was. She could always try to get herself pregnant, by losing her virginity either to one of the Farnleigh sixth formers or to Mr. Stuart (Latin and Greek), who seemed willing. But a step like that would create a lot more new problems, for which she wasn't yet ready. Though, if the worse came to the worst, pregnancy would answer. It remained an option. (213)

As an intended progress, Chrissie means to "break the pattern and escape." Yet, her future fate of marrying because of an unintended pregnancy makes her "repeat" and "get things wrong."[9] Chrissie reproduces her mother's unsatisfying life as a wife and a mother, an ironic result of her original escape scheme toward liberation and progress. When all things go wrong and Chrissie suffers tremendously from her first husband's infidelity, Chrissie does not and cannot escape but becomes like her mother, being trapped in an unhappy state of marriage. Rather than marching into progress, Chrissie plunges herself into repeating her mother's life. In addition, her second marriage with an archaeologist, although they apparently have a happy marriage, ironically brings Chrissie again back to the first track she has chosen in an attempt to escape.

But does Faro the granddaughter "break the pattern and escape?"[10] Drabble does not give us a full account of Faro's life except Faro's preoccupation with the scientific discovery of her ancestral matrilineage, motivated both by her occupational and personal needs and interests. Referring back to a series of questions raised by Drabble at the end of the prologue: "Is she [Faro] one who got away? Is she a freak, or is she the future?"(3), the enquiry about whether the Cotterhall Man's descendants will become extinct remains uncertain. What seems to be worrying is that "If Faro does not have a daughter, her mitochondrial DNA will perish with her and the chain will be broken. It is already getting late in the biological day. She is in her thirties, and the hours hasten" (327). Faro is later put into a dilemma of choosing between two men, Sebastian, whose idiosyncrasy and obsession with Faro intimidates and appalls her, and Steve Nieman, whose irresistible charm and sincerity spark Faro's passion for him. This dilemma is resolved in her final decision to leave Sebastian, implying Faro's avoidance of following her female ancestors' footsteps by choosing the wrong man. Notably, Faro's romance with Steve, who discovers the skeleton of her suspected ancestor and is also part of Faro's incentive to visit her matrilineal site, serves as an enhancement to materalize and consolidate her inevitable connection with her matrilineage and ancestry in Breaseborough. When the DNA result is finally announced, and Faro is confirmed to be a direct descendant of the Cotterhall Man, Faro's matrilineage becomes emblematic of the kind of peppered moth that can "adapt to a changing environment and survive."[11]

When, toward the end of the novel, Faro goes back to Breaseborough on behalf of her mother to visit her Aunt Dora, who is sent to the hospital because of a stroke, Faro goes to her aunt's house on her aunt's request to fetch things for her. In it, she discovers hidden treasures of her matrilineage: one of her aunt's books called *Faro's Daughter* written by Georgette Heyer, Aunt Dora's golden bracelet, her great-grandfather's silver watch, her great-grandmother's engagement ring, and, most notably, a wedding photograph of her grandmother, Bessie, with her Aunt Dora. As Faro looks more closely at the photograph, she discovers something alluring and intriguing:

> She examines it through the magnifying glass, and it seems that through the curve of the thick plastic lens, round the receding edges of the image, she begins to see movement. It is as though the frozen moment lives again. Somebody is standing behind Bessie and Dora Bawtry, in the shadows. Who is it? Will this person come out of the shadows? Who is there, with these young women? Is it their redeemer? (388–9)

Is it purely Faro's hallucination or is there really someone hidden behind her grandmother and great-aunt in the shadows? We do not know. Yet, what we do know is that it could be, metaphorically speaking, Faro who is hidden behind her female ancestors in the shadows. Seeing the photograph "through the magnifying glass" signifies Faro's participation in the scientific project of retrieving her mitochondrial DNA through which her matrilineage becomes alive and their lives begin to move again in Faro. Faro is undoubtedly a redeemer. Her accidental discovery of a silver sixpence lying on the stairs on her way down reminds her of the Christmas pudding her grandmother, Bessie Barron, provided for them in their last family gathering at Christmas. This family event is recalled by Faro as a happy memory in contrast to the often tense and agitated relationship between her grandmother and mother:

> Faro stands stock-still on the seventh step, for she can see Grandma's happy face, smiling, as Faro cries out and unwraps the silver treasure. Grandma Barron had always made a good Christmas pudding. Faro had always enjoyed the Surrey Christmas. She felt safe there, in that large, bright, clean house. Like a proper child. (389)

Faro's enchanting recollection of her happy moment with her grandmother, as this excerpt shows, helps redeem and restore the mother-daughter relationship between her grandmother and mother. This resolution of matrilineal ambivalence in a grandmother-granddaughter relationship mirrors Edelman's study discussed previously.[12] It also reflects Drabble's narration in the interview: "It strikes me that it's no coincidence that the novel spans three generations. You need this for some kind of understanding. The set-up, the tension and the forgiveness."[13]

So what does mitochondrial DNA—a signifier for "the transmission of female behavioral patterns from one generation to the next," as Mackenzie aptly defines it[14]—mean for Bessie, Chrissie, and Faro? It means not only an affirmation of their biological connection and closeness. It means also, in a more meaningful context, the recycling of their common "female behavioral patterns" in their grandmother-mother-daughter triad, rescued and redeemed by Faro the (grand) daughter's recovery project, which breaks the spell of their generational repeating and suggests likely progress. To a certain extent, however, Drabble presents her *Peppered Moth* as an antiromance in which a difficult mother-daughter relationship between grandmother (Bessie) and mother (Chrissie) cannot be seen as being fully resolved. It is only when Drabble confesses during her talk with Mackenzie that she begins to assert her identification with her mother:

> My mother was my mother, and I am undeniably a product of my mother. I would have liked my mother to have been happy. But whatever she was, she was my mother and there is no other mother I could have had. So I don't deserve a better mother. I feel intimately and closely connected to that woman who was my mother.[15]

Alluding to the biological premise of mitochondrial DNA, Drabble's construction of a matrilineal romance rescripts both Freud's family romances and Lawler's female family romances by confessing that she does not "deserve a better mother." In so doing, Drabble retains her mother's subjectivity as she accepts "whatever she was" rather than transforming her mother into a better person.

There is a strong sense of biological determinism in Drabble's use of mitochondrial DNA as a metaphor in her book. Although each of the three generations of women in *The Peppered Moth*, consciously or unconsciously, tries to escape and break away from their mother and ancestry in order to make progress in their life, they are still subject to repeat or reproduce their mother's life, which binds them inevitably to their matrilineal past. Although the culmination of the book is the (grand)daughter's recovery of her matrilineage, especially focusing on the reclamation of the grandmother, the mother-daughter relationship as presented in the grandmother-mother dyad is still contaminated by matrophobia and their difficult relationship is never totally resolved by means of mutual understanding and recognition. Indisputably, Drabble's construction of a matrilineal narrative as "negative" and "matrophobic" is, in Cosslett's words, "often also present as a possibility."[16] Yet, Drabble's *The Peppered Moth* cannot be strictly seen as a matrilineal romance even though there is a celebratory moment of matrilineal recovery at the end of the novel. The resolution of Drabble's unhappy female family romance only dawns on us when we read her confession in the recent interview conducted by Mackenzie that Drabble does not wish to denigrate or disavow her mother. What Drabble has admitted to in this interview is reconnecting with her mother who has been lost to her because of their difficult relationship and also the daughter's desire to retain her mother's subjectivity.

Notes

1. Margaret Drabble, *The Peppered Moth* (London: Viking, 2000). Hereafter, page numbers to this volume are cited parenthetically.
2. Suzie Mackenzie, "Mothers and Daughters," *Guardian Weekend*, December 16, 2000, 41.
3. Ibid.
4. Ibid., 39.
5. See the discussion with regard to rivalry and ambivalence between generations of women in chapter 1, 22–5.
6. Mackenzie, "Mothers and Daughters," 39–40.
7. Tess Cosslett, "Matrilineal Narratives Revisited," in *Feminism and Autobiography: Texts, Theories, Methods*, ed. Tess Cosslett, Celia Lury, and Penny Summerfield (London and New York: Routledge, 2000), 146.

8. Mackenzie, "Mothers and Daughters," 41.
9. Ibid.
10. Ibid.
11. Ibid.
12. Hope Edelman, *Mother of My Mother: The Intricate Bond between Generations* (New York: Dial Press, 1999), 202–15.
13. Mackenzie, "Mothers and Daughters," 43.
14. Ibid., 41.
15. Ibid., 43.
16. Cosslett, "Feminism, Matrilinealism, and the 'House of the Women' in Contemporary Women's Writing," *Journal of Gender Studies* 5, no. 1 (1996): 8.

Chapter 8
A Poetics of Matrilineal Narratives

In relation to the previous chapters in this part, I would like to conclude by suggesting possible links. In particular, for the purpose of elucidating what a poetics of matrilineal narratives could mean in the context of the grandmother-mother-daughter triad, I will first elaborate on what commonalities and differences can be drawn from my readings of the four matrilineal narratives discussed in this part. Then, I will go on to illustrate the narrative structures of these new feminist family romances by drawing a series of diagrams. Although I have done a separate textual analysis of each of the four matrilineal narratives presented, there are, undeniably, several recurrences of thematics among these texts that are worth mentioning, although these thematic recurrences do not always appear in every text. In what follows, I shall elaborate on a discussion of these themes as explicated in the four previous chapters.

The Assignment of a (Grand)daughter as a Biographer-Researcher and the Use of Storytelling as Inspired by Her (Grand)mother

In Marianne Fredriksson's *Hanna's Daughters*, we have Anna the (grand)daughter, who is also a (grand)mother herself, as a researcher and writer of her matrilineage. She aims to write three books, on Hanna, Johanna, and Anna, which she does finish at the end of the novel. Anna's triple identity as daughter, mother, and grandmother, which establishes a maternal paradigm that preserves matrilineage, well equips her with agency and authority as the ultimate storyteller to pass on her version of matrilineage to her female descendants. In both *Wild Swans* and *Hidden Lives*, we have obviously the two writers who position themselves as (grand)daughterly researchers and biographers. In the case of *Wild Swans*, the author, Jung Chang, is inspired by her mother's storytelling that impels her to conduct further research and hence write the book. For Margaret Forster, the motivation behind her writing is triggered by her need to uncover her hidden matrilineage and its accompanying social and political issues. What Forster has acknowledged in her recovery project is the irrecoverability of her grandmother's early life and the hidden life of her Aunt Alice, whose stories Forster has refused to fictionalize.[1] In Margaret Drabble's *The Peppered Moth*, although the reader is informed in the epilogue that the novel is based on Drabble's mother's life, Drabble chooses not to divulge her identity as a daughter biographer in the book by creating instead her heroine, Faro, as the figure of a (grand)daughter who recovers her matrilineage.

The Writers' Concurrent Engagement with Recovering Maternal Subjectivity

In the process of reinterpreting and re-creating their matrilineal narratives, almost all these writers, with the exception of Drabble, have concurrently attempted to retrieve maternal subjectivity even though their approaches vary accordingly. In Fredriksson's *Hanna's Daughters*, the way in which the (grand)mother's subjectivity is retrieved is through the (grand)daughter's use of dreams, memories, and photographs, especially because by the time when Anna starts writing her matrilineal narrative, the mother, Johanna, is on the brink of dying and the grandmother, Hanna, has already died. As a consequence, the appearance of dreams, memories, and photos in the text functions significantly as these are vehicles for resurfacing and even reviving the maternal subjectivity that has been lost due to the circumstances happening to both mother and grandmother. Furthermore, Fredriksson prioritizes maternal subjectivity by setting and narrating her matrilineal stories before her quest for matrilineage is introduced.

In *Wild Swans*, Chang resorts to a more conventional way of approaching maternal subjectivity by presenting a detailed description of her grandmother's and mother's lives in China. Even though their life narratives, her grandmother's and mother's, respectively, are not depicted from a first-person perspective, the realistic re-presentations Chang brings to light in her delineations appear to equip the reader with a reliving of the lives her two immediate female forebears have led, thereby assisting in resurrecting their maternal subjectivity in their own generational contexts. In *Hidden Lives*, Forster refers to a more creative means of retrieving the mother's subjectivity by revealing her consciousness of the "I" voice at the age of five when her subjectivity "intrudes" into the narration of her matrilineal narrative. Although Forster perceives this act of announcing the "I" voice as "dangerous," it is exactly through her introduction of the "I" personal pronoun that her mother's subjectivity is then brought to the surface, that the mother "refuses to fit the story Forster is composing for her."[2] In Drabble's *The Peppered Moth*, there is no sign of retrieving the mother's subjectivity in the text, especially because the mother-daughter matrix as portrayed in the relationship between grandmother and mother is strained and ends without being fully reconciled. As Drabble herself submits in the recent interview with Suzie Mackenzie, the inspiration for her book *The Peppered Moth* is derived from her mother's life and their unresolved mother-daughter relationship. Nonetheless, Drabble makes a striking comment toward the end of the interview by confessing that she hopes to retain her mother's subjectivity, "whatever she was."[3] No matter how these writers (re)present their retrieval of the mother's subjectivity, they all participate in enacting the intersubjective attunement through writing their own genograms or matrilineal narratives. It is also this art of intersubjective attunement that aligns them with a common goal of the recovery of the mother.

The Disclosure of Matrilineal Ambivalence and the Different Rewritings of Family Romances

Except Chang's *Wild Swans* where matrilineal ambivalence barely exists, the rest of the matrilineal narratives in varying degrees entail misunderstandings and feelings of resentment, anxiety, and ambivalence between mothers and daughters. In Fredriksson's *Hanna's Daughters* and Forster's *Hidden Lives*, the separation or gap between generations of mothers and daughters has to do with class, caused by education the granddaughter is privileged to earn. While Fredriksson does not disclose matrilineal ambivalence to its full extent, Forster elaborates on the topic both extensively and intensively in delineating the paradoxical triad of grandmother, mother, and daughter. In Drabble's *The Peppered Moth*, although the main concern of the novel is not specifically on an examination of ambivalence and/or resentment between generations of women, the pervading message of "break away and escape" from the previous generation produces a similar sense of ambivalence in a generational cycle.

The way in which matrilineal romances, as constructed in the texts of Fredriksson and Forster, differ from the extant discourses of family romances, both Freudian and feminist appropriation, is in their resolution of matrilineal ambivalence through recognition of both mother-daughter resonance and differences. With the exception of Chang's *Wild Swans* where there is no revelation of defining characteristics of either a female family romance or a matrilineal one, the other three texts exhibit certain features of romances despite the fact that all of them do not follow the exact formula of a family romance, either Freudian or feminist adaptation. In Fredriksson's *Hanna's Daughters*, Forster's *Hidden Lives*, and Drabble's *The Peppered Moth*, the mother-daughter recognition or reconciliation is often initiated by the (grand) daughter as all of them assign her as the important figure in recovering her matrilineage.

In Forster's *Hidden Lives*, there are textual representations of Steph Lawler's female family romances in which the daughters in her study who have moved their social status from a working class to a middle class exhibit their phobia of "inhabiting" the world of their working-class mothers and their aspiration to be like other women who are better than their mothers are. However, the ways in which Forster's construction of her female family romance differs from that in Lawler's research are in not seeking a replacement of her mother with a superior mother but her recourse to higher education and a career outside the domestic space, which exempt her from reproducing her mother's life or the lives of her female ancestors. More noteworthy, however, is Forster's later-in-life realization and assertion of her strong identification with her mother in terms of being a wife and a mother. That is, following her resentment of her mother's life and her liberation from leading a life like her mother's, there is also the resolution of her matrilineal ambivalence and the reconnection with her matrilineal past. Drabble, likewise, admits her reluctance to fulfill her fantasy of replacing her mother with a better one in the recent interview with Mackenzie. What Drabble intends is to keep her mother's subjectivity the way she always was. The manners in which all these different rewritings of family romances have been presented suggest the emergence of new feminist family romances, narratives that yield a great capacity for creativities and transformations.

The Tension between Recovery and Progress

The tension between recovery and progress in these four texts is bound up with the undertaking of journeys and migrations. Almost all the female protagonists in these texts take on journeys or migrations to the places of their origins and/or places away from home. The journey back home often signifies recovery of matrilineage whereas the migration to foreign places usually indicates progression from the motherline. In Chang's *Wild Swans* and Forster's *Hidden Lives*, the progress is intricately related to a (grand)daughter's revision and superseding of her (grand)mother's life. For Chang, in order to make progress, she needs to "take wing" by embarking on a journey to the West. Chang's mother, marrying and being a devoted and successful communist officer, is also propelled to make successive arduous journeys both by choice and circumstance, which make her life progress from her mother's stabilized and stale life. Forster's progress from the lives of her immediate female ancestors is constantly unfolded in her resentment against the lives her grandmother and mother are leading. She fulfils her progress by opting into receiving better education, thus migrating from her place of origin, Carlisle, and then leading a life of her own choice. The tension between recovery and progress exerts its paradox when Forster displays her matrilineal ambivalence, which problematizes the division between self and (m)other, in her "conflict between nurturance and autonomy" in relation to her mother.[4] However, it is exactly Forster's recognition and then resolution of her ambivalence toward her matrilineage that not only reconnects her with her matrilineage but also reaffirms her recovery project of writing a genogram. The tension between recovery and progress is exercised in a state of flux in Drabble's composition of the interrelation between generations of women in *The Peppered Moth*. Faro's constant journeys back and forth, in and out of, the place of origins, Breaseborough, depict the interaction between recovery and progress as instantaneous and synchronous. The performance of recovery and progress does not, as in Chang's and Forster's texts, stretch into a long sequence of chronology and progression. The sustained and intensive tension between recovery and progress can only cease and be resolved by the (grand)daughter's final retrieval of her matrilineage.

The Use of Photographs and Mother-Daughter Mirroring as Manifestations of Their Identification and Differences

The use of photographs and mother-daughter mirroring, either described in the narratives or inserted in the books, appears in all these four texts. In Chang's *Wild Swans* and Forster's *Hidden Lives*, family photos are used to provide visual parallels to their literary representations. They afford truthfulness to the narratives recollected and justify the credibility of the narratives or memoirs. In Fredriksson's *Hanna's Daughters* and Drabble's *The Peppered Moth*, the family photos, specifically the photos of grandmothers, are discovered by granddaughters and then described in the books. The granddaughters' discovery, often accidentally, of their grandmothers' photographs has its matrilineal significance; it is often the crucial moment when the granddaughter, as the conciliator of matrilineal ambivalence, begins to recognize her female ancestor and the importance of such a matrilineal figure as the grandmother in preserving matrilineage.

Beyond the Triangular Configuration: The Narrative Shapes of Matrilineal Narratives

What the aforementioned thematic recurrences have demonstrated is a textual trajectory of moving from mother-daughter separation to connection. This transition from separation to connection, as performed through the working and reworking of these thematics, shapes and reshapes the narrative structures of these matrilineal narratives. Although the four matrilineal narratives concerned here are founded on the triangular relation among grandmother, mother, and daughter, the fluidities, flexibilities, and complexities they show suggest their evolution from the triangular configuration. Referring back to my original proposition beginning from Sigmund Freud's family romances, Marianne Hirsch's feminist family romances, and then Audre Lorde's grandmother-mother-daughter triad, we can see clearly their revisions and transformations as shown in the following three diagrams:

1. Freud's Family Romances

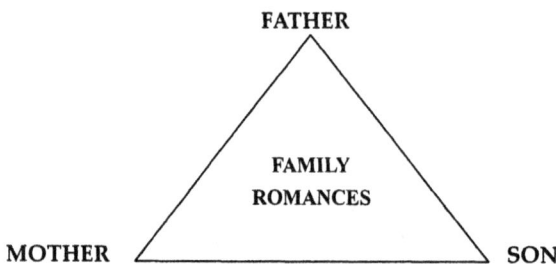

2. Hirsch's Feminist Family Romances

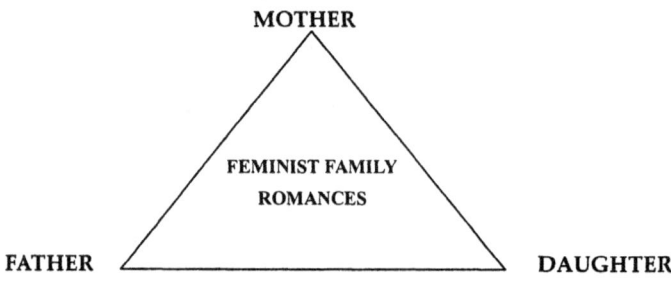

3. Lorde's Grandmother-Mother-Daughter Triad

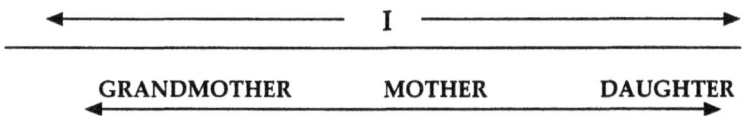

As mentioned at the beginning of this part, there are three points I would like to highlight emerging from a reading of these diagrams. First, there is a gradual disappearance of the father from the center to a secondary position and finally to complete erasure. Second, there is the positioning of the mother in the center, highlighted by and culminating in the emergence of the grandmother. The disappearance of the father figure does not imply absolute failure. Neither does the appearance of the grandmother point to the substitution of another powerful, hierarchical familial figure. What needs to be emphasized here is that women writers' preoccupation with mother-daughter relationships has resulted in the relative obscurity of the father figure and has explored the interrelations between women within a primarily female network. These women writers have envisioned a process of female development and have situated this development in the context of relationships between women without male intrusion. Third, there is a transformation in terms of narrative shape from triangle to line. Lorde's depiction of the grandmother-mother-daughter triad as a straight line diminishes, on the one hand, the tensions created in a triangular shape and engenders, on the other hand, further graphing of different possible narrative threads and shapes as illustrated in contemporary women's creative writing. In linking Lorde's grandmother-mother-daughter triad with Cosslett's two frameworks of time of feminist matrilinealism, the diagram can also be drawn as follows:

4. The "Two Time-Frames" of Cosslett's Feminist Matrilinealism

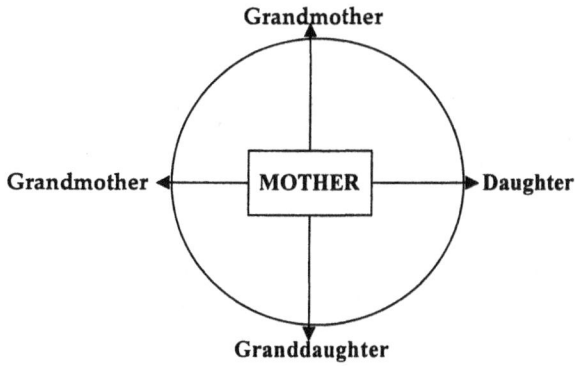

118   Mother, She Wrote

The scale Lorde has delineated in her triad seems to suggest only "a synchronic, horizontal plane, on which the generations of women are united by a common femaleness."[5] What the two frameworks of time of Cosslett's feminist matrilinealism have added to Lorde's three-generational triad is the coexistence of both synchronic and diachronic frameworks, which execute the concurrent operation of both female solidarity and liberation and feminist recovery and progress.[6] What I am interested in pursuing further in relation to this woman-centered development within literature and, in particular, contemporary women's writing, is the reshaping of the three-generational triad among grandmother, mother, and daughter. I would like to explore the different narrative shapes of these new feminist family romances, beyond the simple triangular structure I have been using so far. The diagrams that follow represent my tentative suggestions.

5. Marianne Fredriksson's *Hanna's Daughters*

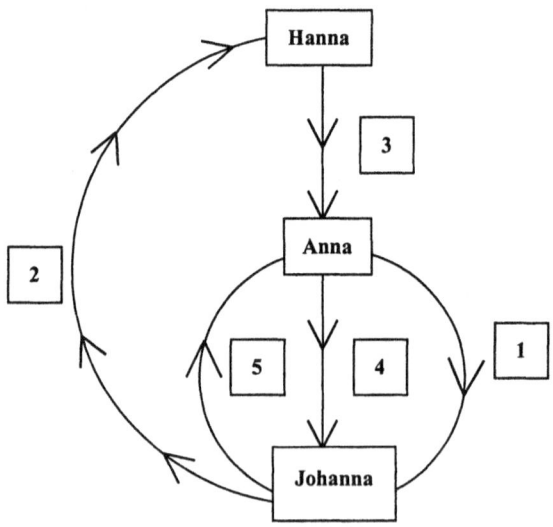

In *Hanna's Daughters*, "the 'I' at its eternal core"[7] is the daughter, Anna. Anna's narrations in the introduction, interlude, and epilogue oscillate between the two narratives of Hanna and Johanna. In the introduction, Anna first goes back to her mother, Johanna, by resurrecting her dying mother's subjectivity through recounting in memory the mother's narration of her own childhood experiences and also through the mother's dreams (trajectory 1). Then, the book proceeds to a lengthy third-person narrative on Hanna's life (trajectory 2). In the interlude, which stands between the two narrations on Hanna and Johanna, Anna explores her writing journey as a biographer of her matrilineal narrative (trajectory 3). The interlude is then succeeded by Johanna's first-person narration of her life (trajectory 4). Finally, in the epilogue, Anna completes her writing task after the death of her mother, and her recovery project ends with her transmission of matrilineage to her daughters (trajectory 5). As a consequence, the insertion of the trilogy of introduction, interlude, and epilogue with Anna's first-person narratives in them provides a linkage among narratives of grandmother, mother, and daughter. It also produces a circular movement of the narratives with Anna's tripartite narratives connecting that of Hanna and Johanna, respectively, thus linking grandmother, mother, and daughter together as a triad.

6. Jung Chang's *Wild Swans*

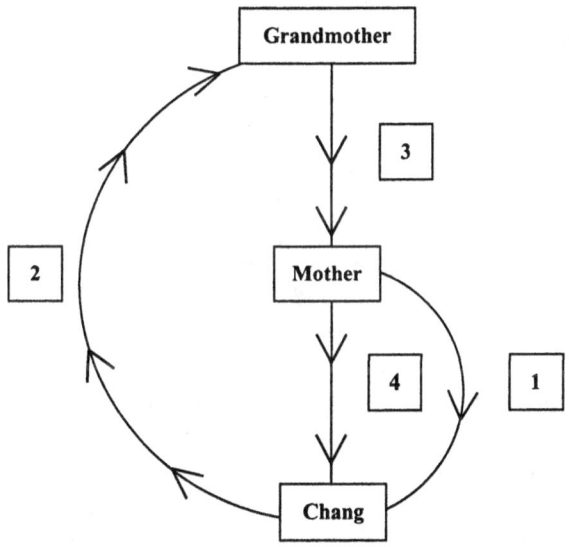

In *Wild Swans*, Chang's mother's stay in London sets Chang off to China to commence her recovery project of matrilineage (trajectory 1). Chang's retrieval of her matrilineage begins first with the grandmother by going back to her times (trajectory 2). When she later launches into writing her matrilineal narrative, she follows a linear, chronological order, beginning from her grandmother, then her mother, and finally herself (trajectories 3 and 4). The story line in *Wild Swans* is basically composed in straight and progressive lines, in a similar manner to the tense straight lines of the triangle. Yet, Chang's writing of her genogram as a unification of the three-generational triad in her matrilineage suggests the possible shape of a circle. The loving, supportive relationships among these three generations of women also reinforce the round and encircling shapes, which tie them together.

7. Margaret Forster's *Hidden Lives*

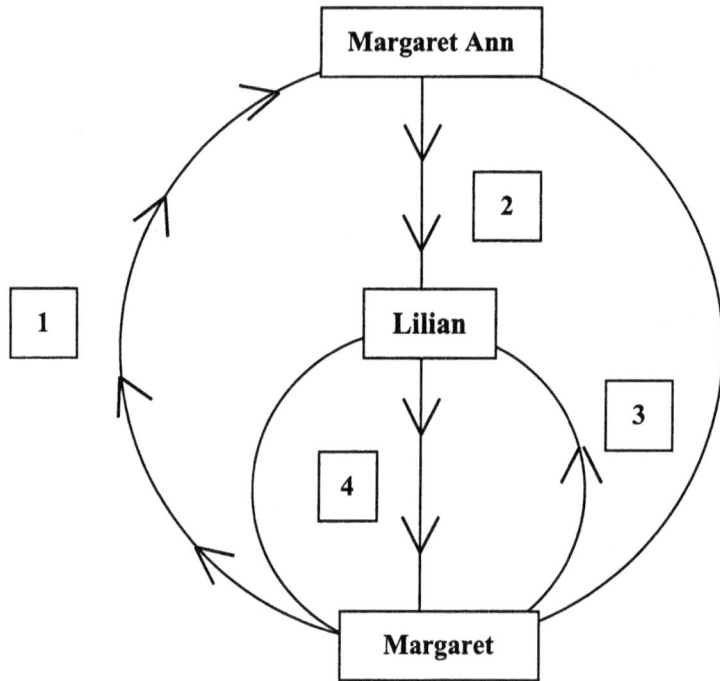

In *Hidden Lives*, Margaret begins her investigation of her grandmother's life, including her attempt to find out her mysterious Aunt Alice who is allegedly her grandmother's illegitimate daughter (trajectory 1). Following a linear and chronological order, the mother's life is narrated in the middle (trajectory 2). However, Margaret with the authorial I begins to emerge in the middle of her matrilineal narrative when she unfolds her conscious memory of her family at the age of five (trajectory 3). Forster continues her remaining narrative on her mother, Lilian, followed by an ending with Margaret's own life narrative (trajectory 4). Although *Hidden Lives* is basically constructed in a linear shape, the daughter's narrative does interrupt and intrude into the line in the middle and then goes back and forth between mother and daughter. More notably, the multiplication of the angles, as shown in the text, commences at the moment of Margaret's disclosure of her "I" voice in the middle of the narrative on her mother, Lilian, through which a different voice and perspective of the mother is to be heard thereafter.

8. Margaret Drabble's *The Peppered Moth*

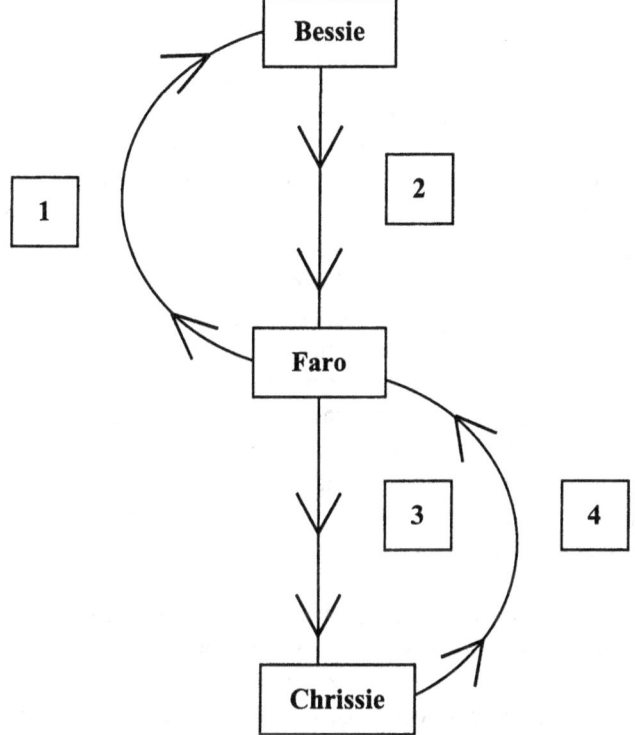

In *The Peppered Moth*, "the 'I' at its eternal core"[8] is the (grand)daughter as she is the key person who recovers her matrilineage and her narrative shuttles between her grandmother and mother. The narration goes back to the grandmother's life narrative first but also moves at intervals to the granddaughter's present time when the scientific project of matrilineal retrieval initiated by Dr. Hawthorn is progressing (trajectories 1 and 2). This similar pattern of alternating between two narratives recurs later and is shifted to that between the mother and the daughter (trajectories 3 and 4). The (grand)daughterly "I" who moves "back and forth flowing in either or both directions as needed"[9] connects her grandmother and mother together. This traversing between two narratives has its significance especially when the motherline linking grandmother and mother is severed. The granddaughter's investigation of her matrilineage both begins and ends with the grandmother, symbolizing the circuit of matrilineage around the three-generational triad. Despite the tense and conflicted angular relation between grandmother and mother, the circular movement that spins from grandmother to mother to daughter and then closes with the granddaughter's recovery of her grandmother transforms the strained and trichotomous relation into a harmonious and nonhierarchical relationship.

When applying Lorde's concept of "the 'I' at [the] eternal core"[10] to a reading of the narrative shapes of matrilineal narratives discussed in this part, the "I" in the grandmother-mother-daughter triad can refer to any one of them. In both Fredriksson's and Forster's novels, the granddaughters are also mothers themselves at the time of writing their genograms. As a result, their embodiment of double or triple identity in their matrilineal relations ties them strongly with their motherlines, which bespeak their significances in being positioned "at [the] eternal core" of their matrilineal triad. Further, even though the four diagrams, as developed from the texts of Fredriksson, Chang, Forster, and Drabble, are illustrated on "a diachronic, vertical axis," they can also be shown on "a synchronic, horizontal plane."[11] Revolving around the "diachronic, vertical axis" are the circular trajectories, denoting the space-time continuum accomplished through "the 'I' moving back and forth flowing in either or both directions as needed."[12]

What all these different narrative patterns have illustrated, as elaborated in the four diagrams, is the heterogeneity of matrilineal narratives. However, what I do not want to do by drawing these diagrams is to construct other powerful alternatives for replacing the existing paradigm of Freudian family triangles. The complexities of these different narrative shapes of new feminist family romances work and rework Lorde's grandmother-mother-daughter triad. Significantly, in response to the triangular relationship of family romances, both Freudian and feminist appropriation of it, the narrative structure of family romances has been altered and reconceptualized in forming and re-forming relationality from dyad or triad to the transfiguration of angular forms or the less threatening and nonhierarchical shapes of curved and enclosing circle. The literary configurations of these narrative shapes in matrilineal narratives shed new light on the theoretical parameter of Jessica Benjamin's intersubjectivity as the formation of the grandmother-mother-daughter triad apparently complicates and diversifies the mother-daughter dyad, from which the theory is developed. The aforementioned thematic recurrences have also contributed to these transformations of narrative structure. Indeed, the emergences of all these characteristics, which I might call a *poetics* or *syntax* of mother-daughter writing—the relative obscurity of the male figure, the participation in a maternal voice, and the working through of ambivalence and tensions toward a sense of connection, to name a few essentials—combine to form a new kind of matrix within which these writers can express their feminine creativity and their feminine voice. The poetics of matrilinealism as created by these texts is, I would argue, new feminist family romances.

Notes

1. Tess Cosslett, "Matrilineal Narratives Revisited," in *Feminism and Autobiography: Texts, Theories, Methods*, ed. Tess Cosslett, Celia Lury, and Penny Summerfield (London and New York: Routledge, 2000), 147.
2. Ibid., 150.
3. Suzie Mackenzie, "Mothers and Daughters," *Guardian Weekend*, December 16, 2000, 43.
4. Jane Flax, "The Conflict between Nurturance and Autonomy in Mother-Daughter Relationships and within Feminism," *Feminist Studies* 4, no. 2 (June 1978): 171–89.
5. Cosslett, "Feminism, Matrilinealism, the 'House of the Women' in Contemporary Women's Fiction," *Journal of Gender Studies* 5, no. 1 (1996): 8.
6. Ibid.
7. Audre Lorde, *Zami: A New Spelling of My Name* (1982; reprint, London: Sheba, 1990), 7. References are to the reprint edition.
8. Ibid.
9. Ibid.
10. Ibid.
11. Cosslett, "Feminism, Matrilinealism, and the 'House of the Women' in Contemporary Women's Fiction," 8.
12. Lorde, *Zami*, 7.

Part 3

Diasporic Matrilineal Narratives in Contemporary North American Women's Fiction

Chapter 9
Diasporic Matrilineal Narratives

For the past two decades, the burgeoning development in diasporic writings by women has been evident in light of the ever-increasing interest in the subject taken by both publishers and literary critics and the consequent attraction of a wider readership. Diaspora, as a heterogeneous entity and group, encompasses vast geographical areas across the globe and a rich diversity of different ethnicities, cultures, and languages. The subject of diasporic writings by women thus grows into an enormous field of study that I will not be able to discuss in full. However, following recent feminist literary critics' interests in this strand of women's writing, I would like to focus on this aspect by highlighting the emergence of two recurring themes—motherhood and mother-daughter relationships—in diasporic women writers' exploration of the intricate affinities between their female identity and their motherlands or mother cultures. Before launching into a full discussion of five diasporic matrilineal narratives assembled in my study, I shall first introduce briefly some of the key concepts and definitions of diaspora given by a couple of postcolonial scholars and critics and then go on to signpost two distinctive feminist literary studies with their focal point on different uses of the maternal in postcolonial and diasporic women's writing. After my examination of these five women's texts, this part will conclude by drawing on their varying manifestations of diasporic matrilineal narratives, thus complicating and diversifying the extant ramifications of these narratives.

Embedded within the discourse of colonialism, the word *diaspora* means "the voluntary or forcible movement of peoples from their homelands into new regions," which reflects a phenomenon in the history of colonization.[1] This diasporic movement has resulted in an inevitable mixture of different races, cultures, and languages. Therefore, the descendants of the diasporic "have developed their own distinctive cultures which both preserve and often extend and develop their original cultures." Moreover, the nature of their "hybridity" and "creolization" is indicative of both their influences over and having been influenced by "indigenous cultures with which they thus came to contact." From a postcolonialist perspective, this distinctive feature of diasporic identity often dismantles and disrupts the concept of "a unified, 'natural' cultural norm, one that underpins the *center/margin* model of colonist discourse." It also problematizes a simpler version of "*nativism* which suggest[s] that *decolonization* can be effected by a recovery or reconstruction of pre-colonial societies."[2]

This definition of *diaspora* in terms of colonization can be traced back to the Greek origin of the word as *sowing over*, denoting expansion and settlement during the periods of Greek colonization in ancient times.[3] As indicated earlier, beyond this colonization of the term *diaspora*, as "a forcible movement of peoples from their homelands into new regions" such as the African diasporas, there is also a "voluntary" migration of diasporas; for instance, some diasporas migrate for work, trade, and better life.[4] Even the Jewish as the prototype of *diaspora* embodies the duality of "voluntary" and "involuntary" migration in historical delineations of the wandering Jews.[5] The definition of diaspora given by Bill Ashcroft, Gareth Griffiths, and Helen Tiffin is specifically one that is looking from the perspectives of colonialism and postcolonialism. Their description of the migration of diasporas as either "voluntary" or "involuntary" is an indicator for distinguishing different or diverse groups of diasporic communities around the globe. Yet, the formation of diasporas as a phenomenon in the history of colonization, as articulated by Ashcroft, Griffiths, and Tiffin, can only reveal a certain proportion of the ever-increasing and evolving globalized diasporic population.

With these telling classifications of diasporic groups, the development of diasporic communities outside their natal countries either by choice or by circumstances is more or less contaminated by their traumatic experiences. While there are some diasporas who assimilate into the mainstream society, there are also others who distinctly form their own collective identity, culture, and language in marked contrast to the dominant or hostile society surrounding them, thereby aligning them with a collective memory for their real or imagined co-ethnic home country.[6] However, having made this distinction between assimilation and resistance in terms of the formation of a diasporic identity does not indicate that these two notions should be seen arbitrarily as the opposition between the colonizer and the colonized or the dominant and the subjugated. The supposed opposition between the two has evolved to the extent that their mutual influences are undeniable and cannot thus be construed as binarism. The following definition of syncreticism can be viewed as a more appropriate denomination to capture the identity formation of diasporas in connection with their adopted nations or cultures.

As mentioned before, the core of a diasporic identity lies in the "hybridty" and "creolization" of intermixing races, cultures, and languages. However, as Robin Cohen cautions us, the term *hybridity* tends to be inappropriately used in postmodernist and postcolonialist contexts. Instead of "denot[ing] the evolution of new, dynamic, mixed cultures," "hybrids," in a breeding sense, are in fact inclined to "sterility and uniformity," signifying a completely opposite meaning to its common usage. Therefore, certain postcolonial critics such as Cohen suggest instead a more positive term, *syncretism*.[7] Synergy or syncretic is defined as "the product of two (or more) forces that are reduceable to neither," which accentuates "the positive and energetic aspects of the process of *transculturation* and the equal but different elements that the various historical periods and forces have contributed in forming the modern post-colonial condition."[8] Of all the diasporic groups and communities, the Caribbean diasporas or migranthood can be said to be particularly reflective of this characteristic because the Caribbean has evolved its own culture from interacting with the world through migration. Mary Chamberlain, a recent feminist social historian, gives an informative definition of the distinct identity of Caribbean people: "Caribbean culture has absorbed its world influences and transfigured it into a new syncretic culture, as elements from Africa, Europe, Asia, and the Caribbean became absorbed, worked and reworked into a new and distinctively 'Creole' culture." With respect to the positive, productive and transforming side of Caribbean culture, Chamberlain continues, "it is not a dislocating or disabling condition but an opportunity for creativity, a continuing process of syncretism shaped by, and contributing to, the history of its diaspora."[9]

Two feminist literary and critical works on the topic of diasporic female identity in relation to their motherlands or/and mother countries are Susheila Nasta's *Motherlands: Black Women's Writing from Africa, the Caribbean, and South Asia*[10] and Simone A. Alexander's *Mother Imagery in the Novels of Afro-Caribbean Women*.[11] In the introduction to her book, Nasta points out that the notions of "motherlands," "mothercultures," and "mothertongues" have been employed by African, Caribbean, and Asian women writers to contest and destabilize "the illusion of the colonial 'motherland' or 'mothercountry'" whereas there is also a need to "rediscover, recreate and give birth to the genesis of new forms and new languages of expression." In conjunction with these themes is a proliferation of black women writers' concern with the subjects of motherhood, mother-daughter relationships, and female identity formation and development.[12] That is to say, as manifest in the critical studies included in Nasta's collection, motherhood and mother-daughter relationships serve as a catalyst for black women writers' literary experimentation with both their personal and political changes.

Published nearly a decade later, Alexander's book pursues this topic further by distinguishing her definitions between "motherland" and "mother country," the two key concepts Nasta uses interchangeably. Focusing her study specifically on the novels of three established Caribbean women writers, Alexander makes an important distinction between "motherland," which denotes the Caribbean and, by extension, Africa, and "mother country," which refers to "the dominant colonial powers" such as "England, France, or the United States."[13] In an effort to explore her redefinition of these crucial notions, Alexander goes on to highlight the trichotomous relationship among mother, motherland, and mother country in her study. She argues that in addition to "the notion of a triad," the "triangular relationship" among the three is also contaminated by "conflict" and is hence divided "into three distinct parts."[14]

In an analogous fashion to her predecessor Nasta, what preoccupies Alexander is the pivotal role the mother plays in sustaining "the triad" and "the trichotomy."[15] In Alexander's view, a daughter's relation to her mother, irrespective of being either harmonious or strained, often prefigures or determines "her relationships with the motherland and, to a lesser extent, with the mother country."[16] In short, Alexander's overall argument is that the centrality of the mother figure in Caribbean women's writing constitutes the configuration of a triangular relationship among mother, motherland, and mother country, which is often fraught with conflicts and tensions. In spite of their nuances in terms of their arguments and scopes of study, what Nasta and Alexander contend concurrently is the inseparable link between one's mother and mother('s)lands and/or mother countries. The political, social, and cultural conflicts emerging from this dyad (mother-motherland) or triad (mother-motherland-mother country) are especially epitomized in their selected black women writers' exploration of the personal relationship between mothers and daughters.[17]

The diasporic women's writing to which I will refer in my discussion in this part will be chiefly investigated in the American context with a particular focus on literary texts written by North American women of African (Toni Morrison); Caribbean (Jamaica Kincaid); Asian (Joy Kogawa and Amy Tan); and Jewish (Judy Budnitz) origins. The rationales for choosing them are twofold. First, their writings with their diverse coverages of different genres (novel, short story, myth, fairy tales, autobiography, and biography); geographical locations (America, Africa, the Caribbean, China, Japan, Canada, and Eastern Europe); cultures; ethnicities; and races serve as highly contested but enriching sites for both personal and political transformations. Second, these women writers' preoccupation with motherhood and mother-daughter relationships provides more diversified cultural perspectives on the subjects than those stipulated in the homogeny of white Western discourses. The themes of motherhood and mother-daughter relationships as cultivated in the works of diasporic women writers become the groundwork for germinating strategies of survival and resistance against sexism, racism, colonialism, and neocolonialism as apparatus of patriarchal dominance. Significantly, the figure of the mother or even the grandmother in diasporic literature by women occupies a pivotal position in maintaining and transmitting the values of one's particular racial and cultural heritages against erasure by the dominance of colonial discourse. Yet, having said this does not mean that the significance of maternal origin in a diasporic context is equivalent to nativism, which is often seen as in opposition to the immigrants' assimilation into the homogenizing majority culture. The demarcation between nativism and assimilation becomes unfixed and ambiguous as far as certain diasporic matrilineal narratives are concerned; for instance, the mother in Kincaid's *Annie John* is perceived by the daughter as a paradoxical figure in constituting the binary opposition between the colonizer and the subjugated.

Although both Nasta's and Alexander's views on the themes surrounding mother, motherlands, or/and mother countries are illuminating in reading the works of a black woman writer such as Kincaid, which I will explore in one of the following chapters, the trichotomous relationship among these three concepts as proposed originally by Alexander varies when applying it to works written by other diasporic women writers. By saying so, I do not intend to suggest that their studies could be argued against as they have specified the bias and partiality of their selection of black women's texts. Rather, I seek to diversify and complicate their conceptual parameters by bringing more works to the extant studies. The apparent limitation in my selection of diasporic women's writing within the continent of North America is that it does not exhibit the diverse geographical characteristics of a kind of study such as Nasta's collection has proved to be. Yet, despite the geographical and even geopolitical constraints, the fact that these five North American women writers sampled in my study entail a variety of ethnic, racial, and cultural backgrounds will still generate fruitful insights into current feminist study of matrilineage and diasporic women's writing. In addition, I do not concentrate my study only on works written by women of color and on black diaspora; one of the writers included is Jewish and her novel deals with Jewish diaspora.

What links all the five women writers together in my study is that they all live in North America, in the United States and Canada, respectively. The heroines in their novels, whose lives are based on either the writers' own or others' personal experiences or are purely constructed out of the writers' imaginations, all reside in their mother countries with the exception of Annie John in Kincaid's book of the same title who inhabits her motherland, the Caribbean island of Antigua. Yet, the concept of diaspora in terms of cultural and identity politics is never a fixed and unified entity. Strictly speaking, Antigua is not necessarily considered as Annie John's mother('s)land as her mother migrated initially from another Caribbean island, Dominica. Therefore, Antigua can only be seen as a metaphor for the motherland, which complicates the notion of motherland in light of the high mobility of Caribbean diaspora. Furthermore, while Annie John makes her journey back to her mother country, England, at the end of the novel, there are also other female protagonists such as Jing-mei in Amy Tan's *The Joy Luck Club* who accomplishes her self-discovery and self-recognition during her journey back to her motherland, China. What can be inferred tentatively with regard to the construction of diasporic female identity in connection with motherlands is the heterogeneity and fluidity such an enquiry produces.

Another useful idea in Alexander's book that is worth mentioning and will also appear in my discussion of the selected diasporic matrilineal narratives is the concept of othermother. What Alexander means by *othermother* carries two connotations. One refers to "the substitute mother who takes on and takes over the nurturing role from the biological in times of need or crisis, becoming a pillar of strength and support for the estranged daughter." Alexander's other definition of the notion of othermother is linked with the biological mother but extends its meaning to denote the "otherness" in the mother. Put another way, the mother is viewed "as an 'other' mother, an enemy to her daughter, particularly when she appears to advocate colonial habits and mannerisms."[18] Alexander's definitions of othermother are made according to her reading of three Caribbean women writers. They do offer certain credibility in reading other diasporic women's texts, but they are also subject to further formulation and transformation especially in terms of seeing or reading the mother as a racial other. I shall elaborate more on this respect in my succeeding textual discussion.

My discussion of five diasporic matrilineal narratives published between 1981 and 1999 will be divided into five chapters with each of them featuring the work(s) of one particular woman writer. Set in a sequential order of African, Asian, and Jewish diasporas in North America, my rationale for arranging these texts in this manner is to follow their time frames. Morrison's *Beloved* is a neo–slave narrative recounting the devastation of slavery and its aftermath. Under this category of African diaspora, Kincaid's *Annie John* is a post-slavery and postcolonial novel about Annie's early happy and then estranged relationship with her mother on their island home of Antigua in the 1960s when Annie was growing up and her motherland, Antigua, was still under the jurisdiction of British colonial power.

Moving into the Asian diaspora, three texts presenting two strands of Asian Americans, Japanese Canadians, and Chinese Americans, will be added to the discussion. Kogawa's *Obasan*, set during and after the Second World War, is about the Canadian government's racist dispersal of Japanese Canadians from their homes in British Columbia to the interior in Canada, epitomized in the traumatic accounts of a female narrator, Naomi Nakane, about her mother's mysterious absence and the unspeakable sufferings her family has gone through. Tan's novel, *The Joy Luck Club*, deals with a much later stage in the history of Chinese immigrants in America after 1945 but affords a herstory by featuring the mother-daughter stories in the scenario. In the last chapter of this part with Budnitz's *If I Told You Once* in it, an allusion to Jewish diaspora in America during and after the time of the Holocaust is made in the text, which sets itself apart from the aforementioned novels with their overt indication of specific historical and cultural backgrounds. The evasiveness of exact time, location, and people in Budnitz's novel is perhaps a logical outcome of the writer's fairy-tale rewrite of a diasporic matrilineal narrative. As perhaps the most imaginative and magical of them all, Budnitz's *If I Told You Once* is also the most perplexing.

What I would also like to indicate is that my choice of these five diasporic matrilineal narratives is not emblematic either of diasporic women writing in general or of their specific groups. My main purpose in presenting a discussion of their texts is to generate productive readings of these narratives that are infused with the complexities of gender, class, race, nationalism, and cultural politics. While exploring one particular theme within each discussion of the texts to highlight their differences, I will also glean from them important features of similarity and resonance. Congruent with the heterogeneous nature of diaspora, my reading of these matrilineal texts will be subject to further modifications, which reflect the inconclusiveness and openness of diasporic (con)texts.

Notes

1. Bill Ashcroft, Gareth Griffiths, and Helen Tiffin, *Key Concepts in Post-Colonial Studies* (London and New York: Routledge, 1998), 68.
2. Ibid., 70, emphasis original.

3. Robin Cohen, *Global Diasporas: An Introduction* (1997; reprint, London: University College of London Press, 1999), ix. References are to the reprint edition.
4. Ashcroft, Griffiths, and Tiffin, *Key Concepts in Post-Colonial Studies*, 68.
5. Ibid., 1–3, 21–25.
6. Cohen, *Global Diasporas*, 1–29.
7. Ibid., 131.
8. Ashcroft, Griffiths, and Tiffin, *Key Concepts in Post-Colonial Studies*, 229, emphasis original.
9. Mary Chamberlain, "The Global Self: Narratives of Caribbean Migrant Women," in *Feminism and Autobiography: Texts, Theories, Methods*, ed. Tess Cosslett, Celia Lury, and Penny Summerfield (London and New York: Routledge, 2000), 154.
10. Susheila Nasta, ed., *Motherlands: Black Women's Writing from Africa, the Caribbean and South Asia* (New Jersey: Rutgers University Press, 1992).
11. Simone A. James Alexander, *Mother Imagery in the Novels of Afro-Caribbean Women* (Columbia and London: University of Missouri Press, 2001).
12. Nasta, *Motherlands*, xix.
13. Alexander, *Mother Imagery in the Novels of Afro-Caribbean Women*, 3–4.
14. Ibid., 18.
15. Ibid., 3–4.
16. Ibid., 18.
17. Although not specifically focusing on the triad of mother-motherlands–mother countries, two other critical works that also have mother-daughter relationships as their subject matters in the writing of women of color include Elizabeth Brown-Guillory, *Women of Color: Mother-Daughter Relationships in Twentieth-Century Literature* (Austin: University of Texas Press, 1996), and Wendy Ho, *In Her Mother's House: The Politics of Asian American Mother-Daughter Writing* (Oxford: Altamira, 1999).
18. Alexander, *Mother Imagery in the Novels of Afro-Caribbean Women*, 7.

Chapter 10
Toni Morrison's *Beloved*

One recurring theme that runs throughout most of the texts written by women in the African diaspora is the mothers' strength and perseverance in protecting their daughters and sons against forces within societies that are usually gendered, sexualized, and racialized. My discussion of five other matrilineal texts by American diasporic women writers in the succeeding chapters of this part will also corroborate this view. For instance, in both *Annie John* and *The Joy Luck Club*, the mothers utilize and transmit the technique of storytelling to their daughters in an effort to protect and even perpetuate their cultural heritages and identities of origin, although in *Annie John* the representation of the mother appears to be more complex and is encoded in an ambiguous tone. The mothers' employments of storytelling, consciously or unconsciously, are also aimed as skills to be passed on to their daughters for survival in the outside cruel and hostile world. In a slightly different manner to *Annie John* and *The Joy Luck Club*, *Obasan* depicts one Japanese Canadian family's protection of their offspring, Naomi, from the burden of sorrow by deliberately hiding from Naomi the truth about her mother's death in Nagasaki's bombing in Japan in 1945, until Naomi is in her thirties. Despite this thematic resonance among these texts, one telling feature of African American matrilineal literature, which differs radically from the others in this part, is that some African American mothers out of their intense maternal love actually murder their children for the sake of protecting them from further destruction.[1]

This incident of mothers killing their own children occurs in Toni Morrison's novel *Beloved*. In *Beloved*, Sethe, the slave mother, commits an appalling crime of infanticide—murdering her baby daughter after her escape from slavery—because she wants to prevent her children from suffering the same pains and miseries she has been through. As a fictional representation of historical precedent in the case of *Beloved*, the motherline or matrilineage in African American literature has been presented in the form of a massive and severe violation and disruption enacted forcefully by large-scale racist expropriation of black women's reproduction and the subsequent inhuman rupture of the bond between black mothers and their children especially under slavery. As a result, to terminate the infliction of slavery and racism on their children, some black mothers opt reluctantly to perform the destructive act of murdering their children.

Taking into consideration the social circumstances of black mothers, an underlying motive for the mother's murderous act is her urgent need to voice her protest against a sexist and racist society that is threatening to the black race. This external, controlling, and paralyzing social force is the main cause of the violation or disruption of a black motherline. For example, within the institution of slavery, since black people were owned as property by their white masters and were not entitled to the status of human subject, in many cases they could not possibly recognize their own family members much less claim their own family lineages. Under such dreadful conditions, slave mothers, whose labor had always been at the disposal of their white masters to care for the well-being of the white race, were deprived of their maternal rights to their own children.[2] Besides this fact of violated black matrilineage, what I would also like to pinpoint in this chapter is that the practices of black motherhood such as othermothering in a black community do play a crucial part in restoring and maintaining the continuity and creativity of black race. In the later part of this chapter, I will use Morrison's text to demonstrate, on the one hand, how the mother-child relationship and the black matrilineage (with a particular focus on mothers and daughters) are interrupted by the fatal destructions carried out by the mothers and by the institutions of racism and sexism, respectively. On the other hand, I will also illustrate how black motherlines are also restored and maintained through other forms of maternity operated mostly in a female-affiliated network and connection.

Jessica Benjamin's intersubjective theory, which has been elucidated in chapter 2, will also be discussed in conjunction with a textual analysis of mother-daughter relationships and othermothering in Morrison's novel. As will be demonstrated later, my reading of Morrison's novel both problematizes and corroborates the relational psychoanalytic tenets of Benjamin. In a neo–slave narrative such as *Beloved*, which is reconstructed from a female and maternal perspective, the disrupted motherline or the severed mother-daughter relationship in the early stage of the human relationship precludes the possibility of mutual recognition in a pre-Oedipal mother-child (daughter) relationship as contended by Benjamin. Surprisingly, however, certain important concepts of intersubjectivity and relationality as advocated by Benjamin reverberate also with Morrison's delineation of black matrilineal narratives. In particular, Benjamin's description of the process of mutual recognition moving from a disruption to its consequent restoration of the tension between negation and recognition among subjects in *Like Subjects, Love Objects* rings true to my thematic investigation of Morrison's novel in this chapter. Before my main textual investigation, however, I will first refer to Patricia Hill Collins's sociological study of black motherhood with the aim of being enlightened by a black feminist perspective. A particular aspect of black maternal practices in the sense of othermothering in Collins's research will be reinforced to highlight my argument in reading Morrison's *Beloved*.

In her article "The Meaning of Motherhood in Black Culture and Black Mother-Daughter Relationships," Collins adopts and advocates an Afrocentric viewpoint on motherhood in counterpoint to a Eurocentric perspective of white motherhood. The rationale for Collins to elaborate on these differences is twofold. First, the Eurocentric ideology of motherhood that has pervaded most of the current maternal discourses, whether feminist or nonfeminist, has not provided an adequate and sufficient model for narrating the existence of other perceptions of motherhood in different cultures and races. Second, in order not to be overwhelmed and manipulated by the existing construction of white motherhood, which often results in a misreading of black motherhood, an Afrocentric notion and practice of motherhood needs to be recovered.[3]

According to Collins, what distinguishes an Afrocentric concept of motherhood from a white one are two important familial and social phenomena with reference to cross-cultural studies of motherhood in African societies. One is that African women fulfill the dual function of being both a provider and a nurturer to their children. Unlike the sexual division of labor with a father as a breadwinner and a mother as a caretaker in a family household, this duality of mothering roles is "interwoven as interdependent, complementary dimensions of motherhood" in the context of African culture. The other reality is that motherhood especially in a West African scenario is never considered as a private matter but more as a public and "collective responsibility" performed within "cooperative, age-stratified, women-centred 'mothering' networks."[4] To a great extent, the West African practices of motherhood have been integrated into most African cultures and societies. The adoption of this West African maternal culture by African American communities, in particular, has its merit in terms of welding it as "a culture of resistance" against the dominant white culture (46).

To make explicit this Afrocentric ideology of motherhood, Collins enumerates four "enduring themes" to characterize this distinct culture of mothering: 1) Bloodmothers, othermothers, and women-centered networks; 2) Providing as part of mothering; 3) Community othermothers and social activism; 4) Motherhood as a symbol of power. Significantly, the familial, social, and political functions of othermothers interlink these four enduring themes. The roles of othermothers are usually played by grandmothers, sisters, aunts, or cousins. The childcare responsibilities taken up by bloodmothers and othermothers contribute mostly to the centrality of women and motherhood in African American extended families. As mentioned earlier, the disruption caused by whatever unforeseen circumstances between biological mothers and their children will always be healed by othermothers. These "collective responsibilities" shared among othermothers create a more generalized sense of care where black women are inclined to extend their nurturing to other black community children as well. At a broader social and political level, the practices of community othermothers also empower black women to be social activists, which generate great cohesion within black communities (46–52). In a word, the significances of bloodmothers, othermothers, and community othermothers render "motherhood as symbol of power" (51) or as an unfailing source of continuity, creativity, and inspiration that guides black communities to survive through most difficulties under slavery and racism. Compared with a Eurocentric ideology of motherhood where mothers are deemed children's affective nurturers, an Afrocentric viewpoint of motherhood where the meanings of motherhood are no longer restricted to the category of biological mother, black motherhood, observed from a recent black feminist perspective, does promise a more revolutionary and liberating aspect of motherhood.

Further, in the later part of her study, Collins also discusses certain critical issues in black mother-daughter relationships when this Afrocentric ideology of motherhood is implemented into the daily life of black mothers and daughters. She states that the contradictions most African American mothers are facing when socializing their daughters are that they entice their daughters into cooperation with systems of oppression for physical survival while at the same time they are also wary of their daughters being "willing participants in their own subordination" (53). This conflict often results in black mothers being less attentive to their children's emotional needs because they have devoted themselves to providing for their children's physical survival. Thus, as Collins elaborates, the portrayal of black mothers as "overly domineering and protective" and determined to raise their children into self-reliant and independent people often appears in fictions and black women's autobiographies (55).[5] Nonetheless, as Collins notes, one essential aspect in the process of black girls' socialization entails the provision for black daughters to deal with this contradiction. That is, being exposed to a wide range of mothering roles within their black communities, black girls learn the multiple survival strategies to combat the social subordination of black womanhood (52–7).

Morrison's *Beloved* is based on the true story of Margaret Garner, an escaped slave in Cincinnati in 1856, who slit her daughter's throat to let her die rather than being taken back to slavery in Kentucky. Placing this appalling occurrence at the heart of her book, Morrison affords a black female version of a neo–slave narrative by exploring further this episode of infanticide during slavery and in the aftermath when the murdered daughter returns as a ghost to haunt her mother with her insatiable female desire for the mother-daughter communion severed by the devastation under slavery. Morrison's naming of the murdered daughter, who dies unnamed, as Beloved, symbolizes "the remembering of the 'sixty million' in one youthful body."[6] The "sixty million" refers to those ancestors of African Americans who had been displaced from their homeland, Africa, to America as slaves during the Middle Passage. Although the murder of Beloved bespeaks a painful, unspeakable past, the "homecoming" of Beloved, to her mother's, Sethe's, house indicates significantly "a mother-quest" with the aim of reclaiming her lost mothers or black matrilineage.[7]

In Morrison's *Beloved*,[8] the violation or disruption of motherline and maternity is conducted at both physical and psychological levels. The physical wounds and devastation are more visible and discernible and are usually expressed in visual signs and symbols whereas the psychological impairment of the black characters in *Beloved* implies a more intense but incomprehensible undercurrent of love, longing, discontent, rage, and destruction. For instance, Beloved's return to her mother, Sethe, with the trauma of murder and slavery, is an obsessive and possessive one haunted by "rememory" through which Morrison delves deeply into the psychological makeup of her black fictional characters. Although the physical pains these black characters suffer can be healed and they as slaves can also escape from their imprisonment and gain their own freedom, the psychological damages and wounds are indelibly etched into their own minds and can hardly be wiped out of their present free life. As Sethe says, "Freeing yourself was one thing; claiming ownership of that freed self was another,"[9] and the major slave characters such as Sethe, Baby Suggs, Denver, Beloved, and Paul D in *Beloved* all have disintegrated and fragmented selves because they cannot recognize their own bodies and do not know how to tell their own stories. They are constantly living in a past that is unspeakable.

For each character, the discontinuation of their family lineages denies and deprives them of any possible link to establish a sense of coherent self in relation with others and black community.[10] Yet, as I shall explore later, Morrison's use of visual signs and symbols in *Beloved* metaphorically and persuasively discloses the psychological wounds inflicted on her characters and also serves as possible means of identification and recognition for characters to form their connection. More significant, with the gradual unfolding of the black slave narrative in the form of storytelling by major black characters in *Beloved*, their voices begin to be heard, their separation healed, and their selfhood restored. In what follows, I shall first enumerate certain episodes regarding disrupted motherlines or broken mother-daughter relationships in *Beloved* to illustrate the problematics of implementing an intersubjective reading of the text. Then, I will go on to demonstrate that with the resurgence of othermothering in repairing the violated black matrilineage and self, the theoretical configuration of intersubjectivity becomes validated and affirmed.

With a slave mother as its protagonist, *Beloved* recounts, in many aspects, the agonizing situation of a maternal figure, Sethe. Being deprived of the status of a human subject, slave mothers such as Sethe and Baby Suggs cannot possibly exert their maternal power as indicated above in Collins's study of the centrality of motherhood in African societies and cultures. This breaking up of motherline and mother-daughter relationships can be discerned in the ensuing passage when Sethe cannot remember where she was born. Neither can she remember who her mother is until another child points her out to Sethe:

> Of that place where she was born (Carolina maybe? or was it Louisiana?) She remembered only song and dance. Not even her own mother, who was pointed out to her by the eight-year-old child who watched over the young ones—pointed out as the one among many backs turned away from her, stooping in a watery field. Patiently Sethe waited for this particular back to gain the row's end and stand. What she saw was a cloth hat as opposed to a straw one, singularity enough in that world of cooing women each of whom was called Ma'am. (30)

Sethe's attempt to recognize her mother is described first with doubt and uncertainty. When eventually Sethe is able to identify her mother aided by an eight-year-old child, the image of her mother is, however, delineated in the form of an object—"a cloth hat." Sethe's mother is objectified because the identification between mother and daughter is not firmly established and recognized. Ironically, even though Sethe's mother can be identified distinctly as a cloth hat, the mother's individual self and subjectivity are still inaccessible. Sethe's intention to seek for her mother's identity could also explain her longing for a mutual recognition between self and the other, namely between herself and her mother. However, if both self and the other do not each have an autonomous, independent self, the task of mutual confirmation between mother and daughter is simply impossible.[11] Thus, the key concept of Benjamin's intersubjective theory—mutual recognition—becomes questionable and problematic in the mother-daughter relationship under slavery. What emerges out of such dehumanization and objectification of slaves is, however, Sethe's effort to reach for identification and recognition between mother and daughter.

Another similar passage of disrupted motherline occurs when Sethe tries to fix up Denver's hair and a question, "Your woman she never fix up your hair?" (60), is posed to Sethe by Beloved concerning Sethe's relation with her mother. Sethe replies:

> "My woman? You mean my mother? If she did, I don't remember. I didn't see her but a few times out in the fields and once when she was working indigo. By the time I woke up in the morning, she was in line. If the moon was bright they worked by its light. Sunday she slept like a stick. She must of nursed me two or three weeks—that's the way the others did. Then she went back in rice and I sucked from another women whose job it was. So to answer you, no. I reckon not. She never fixed my hair nor nothing." (60)

Incessantly and excessively exploited for their labor, a temporary moment of repose becomes a luxury for a slave. Sethe's impression of her mother as working industriously and endlessly in the rice corresponds to the image of a black mother as an economic provider. A slave such as Sethe's mother, whose labor is abused to its full extent, cannot afford to provide her children sufficient nurturance let alone attend to their emotional needs. Nonetheless, the motherline is not disrupted completely as Sethe tells Beloved later that her mother does teach her how to recognize her by pointing out the marks on her skin—"a circle and a cross" (61). Although these marks symbolize the mother's identity as a slave, they are also the crucial signs that tie the mother and the daughter together. Since Sethe desires this mutual recognition between herself and her mother, she responds to her mother by asking her mother to mark her as well.[12] The mother's reply to Sethe is surprisingly a slap on the daughter's face (61). Sethe's mother's reaction can perhaps indicate her intention to protect Sethe from the cruelty of slavery. Paradoxically, the marks etched into Sethe's mother's skin mark her as a profitable object owned by a slave owner but also her crucial identity as a mother. This mother-daughter identification between black female slaves that can only be achieved through markings on their skins ruptures the assumed biological rapport between mother and child, as premised in the subject-relations theory of Benjamin.

A maternal substance such as milk is also used by Morrison to describe the exploitation and violation of motherhood under slavery.

Maternal milk that denotes the essence of motherhood is a channel through which a natural link between mother and child can be established and is a birthright that is undeniable. Nonetheless, the exploitation of a slave mother's milk for the use of her masters and its subsequent degradation as an animal's substance suspend the mother's natural right and power to nurture her children and could also put the motherline in jeopardy. Sethe tells about the scarce milk she is allowed to have from her wet nurse:

> Nan had to nurse whitebabies and me too because Ma'am was in the rice. The little whitebabies got it first and I got what was left. Or none. There was no nursing milk to call my own. I know what it is to be without the milk that belongs to you. (200)

In this passage, Sethe's lack of access to her mother's milk reinforces the violation of the black motherline. Sethe is not only deprived of her basic physical nutrition but also her emotional sustenance, the mutual recognition and attunement she can build between herself and her mother when the mother breast-feeds her.[13] Although Sethe as a young child could be constantly malnourished because of her unequal share of the wet nurse's milk, it is, significantly, the wet nurse who acts as a substitute mother or an othermother to ensure and to sustain the continuity of the black younger generation. Similarly, the eight-year-old child who helps Sethe recognize her real mother, as illustrated earlier, facilitates the mother-daughter bond and connection.

Conversely, what draws the attention in Sethe's narration that follows is a mother's claim to her own subjectivity, signaled in her action to reserve her own milk for her own baby: "Nobody will ever get my milk no more except my own children" (200). Later, Sethe reinforces that "I'll tell Beloved about that; she'll understand. She my daughter. The one I managed to have milk for and to get it to her even after they stole it" (200). Sethe's assertion of contributing her maternal milk to Beloved affirms, on the one hand, her maternal identity and claim to her daughter; on the other hand, it implies her attempt to restore a broken motherline factured by her murder of her baby daughter, Beloved. Similar messages of maternal nurturance are also conveyed in Sethe's earlier explanation for the murder of her daughter:

> Why I did it. How if I hadn't killed her she would have died and that is something I could not bear to happen to her. When I explain it she'll understand, because she understands everything already. I'll tend her as no mother ever tended a child, a daughter. (200)

Restoring a broken motherline includes a recovery from

psychological wounds that needs Sethe's maternal identity as a self in relation to ensure that the other self's autonomy and independence are not violated. Paradoxically, in order to maintain and protect her daughter's autonomy and independence, Sethe is forced to commit the crime of killing her own daughter.

Apart from Sethe's endeavor to (re)connect with her mother and matrilineage, her murdered daughter, Beloved, who returns to haunt her, gives evidence of a daughter's desire for the mother-daughter communion. Yet, in her desperation to recover her connection with Sethe, Beloved reverses the mother-daughter role by infantilizing Sethe as a child of her own:

> I am Beloved and she is mine. I see her take flowers away from leaves she puts them in a round basket the leaves are not for her she fills the basket she opens the grass I would help her but the clouds are in the way how can I say things that are pictures I am not separate from her there is no place where I stop her face is my own and I want to be there in the place where her face is and to be looking at it too a hot thing (210)

Beloved's eagerness to be "in the place where" the mother-daughter symbiosis can be reached by the daughter's owning of her mother's face is suggestive of that in an undifferentiated pre-Oedipal mother-child phase. Contrary to what Benjamin has contended as the coexistence of two differentiated subjects in the early development of mother-child relationship, Beloved's insatiable desire for mother-daughter closeness denotes female fusion and merger. Rather than accentuating the interconnection between resonance and difference, Beloved's longing is aimed at establishing the sameness between mother and daughter. Noteworthy, however, is Beloved's precarious status as a ghost who is perpetually locked in her memory of the past. Although appearing as the image of a nineteen-year-old young woman, Beloved's psychological state still lingers at the age of one.[14] As a result, Beloved cannot progress into a later and more mature stage of individuation and independence, which also inhibits her intersubjective attunement with Sethe as a subject in her own right.

Even though the motherline exemplified in the portrayal of mother-child (daughter) relationships is ruptured by the exploitation of slavery, the presence of the so-called othermothers, including a couple of minor characters, assists in the perpetuation and persistence of the black race. In *Beloved*, the role of othermothers is not restricted only to the category of a natural mother and is not assigned only to the black race and a certain gender.[15] One of the othermothers appears in a passage about labor. She is a white woman named Amy Denver who helps Sethe deliver her baby daughter, Denver:

> "Pushed!" screamed Amy.
> "Pull," whispered Sethe.
> She [Sethe] reached one arm back and grabbed the rope while Amy fairly clawed at the head.... Coming to, she heard no cries, just Amy's encouraging coos. Nothing happened for so long they both believed they had lost it. Sethe arched suddenly and the afterbirth shot out. Then the baby whimpered and Sethe looked. Twenty inches of cord hung from its belly and it trembled in the cooling evening air. Amy wrapped her skirt around it and the wet sticky women clambered ashore to see what, indeed, God had in mind. (84)

Acting as a midwife and an othermother, Amy Denver provides both Sethe and her baby with invaluable physical and emotional support. Moreover, Amy Denver's assistance in Sethe's childbirth signifies something else significant as well. This sequence of giving birth unifies these two women of different races and thus generates a sense of sisterhood out of their commonality as outlaws and social outcasts particularly under the hardship of slavery and severe racism: "there on a summer night surrounded by bluefern they did something together appropriately and well" (84). Before leaving, Amy Denver expresses to Sethe her concern about letting the newly born baby know who she is:

> "She's never gonna know who I am. You gonna tell her? Who brought her into this here world?" She lifted her chin, looked off into the place where the sun used to be. "You better tell her. You hear? Say Miss Amy Denver. Of Boston." (85)

Amy Denver's words here indicate her expectation of being recognized and remembered as an othermother who also brings life to a baby girl. As a result, Sethe's baby girl is named Denver. This story of Sethe's giving birth to Denver is also the one Denver always likes to hear from her mother.

Another othermother who functions as a community othermother is Sethe's mother-in-law, Baby Suggs, even though she and her family members also undergo severe devastation. Baby Suggs's role as a community othermother becomes conspicuous when she starts preaching in the Clearing. Baby's summoning of her people before giving her speech to them qualifies her as God Almighty incarnated as matriarch and spiritual leader of the black community:

> The company watched her from the trees. They knew she was ready when she put her stick down. Then she shouted, "Let the children come!" and they ran from the trees toward her.
> "Let your mothers hear your laugh," she told them, and the woods rang. The adults looked on and could not help smiling.
> Then "Let the grown men come," she shouted. They stepped out one by

one from among the ringing trees.
"Let your wives and your children see you dance," she told them, and groundlife shuddered under their feet. (87)

Baby's summons here resonates with Genesis in the Old Testament of the Bible. Baby as a female creator brings life and enlightenment to her black people who have long been hidden under the engulfing darkness of human brutality, suffering, and injustice. The exercise of her maternal life-giving power on her people also entitles her to the status of a black matriarch. Later, when Baby encourages her people to love their own different body parts that have long been neglected, forgotten, despised, violated, and destroyed, she exerts her maternal power to piece the broken fragmented selves of her people into a whole.[16] Further, Baby's assembling of her people to listen to her sermon also positions her as a social activist who intends to uplift her own race to change things. Another similar literary appropriation of community othermother toward the end of the book is the assembly of thirty women in front of Sethe's house to exorcise the ghostly Beloved away from her mother. With their singing of gathering "voice upon voice," Beloved disappears and Sethe, Denver, and Paul D are drawn to the community by joining the group of thirty singing women. This community othermothering thus paves the way for Sethe's reawakening and redemption of her selfhood (261–2).

As said earlier, Morrison's employment of an othermother is not restricted to a certain gender. Counterbalancing Baby Suggs's image as a black matriarch is the portrayal of an old black man named Stamp Paid, alias Joshua. Stamp Paid's significant appearances during certain critical moments when the ruptured black motherline demands assistance entitle him as another community othermother. He is, for instance, the one who aids Sethe and her newly born baby, Denver, with warmth (covering the naked body of the newborn with a jacket) and security (a safe ride across the river) (90–2). Stamp Paid's several visits to Sethe at 124 both before and after Beloved's haunting of the house delineate him as a provider and a nurturer of his black community. One such remarkable description occurs when Stamp Paid carries two buckets of blackberries to 124, feeding one berry to the three-week-old Denver. This bountiful supply of blackberries whose taste makes one feel "like being in a church" and that leads to a grand feasting of the black community (135–7) symbolically depicts Stamp Paid as fulfilling the Afrocentric mothering role of providing both physical and spiritual nutrition to the black race.

Another othermother who comes to rescue Denver from further psychological destruction is Mrs. Jones. When both Sethe and Beloved are caught in a narcissistic obsession with each other in the house at 124, Denver feels suffocated and is afraid of being also submerged in this static but degrading state. Earlier in her discovery of the Beloved-Sethe dyad, Denver has already sensed her need to free herself from this involvement:

> Neither Sethe nor Beloved knew or cared about it one way or another. They were too busy rationing their strength to fight each other. So it was she [Denver] who had to step off the edge of the world and die because if she didn't, they all would. (239)

When Denver summons her courage to go out of 124 to seek help, she cannot conquer the fear of her first encounter with the outside world. Finally, when she is well received by Mrs. Jones, her former teacher in the school, her fear and worry subside:

> "I want work, Miss Lady."
> "Work?"
> "Yes, ma'am. Anything."
> Lady Jones smiled. "What can you do?"
> "I can't do anything, but I would learn it for you if you have a little extra."
> "Extra?"
> "Food. My ma'am, she doesn't feel good."
> "Oh, baby," said Mrs. Jones. "Oh, baby." (248)

Denver's wish to work for Mrs. Jones in exchange for the food her family needs is kindly received by Mrs. Jones's generous offer. In particular, Mrs. Jones's address to Denver as "baby" enlightens Denver: "Denver looked up at her. She did not know it then, but it was the word 'baby,' said softly and with such kindness, that inaugurated her life in the world as a woman" (248). Significantly, Mrs. Jones gives Denver both physical and emotional nutrition especially during the time when her bloodmother, Sethe, can provide neither of them. The word *baby* miraculously turns Denver into being a woman of a mature and independent nature.[17]

This address with the word *baby* to heal a wounded character in *Beloved* also happens in the final reunion between Sethe and Paul D. When Sethe is emotionally deprived and feels completely lost because Beloved will never return to her again, Paul D thus comforts Sethe by calling her "baby":

> "What, baby?"
> "She left me."
> "Aw, girl. Don't cry."
> "She was my best thing." (272)

This dialogue between Paul D and Sethe resembles the one between mother and daughter because it reads as if a mother is attempting to repair her daughter's broken heart. Sethe is a bloodmother, a Demeter who is lamenting the loss of her daughter. Nonetheless, playing the role of an othermother, Paul D reestablishes a mother-child relationship in order to compensate for the loss of Sethe's motherline. Moreover, as Barbara Ann Schapiro indicates, in the final scene of the story, "Paul D's gently touching Sethe's face recalls the touching faces of the mating turtles; the relationship here is not one of merging nor of domination, but of resonating 'likeness' and empathic understanding": "He leans over and takes her hand. With the other he touches her face. 'You your best thing, Sethe. You are.' His holding fingers are holding hers."[18] The analogy, "the touching faces of the mating turtles," drawn here by Schapiro suggests a romantic reunion between Sethe and Paul D, but, more significant, it is the maternal quality manifested in Paul D that not only helps retrieve a lost motherline but also heals and even transforms Sethe's broken, fragmented self into wholeness. In touching Sethe's face with his hand and addressing her with "You your best thing, Sethe. You are,"[19] Paul D also affirms Sethe's autonomy and separateness as her own subject. It is with such assertion of one's self and subjectivity by the other that mutual recognition between subjects or mother and child can be fulfilled.

What has been discussed so far is how internal and external forces can cause the violation or disruption of black motherlines or mother-daughter relationships. These two forces are interlocked to the extent that both are mutually affected. In other words, the internal factors such as mothers' killing of their children out of maternal protectiveness and the lack of emotional interaction between bloodmothers and their children are results of the pressures imposed from the external forces such as the institution of slavery, racism, and sexism. Nonetheless, while recovering from the damage and destruction caused, the existing Afrocentric maternal practices such as othermothering have also supplied black mothers and children with tactics and skills to survive and even resist the oppressive forces outside the black communities. In a black woman's writing such as *Beloved*, the spirit of othermothers can be traced and identified in certain characters. Providing both physical and emotional needs to black people, the othermothers are the binding force to foster the continuity and creativity of the black race. Interestingly, the disruption and restoration of the black motherline also mirrors the theoretical parameter of Benjamin's intersubjective theory, in which it encompasses a "continuous disruption and repair."[20] The black motherline and matrilineage in Morrison's *Beloved* have been constantly violated and disrupted under their different circumstances, but simultaneously there is the working of repair and recovery undertaken by the act of othermothering. In *Beloved*, Sethe's attempt to restore her fragmented self in relation to the (m)other as performed in the process of mutual recognition constitutes a "tension between negation and recognition."[21] That is to say, Sethe comes to terms with the "negation and negativity" in both herself and the "concrete other[s]" in her effort to recognize her mother and her daughter Beloved.[22] To use Benjamin's notion, it is "when the Other intervenes" that intersubjective attunement between subjects can be facilitated and fostered.[23] Proposing this matrilineal reading of othermothering in Morrison's novel inadvertently runs the risk of thwarting the maternal agency and authority of bloodmothers. However, what I want to emphasize is that the Afrocentric cultural practice of othermothering, as a vital means for safeguarding and sustaining the continuity and creativity of the black race, especially when motherline and mother-child relationships are under drastic violations, suggests instead the reinstatement of the maternal at the center.

Notes

1. Elizabeth Brown-Guillory, "Disrupted Motherlines: Mothers and Daughters in a Genderized, Sexualized, and Racialized World," in *Women of Color: Mother-Daughter Relationships in Twentieth-Century Literature* (Texas: University of Texas Press, 1996), 188–9. See also Barbara Offutt Mathieson, "Memory and Mother Love: Toni Morrison's Dyad," in *Narrating Mothers: Theorizing Maternal Subjectivity*, ed. Brenda O. Daly and Maureen T. Reddy (Knoxville: University of Tennessee Press, 1991), 214–6.
2. Erica Lawson, "Black Women's Mothering in a Historical and Contemporary Perspective: Understanding the Past, Forging the Future," *Journal of the Association for Research on Mothering* 2, no. 2 (Fall/Winter 2000): 21–30.
3. Collins explicates that "white perspectives on motherhood are particularly problematic for Black women and others outside of this debate" because "the ideal of the cult of true womanhood" in a middle-class nuclear family household—mothers stay at home taking care of their own children and are well provided by male economic supports—cannot be aptly applied to black families (43). In addition, the Eurocentric images of black motherhood such as "the Mammy, the faithful, devoted domestic servant" working in a white household and "the too-strong matriarch" in a black family have misled and misinterpreted the true meanings of black motherhood (44). See Collins's essay "The Meaning of Motherhood in Black Culture and Black Mother-Daughter Relationships," in *Double Stitch: Black Women Write about Mothers and Daughters*, ed. Patricia Bell-Scott et al. (New York: Harper Perennial, 1993), 42–60, first publ. in "Black Women and Motherhood," *Black Feminist Thought: Knowledge, Consciousness, and the Politics of Empowerment* (1990; reprint, New York:

Routledge, 1991), 115–37. See also Nina Lyon Jenkins, "Black Women and the Meaning of Motherhood," in *Redefining Motherhood: Changing Identities and Patterns*, ed. Sharon Abbey and Andrea O'Reilly (Toronto: Second Story, 1998), 201–13, and Andrea O'Reilly, "'I come from a long line of Uppity Irate Black Women': African-American Feminist Thought on Motherhood, the Motherline, and the Mother-Daughter Relationship," in *Mothers and Daughters: Connection, Empowerment, and Transformation*, ed. Andrea O'Reilly and Sharon Abbey (New York: Rowman & Littlefield, 2000), 147–55.

4. Collins, "The Meaning of Motherhood in Black Culture and Black Mother-Daughter Relationships," 45. Hereafter, page numbers to this essay are cited parenthetically.
5. See also Rosalie Riegle Troester, "Turbulence and Tenderness: Mothers, Daughters, and 'Othermothers' in Paule Marshall's *Brown Girl, Brownstones*," in *Double Stitch: Black Women Write about Mothers and Daughters*, ed. Patricia Bell-Scott et al. (New York: Harper Perennial, 1993), 163–72.
6. Caroline Rody, "Toni Morrison's *Beloved*: History, 'Rememory,' and a 'Clamor for a Kiss,'" *American Literary History* 7, no. 1 (1995): 104.
7. Ibid., 105.
8. Toni Morrison, *Beloved* (1987; reprint, London: Picador, 1988). Hereafter, page numbers to this volume are cited parenthetically. References are to the reprint edition.
9. Morrison, quoted in Barbara Ann Schapiro, *Literature and the Relational Self* (1993; reprint, New York: New York University Press, 1994), 134, first publ. under a different title, "The Bonds of Love and the Boundaries of Self in Toni Morrison's *Beloved*," *Contemporary Literature* 32, no. 2 (1991): 191–210. Another useful article that deals with the same theme is Betty Jane Powell's "'Will the Parts Hold?': the Journey Toward a Coherent Self in *Beloved*," *Colby Quarterly* 31, no. 2 (1995), 105–13.
10. Andrea O'Reilly, "Maternal Redemption and Resistance in Toni Morrison's *Paradise*," *Journal of the Association for Research on Mothering* 1, no. 1 (1999 Spring/Summer): 188–9.
11. Schapiro, *Literature and the Relational Self*, 134.
12. In "Mother Right/Write Revisited: *Beloved* and *Dessa Rose* and the Construction of Motherhood in Black Women's Fiction," Carole Boyce Davies discusses how a maternal body such as Sethe's, which bears "multilayered markings" caused by "abuse, pregnancy, motherhood, and other social inscriptions," is seen not only as a site of captivity but also as naming and redefinition (46–7). See her article in *Narrating Mothers: Theorizing Maternal Subjectivity*, ed. Brenda O. Daly and Maureen T. Reddy (Knoxville: University of Tennessee Press, 1991), 46–50.
13. Schapiro, *Literature and the Relational Self*, 131.
14. Mathieson, "Memory and Mother Love: Toni Morrison's Dyad," 213–4.
15. Schapiro, *Literature and the Relational Self*, 138.
16. Ibid., 140.
17. Ibid., 139–40. Though not explicitly using the concept of othermothering, Schapiro also explores the maternal qualities in Mrs. Jones, especially in the assistance she generously offers to Denver.
18. Morrison, quoted in Schapiro, *Literature and the Relational Self*, 141.
19. Ibid.
20. Jessica Benjamin, *Love Subjects, Like Objects: Essays on Recognition and Sexual Difference* (New Haven and London: Yale University Press, 1995), 47.

21. Benjamin, *Shadow of the Other* (New York and London: Routledge, 1998), 96.
22. Ibid., 105.
23. Ibid., 99.

Chapter 11
Jamaica Kincaid's *Annie John*

As graphically portrayed in Jamaica Kincaid's *Annie John*, the strength and vibrancy but also the animosity and ferocity of the mother-daughter relationship intrigue and attract a host of literary scholars and critics to investigate the intensity and complexity of this female development. Among critical studies of Kincaid's novels, *Annie John* in particular, a clear majority unanimously concentrate on a psychoanalytic interpretation of how the formation of a female identity is established through either a separation/differentiation from or a strong identification with the mother, who is often construed as a symbolic embodiment of the other, seen in terms of cultural and racial differences. The fact that Kincaid's *Annie John* elicits predominantly psychoanalytic readings is bound up with the prevalence of pre-Oedipal mother-child symbiosis and fusion and Oedipal conflict and identity crisis, as delineated progressively and developmentally in the initial connection and the subsequent separation between Annie and her mother. While psychoanalytic examinations of Kincaid's novel generate fascinating and worthwhile studies, the two paradigmatic premises, which rely on either a masculine or a feminine model of personality development, constrict or disguise a holistic and integrative reading of the text, which I will argue in this chapter, by adding the combination of the postcolonial element, syncretism, and matrilinealism to the extant psychoanalytic frameworks.

With regard to the development of female identity in *Annie John*, as noted, there are two contrasting critical views in readings of the text. One regards the gradual separation between Annie and her mother, as exacerbated particularly in Annie's rebellion against her mother during the period of adolescence, as a necessary process for Annie's maturity in obtaining an independent and autonomous selfhood. This viewpoint rests on a masculine paradigm of psychological development.[1] The other standpoint opposes this model of masculine identity by stressing the mother-daughter bond in the text as a springboard for the female protagonist to leap toward her maturity instead of her individuality.[2]

Nonetheless, what I want to pinpoint here is that a masculine-based reading of Annie John's eventual separation from her mother, culminating in her significant journey to England, far away from her island home, Antigua, effaces the matrilinear bond that ties Annie so strongly to her female relations and her motherland. Simultaneously, an empathic reinforcement of the mother-daughter bond, as developed from a feminine-based model, avoids the conflict, anguish, and ambivalence of this female relationship, as openly revealed by Kincaid in the novel. Drawing on the aforementioned two propositions, I suggest that the mother and daughter in *Annie John* actually undergo three phases in the development of their relationship: connection, separation, and reconnection through separation by instigating a Caribbean diasporic cultural concept of matrilineal syncretism. That is, by going through this triadic trajectory, Annie is able to restore the loss of her self-identity by integrating matrilineal syncretism within herself, her mother, and her grandmother, from which a more viable depiction of Caribbean female subjectivity is developed.

To read the concept of matrilineal syncretism, one needs first to refer to the historical, social, and cultural milieu in which Kincaid contextualizes *Annie John* in Antigua in the 1960s when it still remained as one of the British colonial islands in the Caribbean, which renders the novel as undeniably a postcolonial and diasporic text. According to Mary Chamberlain's clarification of Caribbean "syncretic culture," as noted at the beginning of this part, the Caribbean islands have been occupied, inhabited, but also vacated by a massive and continuously flowing number of traveling migrants from all over the world, including white settlers and colonizers, Indo-Caribbeans and Afro-Caribbeans who had been treated as either indentured laborers or slaves for hundreds of years, and descendants of Caribbean immigrants, many of whom later either emigrated to Europe (such as Britain, France, and the Netherlands) or returned to their "places of origin" such as Africa and India. Even among different Caribbean islands, inhabitants migrate for various reasons. Throughout all the years until now, the migration of Caribbeans home and abroad is still in a state of flux like the ebb and flow of the tides moving along the shores of the Caribbean islands. Yet, it is precisely this cosmopolitan characteristic of Caribbean migranthood that cultivates its distinct diasporic syncretism.[3] In her more recent study of the life narratives of Caribbean migrant women, Chamberlain enumerates a few examples of literary manifestations of Caribbean cultural syncretism specifically written by Caribbean women writers. She points to an inextricable interrelationship between a Caribbean woman's "'syncretic' self" and her matrilineage.[4] That is to say, a Caribbean woman will often find within herself a voice indistinguishable and inseparable from those of her mother and grandmother. In saying this, Chamberlain specifies that the multiple subject positions of Caribbean migrant women should be viewed as their collective identity, a type of identity formation different from that of the Western, masculine-oriented notion of autonomy and independence. This collective identity of we-ness especially plays a pivotal role in supplying an unfailing source of cohesion between Caribbean groups home and abroad, linking the ties of kinship, lineage, and family firmly together.[5]

Chamberlain's concept of syncretism is illuminating and useful in reading Kincaid's novel *Annie John* because there is an interesting connection between syncretism and matrilinealism in the text. In relation to her mother and grandmother, Annie John as the female narrator in the book has an Afro-Caribbean identity and matrilineage. At the age of sixteen, Annie's mother migrates from her home island, Dominica, where Annie's maternal grandmother lives, to Antigua where Annie's mother marries and establishes a family on the island. Annie's grandmother, Ma Chess, who is of African descent, marries a Caribbean Indian, Annie's grandfather whom Annie calls Pa Chess. Yet, Annie's grandmother still retains her African identity and customs as an obeah woman.[6] Annie's mother, who is "part Carib Indian," thus has a fairer skin than does Annie. In fact, the skin color, black, is not racially marked on this island of Antigua, as the majority of inhabitants are descendants of African slaves. The only mention of skin color refers to those with a white or whiter complexion such as Annie's mother and a white headmistress and a girl from England in Annie's school.[7] In light of this composite of homelands, migrations, and cultures, the three-generational relation among grandmother, mother, and daughter in Annie's matrilineage epitomizes what I term *matrilineal syncretism* in which different cultures, identities, classes, and races influence and are influenced, shaped, and redefined in their interactions with one another.

However, this matrilineal syncretic reading of *Annie John* does not mean that the text itself can only be read purely in the sensibilities of postcolonialism. As pointed out briefly at the beginning of this chapter, Kincaid's exploration of the mother-daughter fusion and symbiosis, dreams, Freudian family romances, and mother-daughter ambivalence yields also interesting psychoanalytic readings, which illuminate, in turn, an eclectic or a holistic reading when combined with matrilinealism and the postmodern and postcolonial notion of syncretism.[8] Seen from a feminist psychoanalytic perspective, the loss of the mother or of a symbiotic unification with the mother, for Kincaid's female protagonist, Annie, is the cause of the disintegration of her selfhood. This fragmentation of a female selfhood is also inextricably linked with the disruption of a Caribbean collective cultural identity.[9] In *Annie John*, the intricacies and complexities of the mother-daughter relationship are elaborated to the extent that the intense connection and the subsequent separation between mother and daughter create a mental breakdown in the daughter, Annie, toward the end of the text.

Indeed, for a Caribbean woman, the figure of the mother embodies various cultural significations. In their article "'The Bloodstream of Our Inheritance': Female Identity and the Caribbean Mothers'-Land," Ann R. Morris and Margaret M. Dunn indicate specifically the strong connection between one's mother and motherland in a Caribbean sense: "The land and one's mothers are [, then,] co-joined." This concept of a Caribbean motherland is defined as a Caribbean woman's "island home and its unique culture as well as the body of tropes, talismans and female bonding that is a woman's heritage through her own and other mothers."[10] Therefore, forming close bonding with both her mother and motherland becomes the *sine qua non* in fulfilling a Caribbean woman's self-identity.[11] At varying levels, Annie's relationship with her mother manifests the effects her motherlands—the African roots of her island home and the colonial England—have on her and also her reactions to these influences. Notably, however, Annie's responses to her two major sources of motherlands and mother cultures unravel an underlying paradox of Caribbean global cultural diaspora. In the process of interacting with these two maternal origins, Annie is poised between assimilation and resistance, as epitomized in her ambivalent relationship with her mother.[12] Although these two converse forces are rendered as incompatible and "irreconcilable," Annie's syncretic self as "in transition" facilitates her absorption of "different traditions" and balance of "old and new without assimilation or total loss of the past."[13]

In *Annie John*,[14] the mother-daughter bond is consolidated through the mother's transmission of their African maternal heritages to her daughter. These African traditions include the arts of storytelling and of the obeah woman.[15] The storytelling, in particular, plays a crucial role in the text and has its different functions, which heighten simultaneously the bonding and the disruption of the mother-daughter relationship concerned. In the second chapter of *Annie John*, "The Circling Hand," for instance, Annie recounts a recurring tale her mother often tells her whenever her mother cleans the trunk in which most of Annie's early childhood belongings are stored. The story the mother narrates is about Annie herself:

> As she held each thing in her hand she would tell me a story about myself. Sometimes I knew the story first hand, for I could remember the incident

quite well; sometimes what she told me had happened when I was too young to know anything; and sometimes it happened before I was even born. Whichever way, I knew exactly what she would say, for I had heard it so many times before, but I never got tired of it. . . . On and on my mother would go. No small part of my life was so unimportant that she hadn't made a note of it, and now she would tell it to me over and over again. (21–2)

Analogous to Trinh T. Minh-ha's delineation of the narrative pattern of African women's storytelling, as discussed in chapter 1, the power of the mother's storytelling lies in its repetition as a form of creativity, rather than causing boredom in the daughter as the listener.[16] Through each reiteration, the mother's storytelling can link the past and the present together, creating a continuum of time. Or as Donna Perry specifies, the creativity of storytelling effectuates "timelessness and immortality."[17] It also signals the sharing of collective memory between mother and daughter. In addition, the trunk is a symbol of maternal heritage as it is the trunk that Annie's mother carries with her when she leaves her home island, Dominica, for Antigua.[18] In association with a matrilineal syncretic reading, the trunk in the text, I would argue, denotes their collective Caribbean identity as traveling migrants, as will be unfolded in the final scene when Annie, carrying her own trunk, is ready to depart from her island home to England. The trope of the trunk in this context of matrilineal storytelling also complicates the notion of Caribbean female identity in relation to motherland as fluid and unbound rather than being circumscribed by the fixed geographical location of a land.

In this storytelling tradition, the daughter is not merely a passive recipient. She is also a creator, a teller, and a writer.[19] In the third chapter "Gwen," for example, Annie John describes the autobiographical essay her class is asked to write toward the end of their first day in a new school. In her autobiographical essay, Annie offers an idyllic and ethereal essay about the Sundays she spends with her mother on Rat Island. Apart from demonstrating the inseparability between mother and daughter, Annie also expresses her anxiety about the advent of her unavoidable separation from her mother:

A huge black space then opened up in front of me and I fell inside it. I couldn't see what was in front of me and I couldn't hear anything around me. I couldn't think of anything except that my mother was no longer near me. (43)

However, Annie is able to restore the mother-daughter connection by re-creating the close relationship she has had with her mother before, especially during the time when Annie's mother deliberately tries to break away from her as soon as Annie reaches puberty:

> [T]ears came to her eyes, and, taking me in her arms, she told me all the same things she had told me on the day at the sea, and this time the memory of the dark time when I felt I would never see her again did not come back to haunt me. (44–5)

In a word, the creative power of storytelling can not only transcend the transience of human life but also transform the vulnerability of human relationships—the mother-daughter relationship in this context.

The daughter's inheritance of this storytelling skill is further developed in the fifth chapter, "Columbus in Chains." Once, after reflecting on the colonial history of the West Indies in a history class, Annie is amazed to see a picture of Columbus, the great discoverer of Dominica, being chained at the bottom of a ship: "How I loved this picture—to see the usually triumphant Columbus, brought so low, seated at the bottom of a boat just watching things go by" (77–8). Shortly after seeing this picture, Annie hears her mother reading a letter from her aunt about her grandfather's, Pa Chess's, partial immobility caused by trouble with his limbs. Hearing her mother's contempt for Pa Chess, "'So the great man can no longer just get up and go. How I would love to see his face now!'"(78), Annie imitates and adapts her mother's narration by writing the words "'The Great Man Can No Longer Just Get Up and Go'" (78) under Columbus's picture. By drawing a parallel between these two patriarchal figures, Annie parrots her mother's words and draws the mother and daughter together in demonstrating their "complicity" in resisting the dominance of the patriarchy.[20]

In *Annie John*, the complexity of the mother-daughter relationship is constantly deployed as a locus of contesting the binary opposition between the colonizer and the colonized. As mentioned already, the storytelling is also the device that Annie adopts to voice her resentment against the discipline and civilization both her mother and the dominant colonial culture impose on her. This storytelling is, in particular, expressed in the form of telling lies. As Annie grows older, her relationship with her mother begins to deteriorate. The gaps between the mother and the daughter start to widen because the mother now acts as an agent who colludes with the patriarchy and the colonizer to mutilate her daughter in conformity with the rules of appropriate womanhood and the submission of a dependent subject. Being forced to consent to this process of socialization and, by extension, colonization, brings rebellion and later great agony to the daughter, Annie. Therefore, in order to detach herself from such subordination, Annie the daughter deliberately tells different lies to safeguard her true self in disguise. For example, Annie's friendship with the Red Girl, a sloppy and unladylike young girl of Annie's age, with whom Annie's mother forbids her to socialize, is developed secretly without her mother's recognition. Besides, Annie the daughter is addicted to collecting marbles, a habit that her mother strongly disapproves of by virtue of its unfeminine nature:

> Using the usual slamming-the-gate-and-quietly-creeping-back technique, I dived under the house to retrieve the marble from the special place where I had hidden it. As I came out from under the house, what should I see before me but my mother's two enormous, canvasclad feet. From the look on my face, she guessed immediately that I was up to something; from the look on her face, I guessed immediately that everything was over. (65)

Shortly afterward, Annie's trick is discovered by her mother. Her mother begins searching frantically for the hidden marbles in the house. Nonetheless, being a rebellious daughter now, Annie plays the trick of "storytelling": "'Where are your other marbles?' said my mother. 'If you have one, you have many.' 'Oh, no,' I said. 'Oh, no. I don't have marbles, because I don't play marbles'" (65).

When the mother-daughter relationship reaches its worst in the sixth chapter, "Somewhere, Belgium," Annie the daughter begins to tell her own story in fantasy that she is an orphan or an adopted child of her parents. This retelling of Freudian family romances is, however, accompanied by her ambivalence toward her mother. At one moment, Annie the daughter emphasizes the importance of her mother's presence in her life and the symbiotic relationship between them:

> If my mother died, what would become of me? I couldn't imagine my life without her. Worse than that, if my mother died I would have to die, too, and even less than I could imagine my mother dead could I imagine myself dead. (88)

At the next moment, an opposing feeling toward her mother would emerge in a recurring dream as Annie dreams that "My mother would kill me if she got the chance. I would kill my mother if I had the courage" (89). Annie's ambivalence toward the mother corresponds to the way the postcolonial theorist Homi K. Bhabha has defined the term *ambivalence* as "the complete mix of attraction and repulsion that characterizes the relationship between the colonizer and colonized." In *Annie John*, the mother-daughter relationship as an epitome of the colonizer-colonized relationship is ambivalent because their opposition cannot be determined and finalized. The paradox of the colonized in relation to the colonizer lies in the coexistence of "complicity" and "resistance" as colonial discourse "may be both exploitative and nurturing" at the same time.[21] Annie's relationship with her mother can be conceived figuratively as that between the colonized and the colonizer because her mother has gradually come to stand for the colonial dominance with her maternal power as both "exploitative and nurturing." As a result, Annie is torn between "complicity" and "resistance" in reaction to her mother.

Since Annie can hardly resolve her ambivalence toward her mother in the later part of the story, she then suffers from an inexplicable mental breakdown. In the seventh chapter, "The Long Rain," Annie has been confined to her bed for three months because of a seemingly incurable disease, which is, in fact, her nervous breakdown that resulted from the disconnection between mother and daughter. Miraculously, Annie's illness is eventually cured by the healing power of an obeah woman, her grandmother, Ma Chess, who practices a source of ancient African woman-specific spirituality that her mother constantly consults in the event of ominous happenings. Significantly, Ma Chess takes up the role of a maternal nurturer as Annie's mother has done before:[22]

> Ma Chess settled in on the floor at the foot of my bed, eating and sleeping there, and soon I grew to count on her smells and the sound her breath made as it went in and out of her body. Sometimes at night, when I would feel that I was all locked up in the warm falling soot and could not find my way out, Ma Chess would come into my bed with me and stay until I was myself. . . . I would lie on my side, curled up like a little comma, and Ma Chess would lie next to me, curled up like a bigger comma, into which I fit. . . . Ma Chess fed me food, coaxing me to take mouthful after mouthful. She bathed me and changed my clothes and sheets and did all the other things that my mother used to do. (125–6)

This healing episode symbolizes Annie's return to her mother's womb. Being physically present in the same location, both Ma Chess and Annie go back to a symbiotic state between mother and child. The positions taken up by Annie and Ma Chess such as "a little comma" and "a bigger comma" resemble the shape of a fetus in a womb.[23] More important, the two commas could fit into each other to form a whole. As Annie gradually recovers through this maternal healing, she goes through a rebirth, which engenders her new emerging self. This can be best testified to in Annie's final reconfirmation of her own identity: "My name is Annie John" (130). In announcing her own name, she is not only claiming her own identity but also that of her mother as both mother and daughter share the same name: "She was my mother, Annie; I was her daughter, Annie" (105). Since this matrilineal syncretic self embodies grandmother, mother, and daughter, the triple identities are, hence, dissolved into Annie herself and pave the way for Annie's journey to England, her other motherland or mother country, to bravely embrace her future and pursue their collective Caribbean global migrant culture.

Written from the standpoint of a postcolonial Caribbean diaspora, *Annie John* elicits a matrilineal syncretic reading of the text, which addresses both the strength and imperfection of the mother-daughter relationship, as compounded by the interlocking structures of sexism, racism, and neocolonialism. A reader is then invited to see within and beyond the mother-daughter relationship or matrilineal relation as a microcosm of life in a postcolonial Caribbean world. In particular, Annie's seemingly separable but also inseparable relation to her mother or matrilineage bespeaks a diasporic woman's ambiguous and complex relation to her motherland and mother country. Notably, Annie's eventual separation from her mother and motherland heightened in her embarking on a journey to her mother country, England, cannot be solely read as her liberation from psychological paralysis overwhelmed by maternal dominance. Before her departure from her motherland, Annie has gone through a rebirth by the healing power of her African matrilineal nurturance. In other words, Annie's new self is born with her matrilineal strength and empowerment, and she cannot and does not aspire to an autonomous and independent selfhood. Rather, she incorporates matrilineal syncreticism within herself, linking together a lineage of her female connection, her mother and grandmother in particular. This triple embodiment of matrilineal syncreticism entails what Jessica Benjamin has theorized as an "intersubjective space."[24] where tension is involved in interactions with "the negation and negativity" of the (m)other as the cultural, racial, and colonial other but also the reconciliation and resolution of this tension.[25] Although Benjamin speaks also from a psychoanalytic position, her reformulation of classical, masculine-oriented psychoanalytic parameters allies her basic tenet with that in a postcolonial black woman's writing. Yet, what a black woman's writing such as Kincaid's *Annie John* has added to the theoretical topos are the specificities of gender, class, race, culture, and self-identity and the writer's interrogation of these complexities in her creative textual practice.

Notes

1. H. Adlai Murdoch, "Severing the (M)other Connection: the Representation of Cultural Identity in Jamaica Kincaid's *Annie John*," *Callaloo* 13, no. 2 (1990): 325–40. See also Deborah Mistron, *Understanding Jamaica Kincaid's Annie John: A Student Casebook to Issues, Sources, and Historical Documents* (Westport, Conn.:

Greenwood, 1999), 2.
2. In an endnote to their article, Ann R. Morris and Margaret M. Dunn comment on the critic, Bryant Mangum's reading of the mother-daughter separation in *Annie John* as a necessary process for the formation of self-identity. Contrary to this male appropriation of female development, Morris and Dunn present a psychoanalytic feminist reading of the text by offering a completely different female model of subject formation with an emphasis on the mother-daughter connection. See their article, "'The Bloodstream of Our Inheritance': Female Identity and the Caribbean Mothers'-Land," in *Motherlands: Black Women's Writing from Africa, the Caribbean and South Asia*, ed. Susheila Nasta (New Jersey: Rutgers University Press, 1992), 236–7.
3. Mary Chamberlain, ed., *Caribbean Migration: Globalised Identities* (London and New York: Routledge, 1998), 1–17. A brief definition of syncretism is also given by Robin Cohen in which he makes a careful distinction between hybridity and syncretism. See his book, *Global Diasporas: An Introduction* (1997; reprint, London: University College of London Press, 1999), 131, rpt. in *Caribbean Migration: Globalised Identities*, ed. Mary Chamberlain (New York: Routledge, 1998), 21–35. In addition, the word *syncreticism* is also mentioned briefly by Helen Pyne Timothy toward the end of her essay, in which she elucidates the combination of different systems of belief, European, African, and Caribbean, as syncretism, which has its manifestations in the female genealogy in *Annie John*. See her article "Adolescent Rebellion and Gender Relations in *At the Bottom of the River* and *Annie John*," *Caribbean Women Writers: Essays from the First International Conference*, ed. Selwyn R. Cudjoe (Wellesley, Mass.: Calaloux, 1990), 242.
4. Chamberlain, "The Global Self: Narratives of Caribbean Migrant Women," in *Feminism and Autobiography: Texts, Theories, Methods*, ed. Tess Cosslett, Celia Lury, and Penny Summerfield (London and New York: Routledge, 2000), 161.
5. Ibid., 160–4.
6. "Obeah" means "voodoo" in patois; it's the kind of African religious practice, which involves the use of "magic and sorcery." Annie John's grandmother, Ma Chess, is an individual practitioner of obeah. See Mistron, *Understanding Jamaica Kincaid's Annie John*, 67–70.
7. Mistron, *Understanding Jamaica Kincaid's Annie John*, 4. See also Murdoch, "Severing the (M)other Connection: The Representation of Cultural Identity in Jamaica Kincaid's *Annie John*," *Callaloo* 13, no. 2 (1990): 326–7.
8. It is worthy of note that adopting a psychoanalytic reading for a postcolonial text could be problematic because of the androcentric and ethnocentric nature of psychoanalysis. Although it is politically incorrect to make a universal claim on psychoanalysis, certain important thematics related to psychoanalysis as it emerges in several postcolonial texts cannot absolutely preclude a possibility of psychoanalytic reading. To a great extent, psychoanalysis facilitates delving into the sophistication of a postcolonial text and vice versa. See Allison Mackey, "Return to the [M]Other to Heal the Self: Identity, Selfhood and Community in Toni Morrison's *Beloved*," *Journal of the Association for Research on Mothering* 2, no. 2 (2000): 48–9.
9. In her study of the Caribbean women writers, Laura Niesen de Abruna stresses the significance of strong connections between women in Caribbean women's writing: "The bonding between African-Caribbean women is stronger than the bonding between other women, either between Creoles or between Creoles and African-Caribbean characters" (90). Kincaid's *Annie John* is also illustrative of

this characteristic as the portrayal of matrilinear bonding among grandmother, mother, and daughter testifies. See her essay, "Twentieth-Century Women Writers from the English-Speaking Caribbean," in Cudjoe, *Caribbean Women Writers*, 86–97.

10. Morris and Dunn, "'The Bloodstream of Our Inheritance,'" 219.
11. Ibid., 222–4.
12. As one of the few studies with a feminist postcolonial reading as its focal point, Simone A. James Alexander elaborates on how the delineations of the mother-daughter relationship in Kincaid's two novels *Annie John* and *The Autobiography of My Mother* are also infused with the politics and dynamics of colonial and postcolonial relations, that between the colonizer and the colonized. See her book, *Mother Imagery in the Novels of Afro-Caribbean Women* (Columbia and London: University of Missouri Press, 2001), 45–95.
13. Cohen, *Global Diasporas*, 131.
14. Jamaica Kincaid, *Annie John* (1983; reprint, London: Vintage, 1997). Hereafter, page numbers to this volume are cited parenthetically. References are to the reprint edition.
15. In her essay, "Initiation in Jamaica Kincaid's *Annie John*," Donna Perry mentions three distinct features of West Indian traditions—the storytelling, the obeah woman, and matrilinear bonding—which constitutes the mother-daughter bond in the text. In the rest of this chapter, my reading of the text will be developed from Perry's point. See her article in Cudjoe, *Caribbean Women's Writers*, 245–53.
16. Trinh T. Minh-ha, *Women, Native, Other: Writing Postcoloniality and Feminism* (Bloomington and Indianapolis: Indiana University Press, 1989), 122.
17. Perry, "Initiation in Jamaica Kincaid's *Annie John*," 247.
18. Different critics have their own various interpretations of the trope of the trunk as used in the text. A masculine-oriented critic such as Murdoch views Annie's mother's trunk as "an indicator of repression and discontent," as a symbol of maternal dominance. Murdoch proves his argument later when he points out Annie's possession of her own trunk as a signal of the daughter's liberation from the powerful mother's tyranny and repression. See Murdoch, "Severing the (M)other Connection," 330. A feminist literary critic such as Alexander sees Kincaid's use of the trunk in a more positive sense. It is, according to her reading, an important symbol of female legacy and maternal history, because the trunk is, in effect, passed on from grandmother to mother to daughter as a maternal heritage. See Alexander, *Mother Imagery*, 74.
19. Perry, "Initiation in Jamaica Kincaid's *Annie John*," 248–9.
20. Ibid., 149–50.
21. Homi K. Bhabha, quoted in Bill Ashcroft, Gareth Griffiths, and Helen Tiffin, *Key Concepts in Post-Colonial Studies* (London and New York: Routledge, 1998), 12–3.
22. Resonating with Hope Edelman's analysis of the liberating aspect of grandmother-granddaughter relationships, both Timothy and Alexander concurrently emphasize the "tension-free" relationship between grandmother and granddaughter, which as an important form of othermothering "bridges the misunderstanding and pain between mother and daughter." See Edelman, *Mother of My Mother: The Intricate Bond between Generations* (New York: Dial, 1999), 97–122. See also Timothy, "Adolescent Rebellion and Gender Relations in *At the Bottom of the River* and *Annie John*," 242, and Alexander, *Mother Imagery*, 68–9.

23. Perry, "Initiation in Jamaica Kincaid's *Annie John*," 251. See also Alexander, *Mother Imagery*, 70–1.
24. Jessica Benjamin, *Shadow of the Other: Intersubjectivity and Gender in Psychoanalysis* (New York and London: Routledge, 1998), 95.
25. Ibid., 79–88.

Chapter 12
Joy Kogawa's *Obasan*

Joy Kogawa's *Obasan* is a novel, narrated by its central female character, Naomi Nakane, about Japanese Canadians' experiences of the racist deportation during and after the Second World War. Persistently throughout the novel and in conjunction with this racist dispersal of her co-ethnic community, Naomi is haunted by the specter of her mother's absence, which in fact is her mother's death, a truth that is concealed from Naomi by her relatives in Canada for protective reasons. As a consequence, Naomi is impelled to quest for an explanation of the breaking up of her family and their Japanese Canadian community. To a great extent, Naomi's anxieties and agonies in such a quest are intensified and complicated by her biracial and bicultural (Japanese and white Canadian) and bigenerational (Issei and Nisei)[1] backgrounds. Under such circumstances, Naomi is constantly torn between these two sets of contrasting reactions to this trauma suffered by Japanese Canadians, as represented particularly in the living forces of two female characters, Obasan and Aunt Emily, during Naomi's childhood and adolescence. Obasan, Naomi's elderly Aunt Aya, who was born in Japan and then emigrated to Canada, represents the first generation of Japanese Canadian immigrants (Issei) who still preserve and carry on Japanese traditions and heritages such as perseverance and stoicism. Conversely, Aunt Emily, who was born and raised in Canada, stands for another type of the second-generation Japanese Canadians (Nisei); that is, as a political activist herself, she assimilates to and adopts white Western cultural views and behaviors such as aggressiveness and vociferation. By virtue of these conflicting images created in Obasan and Aunt Emily, Naomi is consequently exposed to the binary opposition between silence and speech with her insistent endeavor to negotiate and strike a balance between these two stances.

Kogawa breaks the imposed silences in the text by writing and publishing *Obasan* as an expression and development of her own poetic language, a book that is derived from her life experience.[2] Yet, the persistence of hidden voices—the different forms of silences—is also meticulously attended to. The inevitability of the silence in the text, as characterized by the absence of the mother in Naomi's life, informs, articulates, and constitutes most of the narration. Speculating on a statement quoted from *Obasan*,[3] "Mother, I'm listening. Assist me to hear you" (288), we can discern the exigency of this silencing mother figure and the daughter's plea to hear her mother. In addressing her mother, Naomi invokes her mother to enhance her vigilance and insight. Although the mother is referred to here as a muse who can only inspire not create, the daughter does attempt to relocate her mother as a subject by listening attentively to her silent mother rather than positioning her as an object of the daughter's desire and fantasy. This daughter's pleading for her mother's voice resonates, in part, with recent Western feminists' concern with discovering the mother's voice and letting the mother speak. One of the contentious issues regarding motherhood within recent feminist scholarship has been focused on constituting maternal subjectivity from the perspectives of mothers.[4]

Nonetheless, within this particular cultural scenario where the mother's absence, which is in fact her death, is "a silence that cannot speak" and "a silence that will not speak" (preface) as Naomi's mother has forbidden her family to tell the truth to her children, the text, *Obasan*, offers an astonishingly different perspective and approach to feminist studies of motherhood and maternal subjectivity. In other words, what and how can feminism deal with a text that has an absent mother in it? Is it necessary and beneficial for feminist maternal researchers to listen to this arbitrary silence of the mother? Can such a silence enlighten or bring any insights into feminist matrilinealism? Although it is crucial to locate mothers as subjects articulating their own discourses in culture and language, what I want to draw attention to here is that this different approach to retrieving maternal subjectivity, as proposed by attending to the silent mother in *Obasan*, signals a different mode of writing and reading the mother that does not necessarily mean that a mother's narrative will be submerged in a child's.

In her later study of matrilineal narratives, Tess Cosslett elicits a pathbreaking thought on the mother's "irrecoverability," generated from a void created mainly by the death of a mother or a daughter's resistance to write her mother in conjunction with herself.[5] Pondering over the early death of her mother, Cosslett avers that "my mother remains an absence, a black hole of longing."[6] With this preoccupation in mind concerning the "unknowability of the maternal," Cosslett revisits her early research into matrilineal narratives and concludes by suggesting her rereading of matrilineal narratives as "a feminist progress narrative, from matrophobia, to speaking for the mother, to allowing her irreducible difference and mystery."[7] The mother's "irreducible difference and mystery" is also what intrigues and haunts

Naomi in Kogawa's *Obasan*.

Reading Cosslett's work in accordance with Kogawa's *Obasan* reminds me of a piece of autobiographical writing I heard in one of the sessions for the seminar "Women's Lives and Life-writing" that I took while I was reading for my master's degree in women's studies at York University, UK, in 1993. In that session, every one of us was supposed to bring along our own autobiographical writings, assigned to be finished prior to the session, when we would share with our whole group. What struck me in the midst of the session is one of my English coursemates, Cathy, and her attempt and failure to read her piece. She uttered painfully a few words from her writing but then paused and ceased abruptly. Detecting the sense of tremendous discomfort from Cathy, my American coursemate, Suzanne, sitting next to her took over the task of reading it instead. With Cathy's heartrending sobs, we began to realize that she had written about her inadvertent but extremely agonizing discovery of the truth about her mother's death. In a similar vein to Naomi's situation in *Obasan*, Cathy's family hid the truth from her about her mother's death; she was not even taken to her mother's funeral. Yet, years later, Cathy accidentally found out the date of her mother's death in her family calendar in a record detailing accurately the dates of birth and death for each of their family members. On the date of her grandfather's birthday, her mother's name had also been written: it is undoubtedly the date of her mother's death.

When a mother's absence becomes mysterious to her daughter, it is very often that this emptiness left by the mother's absence turns into the daughter's continuing quest for an answer. For Cathy, she got it unwittingly. For Naomi in *Obasan*, she conducts a painstaking search for the truth. The truth is then revealed to Naomi later in her life. As Cosslett indicates, Kogawa's composition of her novel with "the mother as absent center" and as a fictionalized character in her book is inextricably linked with her needs as a daughter.[8] This daughter's wish to fill in the gap, resulting from various circumstances of a daughter's relation to her mother and conducted either by a daughter's fictionalization or search for documentary and biographical truth, is exactly the propelling force for women's writing of matrilineal narratives. For Kogawa's *Obasan*, this issue of the mother's inaccessibility is also compounded by the intermeshing structures of race, class, and gender.

In what follows, my investigation of Kogawa's *Obasan* will be divided into three areas. First, I will dip into the immigrant experiences of Japanese North Americans in a broader social and historical scenario in an effort to contextualize and specify the politics inherent in reading a Japanese Canadian text such as *Obasan*.[9] Second, I will explore the extent to which the intricacies and complexities between silence and speech in the text, in negotiation with the political and racial strictures, are worked and reworked to constitute a matrilineal narrative with a silent mother in it. Third, I will envision tentatively what model or paradigm of writing and reading the mother can be possibly developed from the text as a contingency plan or an adaptive strategy to deal with the exigency of social and political strictures.

Unlike their Asian American counterparts such as Chinese Americans, the early Japanese American immigrants between 1885 and 1907 demonstrated their conscious intention to assimilate into the mainstream white culture and society. The incentives for their willingness to be Americanized are, in part, due to the fact that a majority considered their adopted country, America, as a dreamland with more opportunities and prospects for a better life than their natal country, Japan, could have afforded them. Moreover, some of these early immigrants were, to some extent, not totally excluded and discriminated against by the dominant white population in America because their financially sound and well-educated backgrounds gave them a higher status than other groups of Asian American immigrants; they were generally viewed as more "civilized" by the white society.[10] Having this high appraisal, nonetheless, does not mean that these early Japanese American immigrants were immune to racism. The stereotyping of Japanese Americans as "aggressive, cunning, and conspiratorial" by "anti-Japanese agitators" stigmatized and pigeonholed most Japanese Americans to the extent that they were restricted by limited social mobility and were usually confined within the vocations of "agriculture, fishing or domestic service."[11] As indicated already, some of this first generation of Japanese Americans, the so-called Issei, did not usually feel repulsed by such a racist discrimination from their host country. Most of them felt obliged to adapt to their new life as a "guest" or as a newly wed "bride" who treated America as their "mother-in-law" country.[12]

Notwithstanding the Issei's cooperative stance of assimilation, the racial discrimination leveled against them still hopelessly and aggressively inhibited their fulfillment of the American dream.[13] As most of them were denied equal access to a share of social resources such as work and education, they were encircled by their own ethnic groups and did not command the English language at a proficient level. Seeing the prospect of their own future as rather bleak and unpromising, the Issei, thus, placed their hopes on their next generation, the Nisei, who are American-born and -educated. The Nisei, like the Issei or even to a greater degree, assimilated into and identified more with the white mainstream culture and language. Yet, the Nisei's assimilation paradoxically set them apart from their parents whose language, cultural values, and customs were still Japanese.[14] Their division and rift were severely widened at the height of racism targeted specifically against Japanese Americans at the outbreak of the Second World War. With the rise of the Japanese empire in the Pacific and the resultant Allied Forces' declaration of a war with Japan, the Japanese Americans in the North American continent suffered from a forced dispersal of their communities and families to internment in camps under inhumane and brutal conditions. In the case of Canada, the Japanese Canadians were deported from their homes in the West Coast to the interior, resulting in most of the families being scattered in different places. Cognizant of their Japaneseness as a threat to their ultimate survival, both Issei and Nisei, being docile scapegoats of this unexpected calamity, responded differently to declare and verify indisputably their loyalty to America. The Issei remained silent and burned artifacts including their diaries, books, magazines, and letters written in Japanese on the eve of the outbreak of the war in the Pacific. The Nisei, however, pledged their loyalty by joining the American army in exchange for better jobs and opportunities, of which they had been deprived. During the period of internment, most families of Issei and Nisei had, thus, been disrupted to a full extent.[15]

Set against such a traumatic and turbulent period in the history of Japanese North American immigrants, Kogawa's use of "the mother as absent center," to cite Cosslett again,[16] can be seen as a trope for racial silence and annihilation. The significant death of Naomi's mother during the 1945 bombing of Nagasaki, Japan, becomes a hidden signifier of "a silence that cannot speak" and "a silence that will not speak" (preface). As Shirley Geok-lin Lim aptly puts it, "the Japanese mother is the figure not only of maternality but also of racial consciousness." Commenting on her comparative reading of two Japanese North American women's texts, Monica Sone's *Nisei Daughter* and Joy Kogawa's *Obasan*, Lim goes on to explain that the manifestation of racial issues in the figure of the mother as demonstrated in these two texts illustrates a progression from "a move to assimilate" to "a reclamation of the culture of origin."[17] This opposition or *"dialectic,"* as Lim phrases it, is related to "the rejection and reclamation of the mother" in *Nisei Daughter* and *Obasan*, respectively. Lim's reading of *Obasan* as a postwar and postinternment novel situates Kogawa's work as a recovery project of the mother as "political 'integration' has been achieved" after the war and there is, thus, a cultural and psychological need to trace "a lost racial origin."[18]

Although Lim's statement concerning the retrieval of an absent mother in *Obasan* captures the heart of the book, what I also want to advance is further elaboration of the intricacy of "the rejection and reclamation of the mother" represented in the covert opposition between silence and speech, as featured predominantly in the two maternal figures of Obasan and Aunt Emily. Yet, before getting to my main discussion of the text, I would first like to define and clarify the meaning of silence. Being located and embedded in an Asian or, to be more precise, a Japanese tradition and culture, the concept of silence does denote a different meaning from that in a Western tradition. As King-kok Cheung makes clear in her book *Articulate Silences*, "in English 'silence' is often the opposite of 'speech' . . . generally looked upon as passive" whereas in Chinese and Japanese "'silence' is synonymous with 'serenity' . . . it traditionally signals pensiveness, vigilance, or grace."[19] What Cheung has emphasized is that looking from an Eastern perspective, the notion of silence is not necessarily the negative that most Westerners perceive it to be. Instead, it conveys certain virtues and merits, which are culturally positive and highly valued. Taking account of these Eastern perceptions of silence, it will then become more meaningful to attend to the silence in this particular text.

In the novel *Obasan*, the most prominent feature of the silence is shown particularly in the portrayal of certain female characters—Naomi's mother, Obasan, and Naomi herself. Although some male characters such as Naomi's father and uncle also share similar characteristics, the center of the silence is focused more on females rather than on males. In particular, the title registers this link with the female connection. In Japanese, *obasan* means both aunt and woman. Therefore, it refers to not only another central female character, Obasan, as Naomi's aunt in the text but also can be extended to symbolize Naomi's identification with "a lineage of traditional women" in her family, including her mother, Obasan, and Grandma Kato, who always goes back to Japan with Naomi's mother.[20] Or as Gayle K. Fujita indicates, the title establishes and "acknowledges the connectedness of all women's lives—Naomi, her mother, her two aunts."[21]

Due to her absence in Naomi's early childhood, Naomi's mother is constantly portrayed as an obscure family figure. Naomi's memory of her mother comes only from her early childhood experiences with her. Looking at her mother's photographs, Naomi's reflections show her mother as a diminishing and frail family figure. In stark contrast to her sister, Naomi's Aunt Emily, who has "the round open face and the stocky build," Naomi's mother "is a fragile presence. Her face is oval as an egg and delicate. . . . Her eyes, Obasan told me, were sketched in by the photographer because she was always blinking when pictures were being taken" (23). More notably, in describing her mother through recollection, nonverbal expressions such as gestures are reinforced rather than a verbal one such as speech.[22] A remarkable example of this occurs when Naomi places chicks back in the cage with a hen, which to Naomi's astonishment pecks the chicks to death. Immediately after hearing Naomi uttering "Mama," her mother comes to the rescue:

> With swift deft fingers, Mother removes the live chicks first, placing them in her apron. All the while that she acts, there is calm efficiency in her face and she does not speak. Her eyes are steady and matter-of-fact—the eyes of Japanese motherhood. They do not invade and betray. They are eyes that protect, shielding what is hidden most deeply in the heart of the child. She makes safe the small stirrings underfoot and in the shadows. Physically, the sensation is not in the region of the heart, but in the belly. This that is in the belly is honored when it is allowed to be, without fanfare, without reproach, without words. What is there is there. (71)

What is striking about this passage is a unique demonstration of Japanese motherhood manifest in the use of silence. That is, empathy can be easily formed between mother and daughter without necessarily engaging the expression of verbal language. It is the use of body language—the language of the eyes—that speaks more than a thousand words about the mother-daughter connection. The mother's eyes and glances bespeak safety, protection, and understanding. This comforting and tranquil quality of motherhood can be best recognized when being contrasted with the glance of Mrs. Sugimoto that can blatantly reveal Naomi's fear and is intrusive to Naomi's inner world.[23] Although Naomi's mother is, to a certain degree, an ambiguous and mute figure, her absence and silence impresses Naomi in the text.

Another significant silent figure or perhaps the most important one is Naomi's Aunt Aya whom Naomi always calls Obasan. Acting as Naomi's surrogate mother who showers Naomi with her motherly caring throughout Naomi's childhood and adolescence, Obasan, however, embodies certain features and qualities that resemble Naomi's silent mother. In an analogous fashion to Naomi's mother, Obasan hardly speaks at all. Right at the beginning of the book, for instance, Naomi as a grown-up daughter narrates her coming back to visit Obasan on the occasion of attending her uncle's funeral. Describing Obasan now as an old woman whose old age gives rise to her being nearly deaf and blind, it seems even more unlikely to hear Obasan speak after all those silent years:

> She leans her head back to look up at me and her cheeks sink into the cavity of her mouth, making her face resemble a skull. The pulse is a steady ripple in her wrinkled neck. Such an old woman she is. She opens her mouth to say more, but there is no further sound from her dry lips.

> The language of her grief is silence. She has learned it well, its idioms, its nuances. Over the years, silence within her small body has grown large and powerful. (17)

Judging from Obasan's appearance in this excerpt, she is compared to a dead person who symbolizes ultimate and endless silence. As Betty Sasaki remarks, Obasan is "the literal embodiment of silence"; namely, the figure of Obasan represents and personifies the abstract and incomprehensible concept, silence. Therefore, in her quest for her mother's absence and silence, Naomi also needs to attend to and even decipher the silent code of Obasan's language. In Naomi's mind, as Sasaki points out again, "Obasan's silence" resembles "both a barrier and a bridge."[24] In other words, reading Obasan's silence for Naomi is not only the means of finding out the truth about her mother's absence and of comprehending fully the values of her Japanese maternal heritage. It also creates difficulties and even differences for Naomi because, as mentioned earlier, Naomi stands at the intersection between different generations (Issei and Nisei) and different racial backgrounds (Japanese and white Canadian). "This silence," as Malve von Hassell indicates, "culturally rooted in a filial piety, was transformed into a cultural miscommunication between the generations, which created a barrier to the mother's past and cut her daughter off from her own family's history."[25] In light of feminist matrilinealism, this cultural misreading of the silence can jeopardize the motherline.

Thus, Sasaki reminds us that in reading Obasan's silence, we also need to bear in mind the social and historical context in which Obasan is involved. Being an Issei, the first generation of Japanese Canadians, Obasan still adheres to her Japanese cultural values and heritage and does not really blend with the dominant white society. Put more crucially, being "preservers and transmitters of cultural tradition and values," an Issei woman such as Obasan often honors her "extended family and the community over the individual"; hence, in exerting her "duty and obligation to the family," she takes up the responsibility of fulfilling "Japanese cultural values of *gaman* (perseverance in the face of adversity), *giri* (sense of duty and obligation), and a kind of fatalism that decreed the acceptance of conditions that couldn't be helped."[26] In addition, being unable to articulate fluently in English, Obasan's silence is usually interpreted as voiceless and powerless. Because of these barriers caused by culture and language, misunderstandings are likely to occur not only between different generations of Japanese Canadians but also, by extension, between Japanese Canadians and the majority of their white counterparts.

In terms of generational differences, von Hassell raises an

illuminating point that "a general lack of verbal communication about many issues in the relationships of *issei* and *nisei* is connected to a style of speaking in Japanese culture which emphasizes indirectness and silences as a courtesy and a protective device."[27] This protective silence, expressed in a Japanese phrase *kodomo no tame ni* (for the sake of the children), is rehearsed and stressed repeatedly in the course of the novel; it is also the silence that Naomi needs to overcome but also maintain.[28] Although Naomi is, in fact, a Sansei, the third generation of Japanese Canadians, the absence of her mother (a Nisei) and her being brought up by Obasan (an Issei) somehow locate her in between these two generations.[29] The way in which Naomi accomplishes this task of not only overcoming the barrier of silence but also maintaining it as a bridge to her motherline is to attend to, read, and understand her maternal silences, thus being able to restore and then reconstruct her own matrilineal narrative.

Fundamentally, Obasan's silence also demonstrates certain significant characteristics of Japanese matrilineage. In an episode where Naomi describes a journey she takes with Obasan and Stephen, her brother, in a train, Obasan shows her motherly and caring capacities to people around her that greatly affect Naomi's interactions with others. For instance, on realizing that a young Japanese woman has been forced to get on the train right after giving birth to her premature baby and has had no time to bring diapers with her, Obasan immediately offers her help to the young mother by asking Naomi to hand a gift with certain fruits inside to the woman. As Naomi hesitates and then declines because she is not accustomed to expressing herself in a caring role, Obasan goes forward instead, showing in front of Naomi how to do so (134). Later, assisted by an old woman on the train, Obasan takes the old woman's white flannel underskirt, which is made into a diaper for the baby of the young mother:

> "Please—if it is acceptable. For a diaper. There is nothing to offer," the old woman says as she hoists herself onto the seat again. She folds the undergarment into a neat square, the fingers of her hand stiff and curled as driftwood. Obasan bows, accepting the cloth, and returns to Kuniko-san and her baby, placing the piece of flannel on Kuniko-san's lap. Both their heads are bobbing like birds as they talk. Sometimes Kuniko-san bows so deeply, her baby touches her lap.
> Leaning out into the aisle I can see better, and the old grandmother nods, urging me to go to them. Kuniko-san is wiping her eyes in the baby's blanket, revealing the baby's damp black hair. (135)

Understanding and caring for others become a collective activity shared between women, in this case between Obasan and the old woman. Interestingly, as if moved and motivated by their generous behaviors, Naomi follows by offering her favorite ball to Stephen (137).

Judging from what has been described about Obasan's silence, we can discern that it can be deadly and compelling on the one hand but can also be nurturing and beneficial on the other hand. It is worth noting that this ethic of care is a maternal heritage that is passed on from the older generation to the younger generation. In particular, this art of attending to others is a specific form of female communication and networking in Naomi's matrilineage, as Naomi aptly puts it thus:

> When I am hungry, and before I can ask, there is food. If I am weary, every place is a bed. . . . A sweater covers me before there is any chill and if there is pain there is care simultaneously. If Grandma shifts uncomfortably, I bring her a cushion.
> "*Yoku ki ga tsuku ne*," Grandma responds. It is a statement in appreciation of sensitivity and appropriate gestures. (56, emphasis original)

Similarly, this "alert and accurate knowing" of others' needs without the expression of verbal language echoes what has been mentioned previously with regard to the "attentive silence" between Naomi and her mother.[30] This is, as Cheung states, "a maternal tradition" that "Naomi has learned from Grandma, Mother, and her surrogate mother, Obasan."[31]

Nonetheless, Naomi does not just attend to the silences of her mother and Obasan. She is also exposed to the voice of her other aunt, Emily, whose character is best exemplified in the following comparison made by Naomi: "How different my two aunts are. One lives in sound, the other in stone. Obasan's language remains deeply underground but Aunt Emily, BA, MA, is a word warrior" (39). In many aspects, Aunt Emily is the "word warrior" who constantly urges Naomi not to forget and keep silent about the sufferings her Japanese Canadian community has gone through during and after the Second World War. "'You have to remember,' Aunt Emily said, 'You are your history. If you cut any of it off you're an amputee. Don't deny the past. Remember everything. If you're bitter, be bitter. Cry it out! Scream! Denial is gangrene'" (60). Aunt Emily's statement here runs counter to Naomi's understanding and reception of her Japanese cultural values as induced and influenced by the silences of her mother and Obasan. In Aunt Emily's opinion, only through voicing the pain and anger of Japanese Canadians under the hardship of internment can the existence of her people be identified and justified.

Consequently, as a political activist herself, Aunt Emily insistently feeds Naomi with documents and facts, enticing her niece to be a fighter like herself who passionately embraces and incorporates the Western way of thinking and behavior in her life. One visit paid by Aunt Emily and remembered by Naomi is full of Aunt Emily's incessant talk of her experience at a conference called "The Asian Experience in North America" she has just attended. While Naomi is driving with her aunt sitting beside her jammed in traffic during rush hour, Aunt Emily cannot restrain herself from displaying to Naomi her pile of papers about the racist dispersal of their people. However, rather than consenting to and even praising her aunt for her devotion in upholding justice and equality, Naomi exhibits her indifference, giving a critical comment on her perception of her aunt's aggressiveness:

> The conference had obviously been a meeting ground for a lot of highly charged energy. Looking at her wildly gesticulating hair caught in the windows' drafts, I felt she should have electrocuted me. But I was curiously numb beside her.
> People who talk a lot about their victimization make me uncomfortable. It's as if they use their suffering as weapons or badges of some kind. From my years of teaching I know it's the children who say nothing who are in trouble more than the ones who complain. (41)

Naomi's opinion with respect to her attentiveness to her students who are silent and those who are not is analogous to her perception of the different voices in Obasan and Aunt Emily. This analogy drawn by Naomi does not imply that Aunt Emily's vociferation should be despised and ignored. What Naomi attempts to emphasize is that it is more significant and noteworthy to listen to the deep silence of her maternal past as it has always been culturally misinterpreted. One of the weaknesses Aunt Emily and her white counterparts are subjected to is, as Sasaki maintains, that "her [Aunt Emily's] assimilation to the dominant Western culture in which she lives has gained her access to a voice, but at the expense of losing her 'ear' — she cannot hear the subtle, cultural registers of silence that characterize Naomi's, Obasan's, and her sister's languages."[32]

To illustrate the intricacies and complexities between speech and silence further, one of the nightmares Naomi has, which is ironically called a "speaking dream," bespeaks the relation. Naomi is suddenly awakened from this nightmare when a "Grand Inquisitor" is prying open her mother's lips and Naomi's eyes. The nightmare implies intensely Naomi's emotional turbulence in light of her constant exposure to such contradictory states. However, Naomi is later able to regain her consciousness and give her own interpretation of the dream:

> The Grand Inquisitor was carnivorous and full of murder. His demand to know was both a judgment and a refusal to hear. The more he questioned

her, the more he was her accuser and murderer. The more he killed her, the deeper her silence became. What the Grand Inquisitor has never learned is that the avenues of speech are the avenues of silence. To hear my mother, to attend her speech, to attend the sound of stone, he must first become silent. (273–4)

In this passage, a reader is well informed that Naomi finds the solution to her psychological dilemma suffered from the sudden disruption of her family and community. Although, at first glance, silence and speech are two opposing terms and conditions, they are, in fact, interchangeable in terms of Naomi's resolution toward the end of the text. For Naomi, in order to listen to her mother, she has to locate herself in the position of silence. Significantly, in reflecting on her previous obsessive enquiry into the truth about the absence and silence of her mother, Naomi is wary that she might have already invaded her mother's inner world: "At the age of questioning my mother disappeared. Why, I have asked ever since, did she not write? Why, I ask now, must I know? Did I doubt her love? Am I her accuser?" (274).

Eventually when the truth about Naomi's mother's absence is revealed and read aloud from the two letters written and sent by Grandma Kato in Japan but that have been hidden in a gray cardboard folder for many years, "the stone" suddenly "bursts with telling" and "the seed flowers with speech" (preface). As the Anglican priest, Nakayama-sensei, reads on, the event of the 1945 bombing of Nagasaki, Japan, unravels the appalling occurrence that happened to Naomi's mother and their relatives. Ironically, after the years of learning to attend to the silence of her mother, to realize finally the naked truth about her mother's absence is no longer as important as it once had been. What Naomi reconciles out of her quest for her lost mother is the love and empathy she has been sharing with her mother since childhood. Therefore, Naomi remarks:

> I'm thinking that for a child there is no presence without flesh. But perhaps it is because I am no longer a child I can know your presence though you are not here. The letters tonight are skeletons. Bones only. But the earth still stirs with dormant blooms. Love flows through the roots of the trees by our graves. (292)

What Naomi tries to convey in the passage can be encapsulated in the word *love*. In analyzing how the ostensible opposition between silence and speech is dissolved into Naomi's rendition of "the two ideographs for the word 'love,'" Cheung illuminates for us: "The first contained the root words 'heart' and 'hand' and 'action'—love as hands and heart in action together. The other ideograph, for 'passionate love,

' was formed of 'heart,' 'to tell,' and 'a long thread.'"[33] Put more crucially, silence and speech are blended together in the ideograph of love. Naomi has to learn to attend to her mother's silence, then she will be able to "tell" the hidden "voice" of her silent mother and finally to "reweave" and "restitch" the thread of their "scattered nikkei community into the tapestry of Canadian history."[34]

As elaborated, the complexities and diversities a text such as *Obasan* has demonstrated to us are mainly determined by its exposure and subjection to a multilayer of cultural, social, and historical strictures. Within this particular political, social, and cultural scenario, *Obasan* does provide us with a different configuration of feminist matrilinealism. In counterpoint to a cultural and racial norm of protective silence that has been imposed on Naomi at both physical and psychological levels since childhood is her employment of attentive silence. What I would like to add with respect to the opposition or tension between silence and speech is the intricate relation between "the rejection and reclamation of the mother" in *Obasan*.[35] The oppressive and protective silence, as conveyed in Naomi's interactions with her absent mother and Obasan, can be perceived as the site for enacting both the repudiation and recuperation of the mother as a racial other. Aggressive and imposing speech, as figured in Naomi's Aunt Emily, can also be read in this light. As noted, Naomi's subjection to the equal but opposite pulls and forces of silence and speech does not make her fall prey to the destructive division between the two. These two conflicting forces of silence and speech or the disavowal and recovery of the mother become, instead, interchangeable and "*complementary*," to use Cheung's word.[36]

In many aspects, Naomi situates herself in a motherline by first attending to the silence of her (m)other and finally weaving together a tapestry of her matrilineal narrative, linking her female connection into a whole. Although the advantage of having the mother speak is unavailable in *Obasan*, Naomi has metaphorically enabled her mother to speak by adopting the concept of maternal thinking herself, effectuated particularly in the form of attentiveness. By means of thinking maternally, Naomi has already placed herself in the position of her mother. Her adoption of attending to her silent (m)other, which eventually culminates in the word *love*, strikes a chord in the following passage:

> Attentive love, in short, is a habit of mind one might also describe as loving detachment. This way of thinking seeks to understand difference but not to change it, to recognize the immutable separation of knower and known without trying to subsume the other into the self. Attentive love, then, is a

useful stance for readers of texts originating in cultures different from their own, as it offers a position from which to "dwell upon the *other*, and let otherness be." This stance allows the reader to interact with the text, not simply attempt to fix the text to preexisting frameworks.[37]

As emphasized, the significance of Naomi's attentive silence or "attentive love," to use Maureen T. Reddy's phrase, lies in its capacities to "understand difference" and "recognize" and embrace others, thus establishing a mutual and dialogical relationship between self and others. Concomitantly, readers of the text *Obasan* are also invited to adopt a reading strategy of attentiveness in order to read beyond "preexisting frameworks."[38]

Significantly, the concluding sentence in Cosslett's chapter "Matrilineal Narratives Revisited" tells us more about this compelling and contentious issue regarding the mother's absence and silence. Cosslett articulates thus: "To have an intersubjective bond with someone unknowable and full of new possibilities is an exciting idea."[39] As elaborated in my earlier discussion of *Obasan*, Naomi does exhibit her concern with intruding into her mother's silence and subjectivity in her attempt to make discernible and present her mother's absence. However, it is also this process or exercise of relocating herself with the (m)other in an "intersubjective space," to use Jessica Benjamin's term, that a daughter such as Naomi realizes the mother's irrecoverability.[40] To develop Benjamin's concept further, this "intersubjective space" is also the locus of recognizing the mother's racial otherness in which resonance and difference, absence and presence, and recoverability and irrecoverability coexist to constitute different subjectivities and othernesses. To write and read the (m)other in *Obasan* requires taking a different stance from that of the 1970s Western feminists' recommendation—speaking for the mother. Indeed, when taking into consideration the complexities and diversities created by differences in culture, race, class, and language, what has been gained from *Obasan* can bring fruitful and promising insights to the formation and re-formation of feminist matrilinealism.

Notes

1. Issei refers to the first generation of Japanese American or Canadian immigrants while Nisei denotes their second generation. The children of Nisei, the third generation, are called the Sansei. Further explanation of Issei, Nisei, and Sansei will be made later as more elaborations of the text unfold.
2. Janice Williamson, "Joy Kogawa: 'In writing I keep breathing, I keep living....,'" in *Sounding Differences: Conversations with Seventeen Canadian Women Writers*

(Toronto and London: University of Toronto Press, 1993), 156–7.
3. Joy Kogawa, *Obasan* (1981; reprint, New York: Anchor, 1994). Hereafter, page numbers to this volume are cited parenthetically. References are to the reprint edition.
4. Susan Rubin Suleiman, "Writing and Motherhood," in *The (M)other Tongue: Essays in Feminist Psychoanalytic Interpretation*, ed. Shirley Nelson Garner, Claire Kahane, and Madelon Sprengnether (Ithaca: Cornell University Press, 1985), 356–8. See also the discussion of recent feminist scholarship on the topic of maternal subjectivity in the introduction, 7.
5. Tess Cosslett, "Matrilineal Narratives Revisited," in *Feminism and Autobiography: Texts, Theories, Methods*, ed. Tess Cosslett, Celia Lury, and Penny Summerfield (London and New York: Routledge, 2000), 141.
6. Ibid., 142.
7. Ibid., 151.
8. Ibid.
9. In the ensuing two paragraphs, I will use historical precedents of Japanese American immigrants to offer a general idea of what their lifestyles and perspectives were like, as derived from their earlier immigration to America commencing from the late nineteenth century to the aftermath of the Second World War. I am aware that my presentation of Japanese American immigrant experiences runs the risks of conflating theirs with those of their Japanese Canadian counterparts and could also be accused of colluding with American imperialism. Although there are certainly nuances between these co-ethnic communities in America and Canada, my intention here is to draw a parallel between the two and highlight their commonalities of sharing a mutual fate and the trauma of racist deportation and internment during and after the Second World War.
10. Elaine H. Kim, "Japanese American Family and Community Portraits," in *Asian American Literature: An Introduction to the Writings and Their Social Context* (Philadelphia: Temple University Press, 1982), 122–4.
11. Ibid., 123–5.
12. Ibid., 125–6.
13. Ibid., 126.
14. Mason Harris, "Broken Generations in *Obasan*: Inner Conflicts and the Destruction of Community," *Canadian Literature* 127 (1990): 42.
15. Kim, "Japanese American Family and Community Portraits," 133–7.
16. Cosslett, "Matrilineal Narratives Revisited," 141.
17. Shirley Geok-Lin Lim, "Japanese American Women's Life Stories: Maternality in Monica Sone's *Nisei Daughter* and Joy Kogawa's *Obasan*," *Feminist Studies* 16, no. 2 (Summer 1990), 293.
18. Lim, "Japanese American Women's Life Stories," 293–4.
19. King-kok Cheung, *Articulate Silences: Hisaye Yamamoto, Maxine Hong Kingston, Joy Kogawa* (Ithaca: Cornell University Press, 1993), 127.
20. Harris, "Broken Generations in *Obasan*," 45.
21. Gayle K. Fujita, "'To Attend the Sound of Stone': the Sensibility of Silence in *Obasan*," *Melus: Journal of the Society for the Study of the Multi-Ethnic Literature of the United States* 12, no. 3 (Fall 1985): 41.
22. Helena Grice affords a valuable and detailed analysis of the use of nonverbal expression in *Obasan*. See her article, "Reading the Nonverbal: the Indices of Space, Time, Tactility and Taciturnity in Joy Kogawa's *Obasan*," *Melus* 24, no. 4

(Winter 1999): 93–105.
23. Betty Sasaki, "Reading Silence in Joy Kogawa's *Obasan*," in *Analyzing the Different Voice: Feminist Psychological Theory and Literary Texts*, ed. Jerilyn Fisher and Ellen S. Silber (New York and Oxford: Rowman & Littlefield, 1998), 129. See also Grice, "Reading the Nonverbal," 102.
24. Sasaki, "Reading Silence in Joy Kogawa's *Obasan*," 123.
25. Malve von Hassell, "*Issei* Women: Silences and Fields of Power," *Feminist Studies* 19, no. 3 (Fall 1993): 550.
26. David O'Brian and Stephen S. Fugita, quoted in Sasaki, "Reading Silence in Joy Kogawa's *Obasan*," 124, emphasis original.
27. von Hassell, "*Issei* Women," 562.
28. Sasaki, "Reading Silence in Joy Kogawa's *Obasan*," 119, 124, emphasis original.
29. Harris, "Broken Generations in *Obasan*," 41–2.
30. Quoted in Cheung, *Articulate Silences*, 20.
31. Cheung, *Articulate Silences*, 148.
32. Sasaki, "Reading Silence in Joy Kogawa's *Obasan*," 132–3.
33. Cheung, *Articulate Silences*, 165.
34. Ibid., 166.
35. Lim, "Japanese American Women's Life Stories," 293.
36. Cheung, *Articulate Silences*, 165–6, emphasis added.
37. Maureen T. Reddy, "Maternal Reading: Lazarre and Walker," in *Narrating Mothers: Theorizing Maternal Subjectivity*, ed. Brenda O. Daly and Maureen T. Reddy (Knoxville: University of Tennessee Press, 1991), 223, emphasis original.
38. Ibid.
39. Cosslett, "Matrilineal Narratives Revisited," 151.
40. Jessica Benjamin, *Shadow of the Other: Intersubjectivity and Gender in Psychoanalysis* (New York and London: Routledge, 1998), 95.

Chapter 13
Amy Tan's *The Joy Luck Club*

> The story of female development, both in fiction and theory, needs to be written in the voice of mothers as well as in that of daughters. . . . Only in combining both voices, in finding a double voice that would yield a multiple female consciousness, can we begin to envision ways to "live afresh."[1]

The voices of mothers and daughters as "a double voice," articulated by Marianne Hirsch, captures the full spirit of Western feminists' preoccupation with the literature of matrilineage in conjunction with an ongoing feminist pursuit of retrieving maternal subjectivity. The literary representations of mother-daughter voices in contemporary matrilineal narratives, in particular, open up a new chapter in the recent feminist development of repositioning maternal subjectivity from a feminist liberal and individualistic stance—mothers as individuals and subjects of their own—to that of a feminist intersubjective one. This repositioning sheds new light on a feminist revisiting of relationality in the field of feminist maternal scholarship.[2] The integration of mother-daughter voices as "a double voice" bespeaks the mother-daughter relationship as merging and interdependent. But this "double voice," which elicits "a multiple female consciousness," also indicates "the story of female development" with the co-presence of two subjects (mothers and daughters) encompassing both resonance and difference in their interactions with each other.

In contemporary women's fiction, Amy Tan has been for the past decade an acclaimed and prolific writer on mother-daughter relationships. In her creative experiments with storytelling—in particular, in her international bestseller *The Joy Luck Club*—Tan explores mother-daughter voices consistently and persuasively. In accordance with Nan Bauer Maglin's definition of matrilineal literature,[3] Tan deals with not only the mother-daughter conflicts and ambiguities but also the resolution and recognition of matrilineage, especially when accomplished through the act of reclaiming the past.[4] Even though Tan's mother-daughter stories reflect a universal phenomenon, they are also embedded within a specific immigrant culture and experience, Chinese American, one that is invariably bound up with issues of race, gender, and self-identity. Thus, in her text, the complexity of the mother-daughter relationship is compounded by the generational shifts in cultural identity caused by migration. Because of these different cultural backgrounds, the mother-daughter stories in Tan's novel encompass a wide range of subjects and geographical locations. Despite the fact that almost all the stories contain mother-daughter conflicts, the main concern of the novel is with recognizing and affirming the mother-daughter bond. As Tan said in an interview, "separation happens in different ways in different cultures. The feeling is in Chinese culture that [the bond] can never be broken."[5]

It is noteworthy that Tan's matrilineal text does not just respond to a Western feminist concern; it also belongs to an important feature—matrilineal discourse—in the tradition of Chinese American literature, which can be traced back to works written by Chinese American male writers and female writers decades before the publication of Maxine Hong Kingston's *The Woman Warrior* in 1976. A profusion of matrilineal literature, written mostly by Chinese American women writers, also follows the trend popularized by Kingston.[6] Matrilineal themes such as "the recurrent image of the majestic matriarch" in a female-dominated household, the "mother-daughter bonding and induction into the woman's submissive role in the culture," and the "combined ethnic/matrilineal rootseeking journey" are vividly portrayed in the works of most Chinese American women writers.[7]

Locating this matrilineal tradition in a broader context, Sau-Ling Cynthia Wong identifies it in the literature of other Asian American writers[8] where the aforementioned matrilineal themes are still covered and carried on but are expanded into other issues such as "the search for the absent mother, surrogate motherhood" in Joy Kogawa's *Obasan*,[9] which I have discussed in the previous chapter. With reference to Wong's historical survey, the theme of matrilineage does play a crucial part in constituting Asian American literature. But more significant, this "Amy Tan phenomenon," as Wong terms it, entails a level of racial and gender politics because Chinese immigrant mothers have been silenced by white feminists and their Chinese American male counterparts.[10] Addressing the issue of "racial politics within feminism," as Wong goes on to argue, this matrilineal characteristic of Asian American literature should be seen in its own right, not conflated with or dominated by the white matrilineal discourse.[11] Conversely, highlighting the "gender politics within cultural nationalism," she also notes the dangers and pitfalls of silencing female perspectives within this matrilineal Asian American tradition. Reversing the prevalent image of a desolate, neglected, and silent China Mama as an old immigrant woman, as delineated in Frank Chin's play *Year of the Dragon*,

Wong characterizes Tan's portrayal of the Joy Luck mothers, who share equal proportions with their daughters in narrating their own stories, as a "China Mama's revenge."[12]

Drawing from what has been highlighted so far, I would like to explore further the matrilineal narrative in Tan's *The Joy Luck Club*. Placing an emphasis on the elements of storytelling and breaking silence, I attempt to envisage what other form of matrilineal narrative could possibly be derived from Tan's novel based on the multiple female consciousnesses and perspectives she provides for a feminist writing and reading of the mother. As noted previously, the ways that Tan's work can illuminate current feminist thinking and theorizing on maternal subjectivity are the intersubjectivity and the dialogue built on "a double voice" that incorporates both the voices of mothers and daughters, not silencing one or the other or subsuming one under the other.[13] That is to say, Tan's use of storytelling establishes a dialogic relationship between mothers and daughters; this mother-daughter relationship reflects, corroborates, and adds to the concept of intersubjectivity found in the theoretical paradigm of Jessica Benjamin. This intersubjectivity established between mothers and daughters in Tan's novel can especially be discerned in certain episodes and scenes of mother-daughter mirroring when they look at each other's faces and reflections in mirrors and photographs. Nonetheless, even though Tan's mother-daughter writing coincides with Benjamin's paradigm of intersubjectivity, she does go beyond the existing psychoanalytic framework to present a more complex and dynamic poetics of mother-daughter voices. Before commencing a detailed analysis of Tan's matrilineal narratives, I will first introduce her adaptation of Chinese talk story in her use of storytelling between mothers and daughters as a trope for matrilineal reclamation. Then, I will conclude this chapter by making a comparison between Benjamin's and Tan's works with a particular focus on their different explorations of intersubjectivity that generates a new avenue for the working and reworking of feminist discourse on maternal subjectivity and matrilineage.

Tan employs storytelling as a powerful narrative strategy to enable her characters, who are from a minority ethnic group, to reconstruct and make significant and coherent their histories and life stories that they might have lost or forgotten after their emigration to the new adopted country, America. Storytelling seems to bridge the rift between the past and the present. It thus appears as a survival skill with which the older generation of immigrants articulates and authenticates the essence of their own existences and selves and then passes that on to the younger generation to sustain and perpetuate the cultural identity of their motherland. From the viewpoint of feminist matrilinealism, storytelling is an apt literary device that allows the once silent mothers, the Joy Luck mothers, to voice their long hidden secrets of suffering and victimization and transform them into an affirmation of their own strength and perseverance as survivors.[14] More significantly in some cases, by means of telling stories to each other, both mothers and daughters can not only discover their own voices but also reclaim and redefine their own selves.[15]

What is different about Tan's storytelling is that it is cast in the form of talk story—a form of Chinese oral tradition. Linda Ching Sledge defines a talk story as:

> a conservative, communal folk art by and for the common people, performed in the various dialects of diverse ethnic enclaves and never intended for the ears of non-Chinese. Because it served to redefine an embattled immigrant culture by providing its members immediate, ceremonial access to ancient lore, talk story retained the structures of Chinese oral wisdom (parables, proverbs, formulaic description, heroic biography, casuistical dialogue) long after other old-country traditions had died.[16]

In many aspects, talk story meets the need of the mothers in Tan's novel. As E. D. Huntley explains, talk story as a type of storytelling is a means of altering the private voices of these mothers to a narrative of public utterances. Due to their vulnerability as first-generation Chinese American immigrants, the mothers in Tan's novel at first choose to be silent. Their initial silence is not only the result of their sense of shame, guilt, and helplessness experienced from their previous lives in China; it is also their strategy for survival as members of a disadvantaged minority adapting to their new life in America. Talk story provides them with a great sense of security and empowerment. That is to say, in their use of a more culturally familiar means of expression and communication, their miseries and pains related to the past and the present could be disguised and even metamorphosed into artistic forms such as myth and folktales. Most important, the technique of talk story permits the storytellers to keep a distance not only between themselves and the subjects concerned but also between themselves and the audience. Each of Tan's immigrant mothers could thus "maintain the silence to which she is accustomed, as well as to speak out and share with others the important stories that have shaped her into the person that she is."[17]

Notably, despite the liberating aspect of talk story that allows the Chinese American immigrant mothers to be freed from being silenced and stereotyped, the mothers and daughters in Tan's novel go through their agitated moments of struggling with their miscommunications and misunderstandings. The main causes for their sense of disfranchisement are the disparities widened by their different cultural perspectives and identities, Chinese and American, and also by their use of different languages, Chinese and English. Many instances occur in the novel when the Joy Luck mothers cannot articulate fully their meanings and true intentions with their fractured English. The Joy Luck daughters also misread and misinterpret their mothers' messages because these American daughters lack a satisfying command of the Chinese language. In some cases, the daughters perceive their Joy Luck mothers as the racial (m)others whose thinking and behaviors are encoded in the stereotyped imagery of American imperialist discourse or orientalism.[18] Nonetheless, it is also the working out of their miscommunications and misunderstandings in the process of talking story that makes the Joy Luck mothers and daughters understand each other and forge their connection.

What has been pointed out with respect to the functions of storytelling in Tan's text is that storytelling enables Tan's mothers and daughters to find their own voices and selves, especially as this storytelling is performed in the mode of Chinese talk story. This discovery of their voices and selves is important because it leads to an assertion and recognition of their own subjectivities. In the process of telling stories, a sense of mutual recognition is also required and involved. In other words, the storytelling can only become meaningful when the two parties, the teller and the listener, are totally devoted to each other. The act of storytelling is built on mutuality in which the acts of telling and listening are conducted simultaneously: one cannot work without the other. The teller is the one who narrates and the listener is the other who listens, but this is an interactive and dynamic process in which the two parties are creating meanings, and neither party is passive. In many respects, the relationship between a teller and a listener is analogous to that between a mother and an infant. To quote and reinforce Benjamin's argument, this relationship is founded on "the premise that from the beginning there are always (at least) two subjects."[19] In Tan's text, she evokes themes of mutual recognition and self-confirmation alongside the progress of storytelling.

However, some of the stories told by either mothers or daughters in *The Joy Luck Club* are not addressed to their daughters or mothers. Tan's mother-daughter writing does, therefore, require that a reader conduct a responsive and interactive reading to establish a dialogic of voices between mothers and daughters. That is, the intersubjective scheme also operates between author and readers or between readers and the text. In the rest of this chapter, I will continue to explore how Tan centers the themes evolving out of the mother-daughter storytelling on the mutual need between mothers and daughters to recognize and affirm each other and what Tan's mothers and daughters have done to achieve this.

The Joy Luck Club[20] is a collection of sixteen stories told by four pairs of mothers and daughters. Basing her book on her experience with her own mother, Tan is able to create in her fictional characters many different facets of the mother-daughter relationship.[21] Situated in and between two different cultural contexts, four mothers, Suyuan Woo, An-mei Hsu, Lindo Jong, and Ying-ying St. Clair are Chinese women who emigrated to America before the revolution in China in 1949. Their daughters, Jing-mei Woo, Rose Hsu Jordan, Waverly Jong, and Lena St. Clair, are second-generation Chinese Americans, brought up in America. The whole book is divided into four sections titled "Feathers from a Thousand Li Away," "The Twenty-six Malignant Gates," "American Translation," and "Queen Mother of the Western Skies." The first two sections are narrated by the three mothers except Suyuan Woo whose voice is represented by her daughter Jing-mei Woo instead due to her absence caused by her recent death. The third and fourth sections are the American-born daughters' stories. Although the mothers' and daughters' stories occupy different physical space in the text, their stories are closely linked by their relationships.

Jing-mei's relationship with her mother, Suyuan Woo, can be used as an archetype to demonstrate how Tan employs storytelling to resolve the mother-daughter conflicts and even create an aesthetic form for the mother-daughter voice. In the stories "The Joy Luck Club" and "A Pair of Tickets," Jing-mei Woo tells of her mother's Demeter-like quest for her lost daughters in China. Recalling her mother's ability to tell her the "Kweilin story" with a different ending each time, which indicates her mother's skill in talk story improvisation, Jing-mei one day discovers the true version of the story. It is the story of how her mother escaped from Kweilin to Chungking during the Japanese invasion of China in 1944. On her way, the mother becomes so exhausted that she has to leave behind her belongings one by one. At last, she gives up her two baby girls. After the mother is rescued, she begins her ceaseless search for her lost daughters. However, Jing-mei's mother does not succeed, and she dies without seeing her daughters again (20–6, 281–6).

Jing-mei's mother initiates the weekly tradition of the Joy Luck Club. This is an occasion on which Jing-mei's mother and her three aunts play mah jong and have a feast together. The year Jing-mei's mother dies, she was supposed to have been hostess. Jing-mei, as her daughter, is therefore seen as the best candidate to replace her. But when, at this meeting, Jing-mei is asked to fulfill her mother's lifelong wish and meet her mother's lost daughters in China on her behalf, feelings of doubt and confusion arise in her mind. She feels she cannot represent her mother, because she does not think that she knows her well enough. The uncertainty Jing-mei feels highlights not only a generational gap between mother and daughter but also a division between two cultural and national identities:

> In me, they see their own daughters, just as ignorant, just as unmindful of all the truths and hopes they have brought to America. They see daughters who grow impatient when their mothers talk in Chinese, who think they are stupid when they explain things in fractured English. They see that joy and luck do not mean the same to their daughters, that to these closed American-born minds "joy luck" is not a word, it does not exist. (40–1)

Joy luck signifies different things for the mothers and daughters. For the Chinese mothers, the words *joy luck* point to their cultural origins and the past they cherish. But for their American daughters, the words do not mean anything; the concept simply does not exist. Although the Joy Luck Club symbolizes a matrilineal heritage to be passed from mother to daughter, it also signifies the differences that act as a boundary between them.

Jing-mei's obedience to her mother's wish compels Jing-mei to fulfil her mother's quest. However, as the story goes on, we are informed that Jing-mei's presence serves not merely as a replacement for her mother. It is also about her own quest for her mother. In the last story, "A Pair of Tickets," Jing-mei makes a trip to China with her father to meet her half-sisters. On this journey, she confronts a conflict of identities, struggling with her doubts about whether she is Chinese. But a sense of identification and belonging emerges as soon as she reaches China, her mother's home country:

> The minute our train leaves the Hong Kong border and enters Shenzhen, China, I feel different. I can feel the skin on my forehead tingling, my blood rushing through a new course, my bones aching with a familiar cold pain. And I think, My mother was right, I am becoming Chinese. (267)

As if a miracle has happened, Jing-mei feels a transformation in her body and realizes that she has become Chinese on arriving in China. By identifying herself as Chinese, she has also come to identify with her mother. Holding a pair of tickets, just before boarding the plane to Shanghai, she senses that she has come to China as both mother and daughter. The moment she meets her half-sisters at the airport, her impression is confirmed:

> The flash of the Polaroid goes off and my father hands me the snapshot. My sisters and I watch quietly together, eager to see what develops.

> The gray-green surface changes to the bright colors of our three images, sharpening and deepening all at once. And although we don't speak, I know we all see it: Together we look like our mother. Her same eyes, her same mouth, open in surprise to see, at last, her long-cherished wish. (288)

What the daughters see in each other's eyes are multiplications of their mother. Although she is dead, she seems resurrected at this moment of reunion accomplished by the daughters. The quest turns out to be a mutual one between lost mother and lost daughters. Interestingly, propelled originally by her Joy Luck aunts, who function as substitute mothers, to attend to, narrate, and later fulfill her mother's story, Jing-mei has unintentionally established a motherline that stretches both vertically and horizontally, linking mothers, daughters, sisters, and aunts together. This motherline also incorporates different racial, cultural, and national identities, Chinese and American, into one thread of family synergy and identification.

In Jing-mei's storytelling, we have a daughter's quest for or journey to the voices of her mother and herself. Drawing from a similar theme but working conversely, we also have the mother's narration in other Joy Luck stories. Nonetheless, because of the inextricably intertwined lives founded on mother-daughter relationships, a mother does not necessarily confine her voice to that of a mother but refers occasionally to those of her other identities in the process of interacting with her daughter. For example, An-mei Hsu, the mother of Rose Hsu Jordan, speaks first as a mother in "Magpies":

> Yesterday my daughter said to me, "My marriage is falling apart."
> And now all she can do is watch it falling. She lies down on a psychiatrist couch, squeezing tears out about this shame. And, I think, she will lie there until there is nothing more to fall, nothing left to cry about, everything dry. (215)

Commenting on the way her daughter handles her almost broken marriage, An-mei uses her Chinese way of thinking to measure her daughter's behavior. Going through difficult situations in her life, An-mei says that she learns to "desire nothing, to swallow other people's misery, to eat my own bitterness" (215). Seeing that her daughter can only lie down and cry on a psychiatrist's couch and is doing nothing to save her marriage, An-mei resents her daughter's weakness in contrast to her own endurance in working things out. Then, An-mei shifts to a daughter's voice:

> My mother was a stranger to me when she first arrived at my uncle's house in Ningpo. I was nine years old and had not seen her for many years. But I knew she was my mother, because I could feel her pain. (216)

For most of the story, An-mei talks about her reunion with her mother and their life in her mother's second husband's house. Being the fourth wife of a polygamist, An-mei's mother's position in the family is the lowest of the low. Surrounded by an atmosphere of jealousy and competition among the different views in the family, An-mei sees and feels her mother's suffering due to being neglected and despised. Later, An-mei learns about the secret behind her mother's marriage: she was tricked by Wu-Tsing and his second wife to bear them a son. As her mother has been defamed as a seductress, her family is not able to forgive her. Thrown out by the family, An-mei's mother has no choice but to marry Wu-Tsing. An-mei's mother carries this shame with her for the rest of her life, until her suicide. Toward the end, we are able to hear the daughter's anger and resentment against her mother's circumstances. Combining the two voices of mother and daughter, An-mei as a mother impresses on her daughter the strength and courage that she as a daughter receives from her mother's suffering (216–41).

Lindo Jong, the mother of Waverly Jong, speaks also with the two voices of mother and daughter. Like An-mei, she speaks first as a mother:

> My daughter wanted to go to China for her second honeymoon, but now she is afraid.
> "What if I blend in so well they think I'm one of them?" Waverly asked me.
> "What if they don't let me come back to the United States?"
> "When you go to China," I told her, "you don't even need to open your mouth. They already know you are an outsider."
> "What are you talking about?" she asked. My daughter likes to speak back. She likes to question what I say. (253)

In the first part of the story, we learn from the mother about her relationship with her daughter, which involves two cultural identities. In the dialogue here, Lindo Jong denies that her daughter looks Chinese, because she knows that her efforts to combine two cultural characteristics in her daughter have failed; they just cannot work together (253–4).

In a beauty parlor scene, Lindo Jong sees even more clearly the difference between herself and her daughter. Her daughter brings her to have her hair cut by Mr. Rory, making her realize that her daughter is ashamed of her Chinese appearance. Without asking Lindo's opinion, her daughter and the hairdresser decide how they should cut her hair. Not angry at their manipulation, Lindo even cooperates by wearing an "American face" that she describes as "the face Americans think is Chinese, the one they cannot understand" (255). However, when Mr. Rory says to Waverly that she and her mother look alike, Waverly is displeased. But Lindo smiles with her real Chinese face. Looking at their reflections in the mirror, the mother and the daughter suddenly realize their likeness. Although these two faces sometimes appear so different, they are still very much the same. And their sameness reminds Lindo of her own mother and herself.

This recollection of her childhood moves Lindo to speak as a daughter:

> My mother—your grandmother—once told me my fortune, how my character could lead to good and bad circumstances. She was sitting at her table with the big mirror. I was standing behind her, my chin resting on her shoulder. The next day was the start of the new year. I would be ten years by my Chinese age, so it was an important birthday for me. For this reason maybe she did not criticize me too much. She was looking at my face. (256)

Lindo describes how her mother can tell her fortune simply by observing the shapes of her ears, nose, chin, forehead, and eyes. Looking at her mother's face, Lindo discovers their sameness and her desire to look like her mother. This desire stems not only from the mother-daughter bond but also from a collective Chinese identity. But Lindo's face is changed when she emigrates to America. Being in a different culture and society, Lindo has to disguise her Chinese face, her "true self," in order to adjust to her life in America (256–8). Eventually, returning to the mirror scene with her daughter, Waverly, Lindo finds that there are more similarities between herself and her daughter. Being mother and daughter, they have the same crooked nose and being both Chinese and American, they are also both "two-faced" (265–6).

This episode of mother-daughter mirroring expanded at a three-generational level highlights the mother-daughter anxiety about and struggle with their differences caused by migration. Waverly Jong's conspiracy with her hairdresser, Mr. Rory, to have her mother's hair cut in an American style exemplifies the assimilating imposition of the white mainstream American ideology on the immigrants who are racial and ethnic minorities. Aligning herself with such "an 'American mindset'" of disregarding and stigmatizing her mother's true identity and selfhood as a Chinese immigrant, Waverly Jong "sees her mother as 'other,' as 'outsider,' as 'intruder.'" Further, her response to Mr. Rory's comment on her similarity with her mother as shameful and unpleasant denotes the American daughter's matrophobia, because Waverly Jong's mother, Lindo Jong, is viewed as "the outcast Other."[22] Interestingly, as this episode is narrated by the mother, we are able to perceive firsthand her reaction to such enactment of racism and classism. Lindo's playing with her two faces, Chinese and American, accommodates her need to both survive and resist. Her display and mimicking of the two faces blurs the boundary between two national and cultural identities, Chinese and American. They destabilize the West/East, subject/object, and imperialist/subaltern dichotomies. Yet, more significant, the mother-daughter matrix assists in reconciling such a conflict.

Judging from the stories told by the two Joy Luck mothers An-mei Hsu and Lindo Jong, we have, similar to Jing-mei's story, the formation of matrilineal narrative extending across different generations. By referring to themselves as both mothers and daughters in a female descent line, both An-mei Hsu and Lindo Jong have built their own matrilineage, creating a herstory of their own lives. Tan's Joy Luck mothers, to a great extent, also participate in what Hirsch has described as "a double voice" (161). The way Tan presents the double voice in *The Joy Luck Club* is to locate maternity as its center, placing "subjectivity in the maternal" and deploying it as "a pivot between the past and the present,"[23] mother and daughter, and China and America. The significance of this double voice in mother and daughter is that it will not silence the one or the other; it enables the two voices to speak either simultaneously or consecutively. Thus, as Hirsch has envisioned, "the multiplicity of 'women' is nowhere more obvious than for the figure of the mother, who is always both mother and daughter. Her representation is controlled by her object status, but her discourse, when it is voiced, moves her from object to subject."[24]

As previously discussed, the distinctive feature of feminist matrilinealism in Tan's text lies in the intersubjectivity and dialogue drawn from the mother-daughter interactions in the process of telling their own stories and presenting their own voices. The scenes of mothers and daughters looking at each other's faces either in photographs or mirrors resemble the moment when both mother and infant gaze into each other's eyes. Although Tan's mothers and daughters also partake of a search for mutual recognition that has been lost in the process of their migration, the intersubjective paradigm represented in Tan's text is far more complicated and in-depth. Benjamin's intersubjective view is drawn from her findings in extensive clinical research, whereas the intersubjectivity of Tan's mothers and daughters is compounded by the interlocking structures of different cultures, identities, and languages. Benjamin's formulation of intersubjectivity is based on her observation of the mother-infant relationship, and she emphasizes the occurrence of mutual recognition and differentiated identities right at the beginning of this earliest human relationship. Conversely, Tan's novel is concentrated on the relationships between mothers and their grown daughters. Tan also complicates Benjamin's earlier theoretical premise by allowing the mothers and daughters in her book to go through a process of development from misunderstandings to reconciliation and then to final recognition. Yet, Benjamin's later theoretical parameter concerning the subject's negotiation with the other and the intervention of the other in her most recent book, *Shadow of the Other*, is validated in reading Tan's text where the Chinese American immigrant mothers, who are perceived initially as racial (m)others, do speak and interact with their Americanized daughters in their storytelling.

As elucidated, Jing-mei's recognition of herself and her mother does not start right at the beginning; it requires a long journey back to her maternal origin, her motherland, China, to accomplish a quest for lost mother and daughters. And the moment of mutual recognition culminates dramatically in the daughters' anxious gazes at their own photograph taken together. Moreover, the coexistence of resonance and difference as a distinctive feature of intersubjectivity not only manifests itself in the process of mutual recognition between mothers and daughters; it also happens between siblings. The combination of similarities and differences between subjects occurs when Jing-mei and her half-sisters in China see in each other's eyes duplications of their mother. In addition, some of Tan's mothers also embody this intersubjective characteristic in their presentation of the double voice. That is, self and other are not only dissolved into the figure of the mother but are also extended into different generations of women. In one of the mother-daughter pairs, Lindo and Waverly Jong, the mother-daughter voices are activated and complicated by their possession of the two faces. The mirror scene in the beauty parlor also reverses and reexamines Benjamin's concept of "maternal mirroring."[25] Rather than stressing the recognition of mother-daughter difference in a "maternal mirroring," Lindo's double voice, which allows her narrative to move between generations, constitutes the mother-daughter desire for sameness. Although the cause for the mother-daughter separation is the display of two different faces, Chinese and American, this sharp difference is also the commonality that unites Lindo and Waverly as they both possess these two faces. This final mother-daughter identification through mirroring undergoes the "tension between negation and recognition."[26]

Storytelling is a reciprocal process that can only become meaningful through the engagement of the two parties. That is to say, the mother-daughter stories need both to be told and heard at the same time. In *The Joy Luck Club*, for instance, sixteen stories told separately and equally by mothers and daughters bespeak, on the one hand, their own separate individuality and subjectivity. On the other hand, the mother-daughter voices as they emerge in the form of storytelling also let mothers and daughters realize their own important roles in sharing a common history, as the Joy Luck mothers and daughters are all involved in recreating a female version of their immigrant family histories and experiences. In a word, Tan's representation of maternity as performed in the storytelling caters to both motherly and daughterly subjectivities, which suggests a feminist intersubjective bond with the (m)other and a different way of locating maternal subjectivity. Significantly, the intersubjectivity and the dialogue dramatized in mother-daughter storytelling and voices have been transformed into a poetics of mother-daughter writing and creativity, which also invites a constructive, dynamic, and interactive reading for both sexual and racial differences.

Notes

1. Marianne Hirsch, *The Mother/Daughter Plot: Narrative, Psychoanalysis, Feminism* (Bloomington and Indianapolis: Indiana University Press, 1989), 161.
2. See the discussions of recent feminist developments on motherhood and maternal subjectivity in the introduction and chapter 1.
3. Nan Bauer Maglin, "Don't Never Forget the Bridge That You Crossed Over On: the Literature of Matrilineage," in *The Lost Tradition: Mothers and Daughters in Literature*, ed. Cathy N. Davidson and E. M. Broner (New York: Frederick Ungar, 1980), 258. See also my discussion of Maglin's concept in chapter 1, 26.
4. Tess Cosslett, "Feminism, Matrilinealism, and the 'House of Women' in Contemporary Women's Fiction," *Journal of Gender Studies* 5, no. 1 (1996): 8. See also my elaboration of her study regarding matrilineal romance in chapter 1, 26-7.
5. Mickey Pearlman and Katherine Usher Henderson, *A Voice of One's Own: Conversations with America's Writing Women* (New York: the University Press of Kentucky, 1990), 24.
6. Sau-Ling Cynthia Wong provides a brief but useful survey on the literature of matrilineage in the Asian American context. In the case of the development of Chinese American matrilineal literature, Wong uses the year 1965 as a dividing line to describe the matrilineal texts written either before or after this year. Enumerating some of the texts published decades before Kingston's *The Woman Warrior*, Wong redresses the wrongly perceived impression that the unprecedented success and popularity of Kingston's novel spearheaded the genre of matrilineal writings in the strand of Chinese American literature. See Wong's article "'Sugar Sisterhood': Situating the Amy Tan Phenomenon," in *The Ethnic Canon: Histories, Institutions, and Interventions*, ed. David Palumbo-Liu (Minneapolis: University of Minnesota Press, 1995), 177-8.
7. Wong, "'Sugar Sisterhood,'" 177-8.
8. Special care needs to be taken when using the term *Asian American*. Originally, Asian American literature referred to those "published creative writings in English by Americans of Chinese, Japanese, Korean, and Filipino descent"; these writers are mostly the descendants of the first American Asian immigrants (20). This branch of American ethnic literature pinpoints specifically this minority

group in America and Canada. However, with the emergence and rapid growth of later immigrants from other Asian countries such as Cambodia, Vietnam, India, and Pakistan, the category of Asian Americans is hence expanded into a wider scenario. See E. D. Huntley, *Amy Tan: A Critical Companion* (Westport, Conn.: Greenwood, 1998), 20.
9. In an analogous fashion, Asian American women writers also produced a wide-range of matrilineal texts either predating or coming after Kingston's novel in 1976. See Wong, "'Sugar Sisterhood,'" 178–9.
10. Ibid., 178.
11. Ibid., 179.
12. Ibid., 180.
13. Marina Heung, "Daughter-Text/Mother-Text: Matrilineage in Amy Tan's *Joy Luck Club*," *Feminist Studies* 19, no. 3 (Fall 1993): 597–613.
14. Huntley, *Amy Tan*, 15–8.
15. M. Marie Booth Foster, "Voice, Mind, Self: Mother-Daughter Relationships in Amy Tan's *The Joy Luck Club* and *The Kitchen God's Wife*," in *Women of Color: Mother-Daughter Relationships in Twentieth-Century Literature* (Texas: University of Texas Press, 1996), 209.
16. Linda Ching Sledge, quoted in Huntley, *Amy Tan*, 32.
17. Huntley, *Amy Tan*, 32–3.
18. Wendy Ho, *In Her Mother's House: the Politics of Asian American Mother-Daughter Writing* (Oxford: Altamira Press, 1999), 161–71.
19. Jessica Benjamin, *The Bonds of Love: Psychoanalysis, Feminism and the Problem of Domination* (New York: Pantheon Books, 1988), 24.
20. Amy Tan, *The Joy Luck Club* (1989; reprint, London: Minerva, 1990). Hereafter, page numbers to this volume are cited parenthetically. References are to the reprint edition.
21. Pearlman and Henderson, *A Voice of One's Own*, 24.
22. Ho, *In Her Mother's House*, 165.
23. Heung, "Daughter-Text/Mother-Text," 601.
24. Hirsch, *The Mother/Daughter Plot*, 12.
25. Benjamin, *The Bonds of Love*, 24.
26. Benjamin, *Shadow of the Other: Intersubjectivity and Gender in Psychoanalysis* (New York and London: Routledge, 1998), 96.

Chapter 14
Judy Budnitz's *If I Told You Once*

Judy Budnitz's latest novel, *If I Told You Once*, is a matrilineal fiction with fairy-tale rewrites about four generations of immigrant women in America: Ilana, Sashie, Mara, and Nomie. As the blurb on Budnitz's novel suggests, the fables and fairy tales Budnitz writes and rewrites resonate with those in the brothers Grimm and Angela Carter. In tandem with a host of feminist rewriters of fairy tales, Budnitz resorts to matrilineage and mother-daughter relationships in order to recover a much "earlier and more women-centered" version of an oral narrative told predominantly by women.[1] Budnitz tackles a series of matrilineal themes such as the interplay of resonance and difference in mother-daughter relations. The mother-daughter resonance is conveyed in their identification by means of mother-daughter mirroring through looking in an actual mirror, following footsteps, and recognizing their common voice. Their difference, however, is exhibited in daughters' feelings of resentment against their mothers compounded by their different cultural perceptions resulting from migration. Despite reverberating with significant matrilineal features, Budnitz's text elicits an altered reading of matrilineal narrative especially in her "negative, matrophobic construction of it."[2] In what follows, I will first elaborate on Budnitz's textual and thematic exploration of diaspora and mother-daughter relationships and then conclude by looking at how Budnitz composes a matrilineal narrative as an antifeminist family romance in comparison with Margaret Drabble's *The Peppered Moth*, discussed in chapter 7.

As introduced, Budnitz's *If I Told You Once*[3] shows a marked contrast to the revised and censored edition of the brothers Grimm's fairy tales. Budnitz retains the folkloric elements of sex, violence, and incestuous desires and fantasies that have been undermined and closely scrutinized and were considered as psychologically disturbing and culturally forbidden after those tales were converted into written forms centuries ago.[4] In conjunction with these cultural taboos, Budnitz also reverts to a matriarchal or matrilineal state. This can be discernible in Budnitz's delineations of Ilana's mother and the three women in their village. But Budnitz's construction of a matrilineal narrative, as displayed in both the representations of the mother and of the three women in Ilana's home village, is contaminated by daughterly feelings of fear and disavowal of the maternal. Although my discussion of Budnitz's text will concentrate mainly on the matrilineal relations, Budnitz's presentation of a strong brother-sister bond between Ilana and Ari and certain female characters' incestuous desires for their brothers, such as Sashie's for Eli and Wolf and Mara's for Jonathan, suggests another configuration of a family romance rather than a matrilineal one. Budnitz's rewriting of a family romance into an incestuous tale has perhaps to do with her negative construction of a matrilineal narrative. As her female characters preoccupy themselves with their relations with men such as their brothers, their female connections are thus fractured.

At the beginning of the book, Ilana's mother is first depicted as a tremendously powerful maternal figure that is fertile, wise, brave, and resourceful. Ilana's mother gives birth consecutively at yearly intervals and is knowledgeable about her labor and its timing. On such an occasion, Ilana is orchestrated by her mother to observe the whole process of giving birth, a woman-specific bodily knowledge that is succeeded immediately by Ilana's first drops of menstrual blood. Mistaking her menstrual blood as a sign of conception, Ilana, being ignorant of her blooming sexuality and maturity, is terrified by the prospect of giving birth herself. Yet, as a mature and wise woman, the mother initiates Ilana into knowledge of conception, abortion, and contraception (18–9). In addition, Ilana is also taught by her mother how to sew and how to be familiar with roots and herbs, a knowledge that has originally been passed on from her grandmother to her mother. This collective effort of gathering herbs is described interestingly in the image of footprints:

> My grandmother had taught my mother her knowledge of herbs. Sometimes they went gathering together. My grandmother always walked first and my mother followed behind her, placing her feet in the prints my grandmother had made in the snow. When I went with them I walked behind my mother, stepping in the footprints that my grandmother had made and my mother had deepened. (20)

The mother-daughter identification is illustrated in the generational tracking of the same trail. But marks of footprints overlapped and intensified by each succeeding generation also indicate the imprints of their individual differences as the footprints being left and "deepened" each time can never be the same as those of the original. Similar passages of generational footprints recur several times in the text thereafter, which serve as a linking image to portray the nuances of matrilineal relation, but they are also presented as a negative presentation of matrilineage in which generations of women are trapped in their meaningless repetition.

Apart from providing a valuable source of wisdom and strength, Ilana's mother is also the one who arouses the daughter's immense fear. The mother's bravery but also cruelty is shown in her savage revenge on a bandit who frightens Ilana while she is running the errand of gathering the plants for her mother. The bandit is later killed gruesomely because Ilana's mother sets him up as a mistaken target for a she-wolf's bereaved mate to take revenge on. Summoning her courage to the forest again, Ilana stands watching the bandit's defeated and grisly corpse and contemplates her mother's mercilessness:

> I sat a long time in the snow, looking at the face, holding the sparkling cold hand of a man preserved in ice; and for the first time I saw that I was not of that country, I did not have my mother's fierceness in me, I did not have that fierceness of love that had kept my family alive for generations in that harsh place. It was a blind devotion, a vicious bloody animal love, and I wanted no part of it; for the first time I knew that I would leave. (14)

Ilana's disapproval of her mother's brutality prefigures her estrangement from her motherland that prompts Ilana to venture on her solitary journey in quest of a fair dreamland with "a picture of life more refined, more considered" inside a magical egg left for Ilana by the bandit (20). Later, it is also Ilana's mother's "fierceness of love" of rescuing her son Ari from a gang of soldiers, who have found and abducted him, that brings bad luck to their whole village by accidentally having her labor exposed to people in the village, which sets Ilana finally off on her journey as a diaspora (22–3).

In Ilana's village, there is also the primacy of three women who are inextricably linked with the lives of the villagers. Being occupied with their common business of weaving, the three women with the same face, gesture, and even the beating of pulses are marked as indistinguishable and indescribable. Their identities and relations become unclear. They look like sisters, mothers, and daughters, or cousins. None of the categories such as witches or saints can be assigned to them either. In addition to sewing endlessly, the three women are also "telling each other stories" incessantly (15). The stories they tell are age-old; as a result, the villagers render them as "the grandmothers, or great-grandmothers or great-aunts, of everyone in the village" (15). One of the stories the three women tell Ilana is a story about her mother. Strikingly, the power of their storytelling lies in their inseparable attachment to the villagers; even those who deliberately avoid them still sense their presence. And the threads they are sewing are "the hairs of everyone in the village" because all the villagers can feel "the tug" (16). The three women not only know the past and present but also can predict the future "with biblical accuracy" although the villagers all try to ignore their prophecy (16). The specter of the three women comes to haunt Ilana in her later life as an immigrant in America. Sometimes, the image of the three women is transposed to stand for Ilana and her two female descendants, her daughter and granddaughter, Sashie and Mara. These three women represent the reincarnation of the Fates in Greek mythology in which the recurrence of the three women reinforces a deterministic view of matrilineage, from which generations of women cannot escape. I shall return to this aspect in greater detail later.

As noted already, Ilana's reason for going on a journey is triggered by her resentment against her mother's ferocity. This echoes a "familiar formula" of fairy-tale family romances, that "one member of the family disturbs the initial tranquility and renders life at home intolerable."[5] Ilana does not fall prey to her parents' rage, abuse, or abandonment as do most protagonists in the Grimms' fairy tales. Yet, right after she launches into her wandering journey and in the early part of her adventure, she can still feel her mother's omnipresence in monitoring her thought and behavior, that her mother is aware of her running away and later coming home. Ilana's act of leaving home symbolizes her proclaimed independence from her mother and motherland as she professes that "I would give myself a new name, walk among a different sort of people" (28). Nonetheless, her migration is, as Ilana articulates, "still entangled in my mother's plans" (28). As we have seen, Ilana's perception of her mother is tainted by her "fantasy of the perfect mother."[6] The great power of the mother is viewed with awe but despised by the daughter. Ilana's intention to break away from her mother and motherland foreshadows her upcoming fate as an immigrant mother in relation to her Americanized daughters.

Observed from the perspective of diaspora, Ilana's wandering across different places and villages in search of the ideal city within the egg aligns her with the identity of cosmopolitan Jews. In Ilana's solitary journey to a homeland, she goes on a pilgrimage (to her dreamland) as a nomad who is in fact clueless about the exact location of her ideal land. As Ilana continues in her journey, there is a progression going on with a transformation from wood, iron, and steel to gold, indicating the industrial revolution and modern advancement of technology as "a picture of life more refined, more considered" (20). When Ilana ends her journey by settling down and marrying her lover, Shmuel, in New York, her wandering life turns into domestication.

In the years following Ilana's settlement in America, she gives birth to two sons, Eli and Wolf, who are identical twins, and a daughter,

Sashie. Later, Sashie also marries and bears a son and a daughter, Jonathan and Mara. Despite their productivity and prosperity, all the men in their household either die earlier or disappear mysteriously. The succeeding absence of men from their household echoes the matrifocality in Ilana's natal land. However, the mother-daughter relationship in the context of their adopted country, America, is complicated at a multigenerational level. The intricacy and complexity of four generations of women – Ilana, Sashie, Mara, and Nomie – are particularly compounded by migration, culture, and language. Ilana, who takes the initiative in leaving behind her old country in her youth, becomes both the matriarch and the crone in her old age who, like her mother, is despised and misunderstood but also respected by her female descendants. In an analogous fashion to most immigrant matrilineal narratives such as Amy Tan's *The Joy Luck Club*, which is discussed in detail in chapter 11, Ilana's difference from her daughter, Sashie, who insists on being called by her American name, Shirley, is their different cultural identities. Ilana, like the Chinese American immigrant mothers in Tan's *The Joy Luck Club*, does not assimilate into American culture as a whole. She reserves her old world's superstition, custom, dress code, food, and language, all of which are regarded by her daughter as unknown, remote, outlandish, and incompatible to their adopted life in the new world. Their incongruity is further illustrated in their naming of Sashie's daughter. Sashie prefers an Americanized name for her daughter of which Ilana strongly disapproves; eventually they both compromise with the name, Mara.

The complexity of the mother-daughter relation is best demonstrated in the intricate relation between their resonance and difference. Looking at a mirror, Sashie recognizes in herself a reflection of her mother's image. Yet, her matrophobia impedes her acceptance of her mother as she is:

> Still, when I studied myself in the mirror and saw my mother's eyes staring back, I felt a twinge of power, the potential in me.
> But I did not want to be like my mother.
> I did not want to be a force of nature. I wanted to be a *lady*.
> So I avoided my mother's ways, her pugilist stance, her out-thrust chin. I'd paced with books on my head for years, practiced enunciation with a pencil between my teeth. I bought high-heeled shoes; I loved that nice clatter on hard floors. The tap-tap of shoes, a pair of gloves, a precise tight-lipped smile with no vulgar teeth showing: these were the hallmarks of a lady. (142, emphasis original)

Sashie's estrangement from her mother, Ilana, is related to both class and culture. Her perception of Ilana as a crude and low-class woman and her deliberate avoidance of her "mother's ways" divide the mother and daughter into the dichotomy between culture and nature. Enacting her female family romance, Sashie resorts to the lady's class by modifying her appearance, manners, and manners of speech in order to replace the lower, inferior culture that her mother represents.

The mother-daughter incompatibility is also extended and transmitted to further generations. Mara's repulsion from her grandmother, Ilana, which is partly brewed by her mother's attitude toward her own mother, is exhibited in her refusal to eat her grandmother's beet soup:

> That night my grandmother made her beet soup. It was bright red, murky. Amorphous shreds of things settled to the bottom. I pushed the bowl away.
> Eat it, my grandmother said. It will make you strong.
> I looked at her, at the black hair and dark eyebrows. There was something wrong with her, there were not enough lines on her face, I thought. She and my mother looked nearly the same age.
> Eat it, she said sternly.
> I saw what she was up to, what she was planning. She wanted me to become like her. She wanted someone to tell all her horrible secrets to.
> I would not do it. I would not let her. (195)

Conceiving of her grandmother as a witch like crone, affected by the conversation Mara has had with her schoolmate before, the beet soup that Ilana has made for Mara becomes the gristly broth a witch boils in her pot. Misreading her grandmother like her mother does, Mara resolves not to let her grandmother fulfill her evil scheme of storytelling. Yet, the narration followed by Ilana informs a reader of the grandmother's true intention. The grandmother wishes to compensate for the loss of love between mother and daughter by teaching the granddaughter to be strong. Disappointedly, the grandmother realizes that the granddaughter will not necessarily reciprocate (195–6).

As we will see later, the mother-daughter disjunction does gradually separate them from each other. The unnecessary repetition that corners these three generations of immigrant mothers and daughters can be glimpsed again in another recurrent image of the mother-daughter footprints in Sashie's dream:

> I dreamed of a line of women walking in the snow, each one stepping in the footprints of the one before. All around them lay vast stretches of smooth snow, unmarked, unexplored.
> This life of mine was like a loop of film, no beginning or ending, just the same figures going through the same motions in endless repetition. (197)

This recycling of a life with "the same figures going through the same motions in endless repetition" bespeaks neither recovery nor progress. It denotes boredom and stagnation without the possibility of looking back to the past or the prospect of looking forward to the future. This circular movement of repetition indicates only degeneration, not regeneration; it also signals confinement, not liberation.

The inextricably intertwined but repeated lives of mothers and daughters as entrapment to them all are also displayed in the replication of the three women in the village. Ilana, Sashie, and Mara reincarnate the three women in the village by simultaneously taking up a nurturing role of mothering Nomie, their allegedly collective daughter, who is, in fact, the daughter of Chloe, a suspected sea creature disguised in a human form, with whom Jonathan, Sashie's son, is infatuated. In declaring each one of them as Nomie's co-mother, their generational hierarchy as grandmother, mother, and daughter begins to collapse to a common ground of mothering. That is, the two frameworks of time of matrilinealism, "a diachronic, vertical axis of descent," seem to be conjoined with "a synchronic, horizontal plane" in their commonality as mothers.[7] Yet, this collective mothering among Ilana, Sashie, and Mara is not performed on an egalitarian and sharing basis. The three women compete with one another as rivals to win their rights as the only legitimate mother of Nomie. This severe competition for mothering is described by Mara in a comic but fierce way:

> It was a constant, subtle thing. A silent war the three of us waged. One would sterilize and prepare a bottle, and then another would pluck it from her hand and run to the nursery. We all hovered over the cradle as she slept, all wanting to be the first face she saw when she awoke. We elbowed each other aside at the changing table. Even my mother, usually so fastidious, dipped her hand in. (232)

Whether this is a competition between mothers and daughters or their endeavor to reestablish the connection lost to them is not clear. For Mara who unlike her grandmother and mother does not have a daughter, mothering Nomie is, as she professes, her turn to be a mother. Realizing, however, that both her grandmother and mother give birth to daughters who they do not really want, Mara also notes that "it was the last chance for all of us" to forge "a connection" (232). Significantly, this rivalry between mothers and daughters also marks their distinct identities and stances with respect to their needs and interests in mothering Nomie. One more thing that is worth mentioning about Mara's endeavor to claim Nomie as her real daughter is related to Mara's incestuous obsession with her brother, Jonathan. In combating with her female predecessors to win her brother's daughter, Mara opts into an incestuous family romance with brother, sister, and daughter instead of a matrilineal one that contains grandmother, mother, and daughter.

A tangible physical feature that displays their similarity but also difference as mothers and daughters is their sharing of familiar looks and black hair. Both Nomie and Mara have "long black hair and dark eyes and lips," which are all identical to those of Sashie and Ilana except that Sashie's hair is tainted "with gray" while Ilana's remains "an unnatural metallic black" (233–4). Thus, the resonance and difference between mothers and daughters suggest again an interesting interplay of the two frameworks of time of matrilinealism. The sharing of similar physical features amalgamate these four generations of women onto "a synchronic, horizontal plane" whereas the changes or differences of hair color in both Sashie and Ilana mark their different generational identities in "the diachronic descent line."[8]

Another intriguing portrayal of the intersection of "synchronic and diachronic patterns"[9] in feminist matrilinealism is the arrangement of rooms in an apartment inhabited by these four generations of women:

> Ilana lived in the largest room in the apartment, and she kept it so dim you could hardly see its boundaries. Sashie's room was smaller, the walls entirely covered with yellowed pictures of starlets from generations ago. Mara's room was smaller still, it was the room that had once been my father's and she slept there among outdated medical textbooks and pencils she allowed no one to use. My room was the smallest of all, it was encircled by the others, a windowless closet in the heart of the apartment. (258)

The apartment Ilana, Sashie, Mara, and Nomie inhabit now is not "the ancestral house" where Ilana and her now-deceased husband lived when they first emigrated to America.[10] Both Ilana and Sashie move to this new apartment in their old neighborhood when Sashie is going to give birth to a daughter. Reverberating with their sharing of familiar looks and black hair, living in the same apartment brings the four generations of women onto the same "synchronic, horizontal plane." Yet, the size for each of their rooms and their individual belongings hoarded inside their rooms make their rooms distinct from one another, indicating clearly their "diachronic descent line." Moreover, instead of being structured as "a diachronic, vertical" and linear line, the formation and configuration of their four rooms connecting one to another is depicted as circular and curved.[11] Nomie's room located at the heart of the circle is surrounded and enclosed by the three other rooms. This signifies Nomie's relation to her three mothers. As Nomie goes on to narrate, their rooms resemble a matrushka doll with a smaller one being subsumed into its bigger counterpart and are repeated in a cycle: "The rooms were like a series of nesting boxes. Each could fit inside the next. They were like those hollow wooden dolls that can be opened to reveal smaller ones, which can be opened to reveal another. And so on and so on forever" (258). This generative image of "rooms within rooms and stories within stories" is consonant with Naomi Ruth Lowinsky's delineation of the motherline as a cyclic life process circling around "bodies being born out of bodies."[12] Yet, in response to Budnitz's negative construction of matrilineage, this circular shape of their rooms illustrates their pointless and nonliberated matrilineal repetition.

As the specter of the three women in the village returns to haunt Ilana, she can always sense, either in her imagination or consciousness, their presence and cannot possibly get away from them. She vividly describes the persistence of the three women in the following example:

> Those three.
> You see, I traveled so far to escape them. I traveled to this place, where their kind do not exist, where the world obeys different rules. Here where the future is uncertain and the past is far away and you can make both up as you go along if you want.
> I thought I had left them far behind. I stopped hearing them in my head, I had not even dreamt about them for years.
> But now suddenly after all this time they have found me. I have begun seeing them again.
> They have changed, certainly. They are crafty. But I can see through their disguises, I recognize their voices. The trouble is that this city is so full of noise I cannot hear their words clearly. (236)

The three women symbolize Ilana's past and her homeland or motherland in Eastern Europe. They represent the past Ilana intentionally renounces but ironically preserves in her later life as an American immigrant. Yet, what Ilana has perceived as the recuperation of the three women in her life is the mimicking of the three women in her matrilineage. Ilana, Sashie, and Mara are the three women in disguise whose "voices" Ilana can recognize but whose "words" she "cannot hear" "clearly" (236). The three-generational voices are too vibrant and diverse to be heard unobtrusively in a cosmopolitan city such as New York whose noise of cultural displacement inhibits such a hearing.

Nonetheless, Ilana, as the ultimate storyteller in this three-generational triangle, manages to tell her story to her (great-grand) daughter, Nomie. Ilana's stories of her own past answer Nomie's enquiry about "intercourse and conception" (267). Ironically, while Nomie feels more drawn to Ilana's storytelling, both Sashie and Mara devise to send Ilana out of the apartment in order to retain their status as Nomie's mothers. Although Nomie later realizes their plan and protests fiercely against it, Ilana, on discovering her daughter's and granddaughter's wicked plan, disappears mysteriously from the apartment. The last scene of the novel ends with Nomie's visit in Ilana's room. In a similar vein to Faro in Drabble's *The Peppered Moth*, Nomie goes into her great-grandmother's room and rummages through her belongings in order to retrieve her matrilineage. There she studies the magical egg in Ilana's room. At first, Nomie sees a wonderful world inside. But at another glance, Nomie sees only an empty egg except a reflection of her own pupil. As Ilana is gone, so is the vision of the ideal land inside the egg.

Unlike Faro, Nomie sees only backward things and the impossibility of recovery. In many aspects, both Drabble's *The Peppered Moth* and Budnitz's *If I Told You Once* focus on a "negative, matrophobic" construction of matrilineal narratives[13] in which generations of women are fated to be confined within their endless and circular repetitions while at the same time they strive to break away from their motherline. Although the motherline connecting the grandmother and the mother is flawed in *The Peppered Moth*, it can still be healed by the granddaughter's recovery of matrilineage and her choice of the right man breaks the spell of their matrilineal repetition. The four generations of women in *If I Told You Once*, on the contrary, break through their repetition only by separating from one another and thus disrupting their motherline. In addition, the concepts of men and Jewishness vary also in both texts. In *The Peppered Moth*, Steve Nieman, who is part of the Jewish diaspora and assists Faro in retrieving her matrilineage, can be incorporated into the motherline of "mitochondrial DNA."[14] In *If I Told You Once*, the Jewish men, including fathers, brothers, and husbands, are discarded earlier than their female counterparts; their absence from the narrative is a result of either their early death or mysterious disappearance.

In Budnitz's fairy-tale rewrite of four generations of women, *If I Told You Once*, we surprisingly have an amalgam of important features of matrilineal narratives. The mother-daughter resonance and differences, matrilineal ambivalence, female family romances, and the working and reworking of the two frameworks of time of matrilinealism[15] all appear in Budnitz's textual experimentation with magical realism in a matrilineal narrative. Yet, Budnitz's puzzling tragic ending or ending without a definite closure reverses the conventional happy ending of fairy tales. Her writing of a matrilineal narrative is also a failed example of the working magic of mother-daughter mirroring and storytelling in resolving matrilineal ambivalence and affirming mother-daughter recognition. The harbingers of this unhappy ending of a matrilineal narrative are manifest in the strained and not-yet-reconciled matrilineal relation among Ilana, Sashie, and Mara and also in the dramatic transformation of the vision within the magical egg from a picturesque wonderland to despairing delusion. The agitated and unresolved immigrant mother-daughter relations mirror the ambivalence and tension between past and present, old world and new world, nature and culture, and assimilation and resistance. Poignantly, a high price to pay for the mother-daughter disjunction is not only the disintegration of their matrilineage but also the perishing of their supposed ideal homeland. The reincarnation of the three village women in Ilana, Sashie, and Mara bespeaks the illusion of momentary recovery of matrilineage in the mother's land; the haunting of these three phantom-like women in Ilana's later life as an American immigrant heralds the toll of her estrangement and ultimate separation from her female descendants. The disruption of the motherline in conjunction with the disillusionment of an ideal homeland, be it a motherland or a mother country, asserts, in a converse manner, the inseparable link among female identification, matrilineage, and motherland. Paradoxically, while attempting to make a progress from their mothers and mothers' land in Eastern Europe to locate the whereabouts of her dreamland, Ilana and her female descendants also undertake their meaningless repetition in a generational cycle in their mother country, America. As their matrilineal relation becomes static and suffocating without either recovery or progress, they are destined to separate from one another forever. Not only both the mother and the (grand)daughter want to send the (grand)mother away, but the grandmother also takes the initiative in leaving her female descendants behind. As there is no recognition of matrilineage, motherland or mother country thus become nonexistent.

Notes

1. Tess Cosslett, "Fairytales: Revisiting the Tradition," in *Women, Power and Resistance: An Introduction to Women's Studies*, ed. Tess Cosslett, Alison Easton, and Penny Summerfield (Buckingham and Philadelphia: Oxford University Press, 1996), 82.
2. Cosslett, "Feminism, Matrilinealism, and the 'House of the Women' in Contemporary Women's Fiction," *Journal of Gender Studies* 5, no. 1 (1996): 8.
3. Judy Budnitz, *If I Told You Once* (1999; reprint, London: Flamingo, 2001). Hereafter, page numbers to this volume are cited parenthetically. References are to the reprint edition.
4. Cosslett, "Fairytales: Revisiting the Tradition," 82. See also Maria Tatar, *The*

Hard Facts of the Grimms' Fairy Tales (New Jersey: Princeton University Press, 1987), 3–38.
5. Tatar, *The Hard Facts of the Grimms' Fairy Tales*, 72.
6. Nancy Chodorow and Susan Contratto, "The Fantasy of the Perfect Mother," in *Feminism and Psychoanalytic Theory*, ed. Nancy Chodorow (Cambridge and Oxford: Polity Press, 1989), 79–96.
7. Cosslett, "Feminism, Matrilinealism, and the 'House of the Women' in Contemporary Women's Fiction," 8.
8. Ibid.
9. Ibid.
10. Ibid., 9–16.
11. Ibid., 8.
12. Naomi Ruth Lowinsky, *Stories from the Motherline: Reclaiming the Mother-Daughter Bond, Finding Our Feminine Souls* (Los Angeles: Jeremy P. Tarcher, 1992), 12.
13. Cosslett, "Feminism, Matrilinealism, and the 'House of the Women' in Contemporary Women's Fiction," 8.
14. Margaret Drabble, *The Peppered Moth* (London and New York: Viking 2000), 2.
15. Cosslett, "Feminism, Matrilinealism, and the 'House of the Women' in Contemporary Women's Fiction," 8.

Chapter 15

A Poetics of Diasporic Matrilineal Narratives

Thinking over each of my individual discussions of these five women's texts, I would like to amalgamate them together by suggesting some possible links. First, in all of the five texts, there are occurrences of disrupted motherlines under various circumstances and their subsequent restoration (with the exception of Judy Budnitz's *If I Told You Once*, which ends with a separation and an unresolved matrilineal relation). The fact that all of these texts deal with violated or disrupted motherlines could be attributed to their sharing of a common fate, diaspora, in which all the mother-daughter relationships are tainted by their painful, traumatic immigrant experiences in America (although in Jamaica Kincaid's *Annie John*, the background is set in one of the Caribbean islands and the mother-daughter relation becomes only tense and strained when the daughter reaches puberty). In varying degrees, the mothers and daughters in these texts are subject to multiple oppressions of sexism, classism, and racism impinging on them from different structures of patriarchal dominance such as imperialism, colonialism, neocolonialism, and capitalism. Some extreme cases are slavery recounted in both the colonial and postcolonial states (Toni Morrison's *Beloved*) and traumatized recollection of racist deportation of Japanese Canadians (Joy Kogawa's *Obasan*).

Yet, by pointing to the two most traumatized literary examples in my study, I do not mean to preclude other texts with lesser degrees of oppression and trauma. As bitterly and ferociously investigated in the often strained and difficult mother-daughter relationship in Amy Tan's *The Joy Luck Club*, Kincaid's *Annie John*, and Budnitz's *If I Told You Once*, the Americanized immigrant daughters (except Annie John) are all inclined to misread and misinterpret their mothers who originally come from other cultures, speak different languages, and adhere to their lifestyles in the old world. In some instances in Tan's and Budnitz's works, the great division drawn between mothers and daughters is cast in the form of that between American imperialists and subjugated subalterns as those immigrant mothers are very often perceived by their daughters as racial others. Apart from combating sexism and racism from outside their familial-domestic space, the American immigrant mothers also need to struggle with their Americanized daughters' internalized imperialist racism. In *Annie John*, however, the mother-daughter relationship charts a different contour; it is the mother rather than the daughter who acts as an agent for colonial power and dominance by socializing the daughter into a neocolonialized subject. With the involvement of social and political variables and complications, there is no wonder that the motherlines in these women's texts suffer from disruption and violation.

Yet, in spite of the disruption of the motherline or the estranged mother-daughter relationship, what I would like to emphasize in my second point is the restoration of the motherline instigated mostly by a non-Western, nonmainstream cultural practice of othermothering, having existed already in different ethnic, racial, and cultural contexts, which most of these texts have unfolded. In African American literary texts such as Morrison's *Beloved*, Afrocentric meanings and performances of mothering have their manifestations and reverberations in literary representations and creativities. In particular, Morrison experiments with the concept of othermothering by expanding it into different persons, not necessarily restricted to a mature woman who has the capacity of childbearing, and configurations, not always presented in a vertical motherline.

In both Kogawa's and Tan's novels, it is the maternalistic aunts who facilitate the restoration of the motherline or the recovery of matrilineage. In Kogawa's *Obasan*, the presence of two aunts in Naomi's life figures in two rather antithetical manners, but they both add to Naomi's quest for the absence of her mother from different angles and help resolve the daughter's tension between repudiating and recuperating the mother. In Tan's *The Joy Luck Club*, the best example is Jing-mei's recuperation of matrilineage in her family, which is propelled by her Joy Luck aunts. However, having proposed this cultural reading of othermothering in American diasporic matrilineal narratives does not imply the deprivation of the maternal agency and authority. Rather, othermothering accentuates the reinstatement of the maternal at the center.

While the emergence of othermothering in a host of diasporic matrilineal narratives covered in my book elicits the extension of a vertical motherline into a horizontal one, the grandmothers or grandmother-like characters figure considerably in reviving the endangered vertical motherline. In Morrison's *Beloved*, Sethe's mother, who speaks their African mother tongue and represents their African origin, unfolds her maternal identity to Sethe by the marks on her body, and hence she resurrects her severed connection with her daughter who then recounts this incident to her daughters in an attempt to secure their motherline. In Kincaid's *Annie John*, Ma Chess's timely rescue of Annie from mental collapse and her resuming of the maternal function during Annie's mother's absence are excellent examples of the rejuvenation of vertical motherline by the grandmother. In Kogawa's *Obasan*, Naomi's maternalistic aunt Obasan, with her older age and generation, resembles Naomi's grandmother, during whose absence Obasan instills their Japanese cultural values and heritage (including matrilineage) into Naomi. Obasan as a substitute (grand)mother also fills the void left by virtue of Naomi's mother's absence. Therefore, her significant maternal functions facilitate the restoration of the ruptured vertical motherline.

In Tan's *The Joy Luck Club*, when the Joy Luck mothers narrate their stories to their daughters, their mothers' stories are often embedded within theirs, thus forming their female story lines in a three-generational framework with their employment of shifting identities between mothers and daughters. As a result, the grandmother in the process of mother-daughter storytelling constitutes a vital link between mothers and daughters and serves as a valuable reference point of their matrilineal culture and history. Although the repudiation of the (grand)mother and an obituary to feminist matrilinealism are the options in Budnitz's *If I Told You Once*, Ilana's efforts to heal the mother-daughter rupture in her motherline can still be glimpsed in her role as the storyteller who means to pass on her matrilineage to her female descendant in the youngest generation, Nomie, in particular. Ilana's mother, whom Ilana both admires and repudiates, is also represented as a source of inspiration and strength from which Ilana can never get away even after her migration to a faraway land. Although some of these grandmothers are presented as peripheral figures and are not one of the potent forces that constitute the grandmother-mother-daughter triad, they are indisputably the essential lifeblood of most of the diasporic matrilineal narratives.

Another enriching source of revitalizing the motherline or matrilineage is the use of storytelling in the texts. These women writers' employment and deployment of storytelling echo a culturally informed narrative pattern and strategy of, for, and by women. In almost all of the texts, the technique of storytelling functions as a vital vehicle of both survival and resistance for mothers and daughters to counteract their oppressions in a frequently hostile world, either in their motherlands or mother countries. In some cases, it even transforms their feelings of disenfranchisement and powerlessness into those of strength and solidity. In *Annie John*, Kincaid even demonstrates the paradox of storytelling in a mother-daughter (con)text. The technique perpetuates the continuity and creativity of one particular cultural heritage and identity or an amalgam of several, which are vital to the survival of immigrant minorities or colonialized subjects. Nonetheless, it can also be utilized as a tactic of resisting colonial manipulation and exploitation. One such example is Annie John's tactful deployment of storytelling into mastery of telling lies in counterpoint to her mother's colonial tyranny.

In a similar vein, the aforementioned multiple functions of storytelling are also manifest in Tan's novel. Yet, what makes the storytelling technique in Tan's work different slightly from the other texts is Tan's specification of Chinese culture-embedded talk story in which the female characters, especially the mothers, aspire to a more culturally accustomed way of narration that assists in restoring the disruptions between them and their daughters both in cultural and political senses. In Budnitz's *If I Told You Once*, storytelling is also the technique that Ilana deliberately uses to deliver her messages to her great-granddaughter, Nomie, to ensure the continuation of the motherline, especially during the crisis of the likely breaking up of her matrilineage. In Kogawa's, Tan's, and Budnitz's novels, the maternal storytellers also weave elements of myths, fables, and fairy tales gleaned specifically from their different cultural resources into storytelling with the aim of passing on their cultural values of origin to their female descendants in North America. In spite of their different textual explorations of storytelling under different circumstances, the storytelling used and developed by these women writers serves more or less similar purposes.

One unique motif displayed in most diasporic matrilineal narratives such as the five texts under consideration here is these women writers' textual exploration of the sustained relation among mother, motherland, and/or mother country in a creative and transformative fashion. In Morrison's *Beloved*, the vital cultural maternal practice of othermothering drawn from the motherland, Africa, serves as a life-surviving and growth-enhancing political weapon against the mutilation of black matrilineage and race from the mother country, America. In Kincaid's *Annie John*, the ever-increasing and constantly evolving migration of the Caribbean diaspora destabilizes the definitions and geopolitics of motherland and mother country. Antigua as the motherland in *Annie John* elicits both pleasure and pain for the female protagonist, Annie, as the development of her relationship with her mother on their island home testifies. Initially, the motherland, Antigua, provides a source of nurturance and love for Annie whereas it is later seen as analogous to the mother country, England, in her execution of colonial dominance and power over her daughter inhabitant. Yet, the recovery from Annie's mental breakdown caused by the mother-daughter estrangement and, by extension, the tension existing in the daughter's conflicted feelings for both motherland and mother country could only be enacted by a matrilineal healing power emerging mysteriously from her mother's land, Dominica. Significantly, the birthing of Annie's new self by her African matrilineage into a combined matrilineal syncretic self untangles the conflicted trichotomy among mother, motherland, and mother country.

In Kogawa's *Obasan*, Naomi's gnawing anxiety about the absence of her mother and the breaking up of their family also makes explicit the discrepancies between her mother('s)land, Japan, and mother country, Canada. Yet, with the mutual influences of both motherland and mother country on Naomi, personified in her two aunt figures, Obasan and Aunt Emily, and also characterized in the dichotomy between silence and speech, Naomi comes to her reconciliation of the tension so that the two contrasting forces become complementary. In Tan's *The Joy Luck Club*, the mother('s)land, China, appears to be ambivalent to both immigrant mothers and daughters. On the one hand, the motherland, China, is seen as the origin of suffering and victimization for the Chinese immigrant mothers and as a source of culture and language barriers for the Americanized immigrant daughters. On the other hand, it is also viewed as provision of empowerment and strength for the mother-daughter survival in their sexist and racist mother country, America, and also as a bridge for the mother-daughter reconciliation of their misunderstanding occurring in their mother country. In Budnitz's text, the tension between mother('s) land in Eastern Europe and mother country, America, epitomized in a matrilineal tension among three generations of immigrant mothers and daughters, appears to be more complex and unresolved than the other diasporic matrilineal narratives. The intricacy of diasporic female identity in relation to motherland and mother country manifests itself vividly in Ilana's ambivalence toward repudiating and recuperating the mother('s)land. The tension between motherland and mother country also, in turn, exhibits itself in the agonizing matrilineal relation among Ilana, Sashie, and Mara. Yet, ironically, as the matrilineal ambivalence becomes unresolved and their relations unreconciled, gone are the existence and physicality of their motherland and mother country, which should have provided them with identification and belonging. And the vanishing of the imagined community inside the magical egg bespeaks in particular the delusion of motherland and mother country.

Finally, in reading these five diasporic matrilineal narratives, I have discovered in them reverberations of Jessica Benjamin's intersubjective theory. In Tan's novel, the poetics of mother-daughter voices established through the art of storytelling or talk story is performed in an intersubjective mode. Put more concretely, by means of storytelling, mutual recognition between mothers and daughters begins to develop and establish in the ways that resemble Benjamin's theoretical trajectory. More significant, in all of the texts, women writers' textual explorations of the mother as the racial other resonate with Benjamin's later theoretical tenet. Benjamin's more recent theoretical contention points out that the state of mutual recognition is a locus of "struggle and negotiation of conflict"[1] and it entails tension existing "between recognizing the other and asserting the self."[2] In other words, what lies at the heart of intersubjectivity is not a "continuous harmony" but a "continuous disruption and repair" that is inevitably involved with the "negation and negativity" of the other.[3] In Benjamin's view, the other plays a pivotal role in fostering the development of intersubjectivity between self and other or between two subjects. In all of the five texts, the daughters within different cultural, social, and racial contexts have to come to terms with the "negation and negativity" of the (m)other and also within themselves.[4] Such an encounter with the often gendered and racialized (m)other generates tensions and conflicts between mothers and daughters, which leads to "disruption" but also "repair" of the motherline (with the exception of Budnitz's text where the restoration of the motherline becomes difficult and impossible at the end). Benjamin's theorization of the other is described in general and abstract terms. Yet, in these diasporic matrilineal narratives, the mother is presented specifically and concretely as both the gendered and racialized other. While Benjamin's theory serves as a benchmark for intersubjective attunement with the other in general, the diasporic matrilineal narrative materializes, in effect, the theoretical contour of intersubjectivity in which the (m)other speaks and intervenes.

What the five diasporic women's texts have added to a poetics of matrilineal narratives are the narrativity and subjectivity of other (con)texts. The breadth and scope they have charted widen the extant facets of matrilineal narratives. The figuration of the mother-daughter relationship or matrilineal relation serves as the trope for our cultural readings of gender, class, race, identity politics, and postcoloniality. The black mother-daughter relationships discussed in this part are shaped by the construction of their different family structures, such as the female-headed household, with cultural and racial variables, features that are remarkably different from the nuclear family model shown in some of the matrilineal narratives selected for my study. Rather than having class and education as the two main determinants in causing the mother-daughter separation as demonstrated in my examination of the selected four matrilineal narratives in part 2, other contributing factors in the context of diasporic matrilineal narratives include race, culture, language, place, and national identity. In addition, the two different endings, either happy or tragic, of these matrilineal narratives amplify the parameter of a matrilineal romance. Tan's *The Joy Luck Club* and Budnitz's *If I Told You Once*, for instance, are exact illustrations of these two possibilities. In fact, happy and tragic endings are both the options in a romance. When a tragic ending is presented in a matrilineal romance, it is most likely to provoke a sense of displacement and loss for a reader, especially if it is antithetical to a feminist celebratory mode. Yet, what I want to argue here is that the "negative, matrophobic construction"[5] of matrilineal narratives, as appearing in Budnitz's *If I Told You Once*, reinforces in a conversely emphatic manner the significance of the maternal in forming a constitutive relationship with diasporic female identity in association with other signification systems such as the concepts of mother cultures, motherlands, and mother countries.

Notes

1. Jessica Benjamin, *Shadow of the Other: Intersubjectivity and Gender in Psychoanalysis* (New York and London: Routledge, 1998), 23.
2. Ibid., 38.
3. Ibid., 47, 79–88.
4. Ibid., 79–88.
5. Tess Cosslett, "Feminism, Matrilinealism, and the 'House of Women' in Contemporary Women's Fiction," *Journal of Gender Studies* 5, no. 1 (1996): 8.

Conclusion

This book has examined contemporary women's writing of matrilineal narratives from a feminist perspective. This feminist study of matrilineal narratives has invoked a feminist revisiting of relationality in which heated feminist issues such as motherhood and maternal subjectivity have undergone scrutiny and transformation. The constructions of matrilineal narratives, as unfolded in several contemporary women's writings, have suggested one positive and possible solution—the working out of conflicts and ambivalences toward connection—for resolving feminist dilemmas regarding motherhood and matrilineage (the mother-daughter relationship in particular). The textual practices of intersubjectivity or intersubjective mothering, as ably experimented on in matrilineal narratives, have also relocated and reconceptualized maternal subjectivity as intersubjectivity. In my exploration of both feminist psychoanalytic theory and women's texts in this book, I have drawn on not only their similarities but also their significant differences, especially the ways in which contemporary women writers' engagement with matrilineal narratives has contributed to the reformulations of extant theoretical paradigms of feminisms. In what follows, I shall revisit my previous investigation of both theoretical and literary texts and conclude by signposting their relations.

In part 1, I conducted a rereading of psychoanalytic feminisms, Chodorow's and Flax's object-relations theory and Irigaray's and Kristeva's post-Lacanian psychoanalysis, and also approached feminist relationality from the angle of Benjamin's intersubjective theory. In analyzing the works of these feminist theorists, I have demonstrated that the theoretical developments of these theorists have signaled a significant move toward reforging connections between mothers and daughters. This working toward connection has also illustrated a triadic shift in feminist theorization of maternal subjectivity from first seeing the mother as an object, then resurrecting her as a subject in her own right, and finally to repositioning her as an "intersubject", whose subjectivity is not necessarily submerged into that of her child.[1] Developing from the male paradigm of psychoanalysis, both Chodorow and Flax envision separation as a possible problem for both mother and daughter. As we have seen in Irigaray's writing of the mother-daughter relationship, this conflict between separation and connection creates ambivalence. Unlike Chodorow's and Flax's sociological approach, Irigaray attributes this ambivalence between mother and daughter to the "dereliction" of women within the symbolic order.[2] Yet, in observing this problem between mother and daughter, Chodorow, Flax, and Irigaray all perceive the mother as the object or the other from which the child develops his or her own subjectivity. This perception of the m/other is, I have argued, implicated in "the fantasy of the perfect mother."[3] In fulfilling their aspirations, the three theorists paradoxically reinforce mother-blaming. The daughter's need for separation from the mother is dictated either by her fear of being overwhelmed by the mother's power or by her resentment against the mother's powerlessness. Located in this paradigm, the mother-daughter relationship is only articulated by the daughter.

However, another French theorist, Kristeva, adopts the voice of the mother. Her experimental writing of the semiotic enables her to let the mother speak as a subject. Regarding the maternal body as a site of self *and* other, Kristeva points to the discursive position the mother occupies between the semiotic and the symbolic, and the disruptive potential of the semiotic or the maternal to counter the symbolic and the paternal. Linking this site of maternity to the mother-daughter relationship, Kristeva favors it as a privileged aspect of femininity, because she thinks that both being female, the mother and the daughter tend to have an inseparable identity, thus having the capacity to reproduce between themselves the language of motherhood. Nonetheless, talking about the mother-daughter relationship in relation to language, Kristeva, like Irigaray, considers this relationship to be "unsymbolized."[4] In trying to solve these problems for women, the four feminist theorists have devised various strategies. Chodorow suggests shared parenting by men in order to short-circuit the reproduction of mothering among women, whereas Flax emphasizes the importance of the mother-daughter bond in achieving a mutual understanding and sharing between women. As for Irigaray, she advocates experimental women's writing in a common female language generated from and by the existence of love and identification between women. For Kristeva, apart from celebrating the writing of the maternal, she is also in favor of the use of the paternal language within the symbolic order.

In an attempt to accommodate the subjectivities of both mother and child, Benjamin's major contribution to feminist thinking on mothering and mother-child relationships is to provide a theoretical frame of reference about how to situate maternal subjectivity as intersubjectivity. Predicated upon the theoretical axiom of intersubjectivity, the maternal identity as seen through the lens of self-in-relation is *not* rendered only as dependent upon the child's fantasy or desire of the mother as an object. For instance, in her book *The Bonds of Love*, Benjamin postulates her theory on the template of intersubjectivity, in which two subjects coexist in this earliest development of human relationship and their existences are verified by their mutual recognition. As two distinctive but also interdependent subjects, there is a coexistence of "resonance and differences," between them, which is involved in the process of mutual recognition between self and the other.[5] Yet, Benjamin's painting of her intersubjective theory is not necessarily a harmonious picture, it also contains "tensions" and "conflicts" in the interactions between self and the other as described in her later reformulation of her earlier theory in *Like Subjects, Love Objects*. According to Benjamin, to accomplish the ideal state of mutual recognition, both self and the other need to go through their "struggle and negotiation of conflict", which can also lead to a disruption and its subsequent restoration of the tension.[6] In other words, tension or conflict becomes a necessity in this intersubjective drama performed by the persona of self-in-relation. Developing her intersubjective theory of tension and conflict further, Benjamin in her most recent work, *Shadow of the Other*, accentuates the importance of the other in facilitating the interactions, negotiations, and even transformations between self and the other. Benjamin wants to develop an other-inclusive theory in which a self's involvement with the other's negation can call forth multiplicity, which entails "tolerating ambivalence", and an intersubjective "consciousness", which can accommodate both "differences and sameness."[7]

Testing out these speculations, I have discovered important congruences between theoretical approaches to mother-daughter relationships and the quasi-autobiographical and fictional texts of Fredriksson, Chang, Forster, and Drabble in part 2. These congruences are the themes of the relative obscurity of the father figure, the ambivalence between mothers and daughters, the working through of these ambivalences and tensions toward a sense of connection, and the participation in a maternal voice. However, drawing on my evaluation of these congruences, I do not want to assert that the theories have determined the key texts. Situating relationality within the family triangular relationship and elaborating on different versions of family romances—Freudian, feminist appropriation, and modification—I have discovered in these four matrilineal narratives different rewritings and reworking of both Freudian and feminist family romances, which I term *new feminist family romances*. In them, not only the theoretical axiom of relationality and intersubjectivity has been experimented on, but also their literary experimentations have engendered a more complicated contour of relationality, moving from dyad to triad and opening up different narrative shapes and possibilities. Significantly, the triadic formulations of matrilineal narratives have also illuminated what the Stone Center theorists have characterized as a *"power-with"* dynamic of mother-daughter relationships rather than a *"power-over"* one[8] which some feminists have felt disquiet with when using the mother-daughter relationship or matrilineage as a metaphor to denote women's relationships.

Investigating five diasporic matrilineal narratives published between 1981 and 1999, part 3 enters another arena where the themes of motherhood and mother-daughter relationships have been actively explored to politicize the issues of race, migration, cultural and national identities, but have also been used to create personal transformations. The themes which the five selected women writers of diasporas – Morrison, Kincaid, Kogawa, Tan, and Budnitz – have coincidently explored in their textual representations of matrilineage and mother-daughter relationships are the disruption and subsequent restoration of the motherline, the emergence of othermothering or surrogate mothers, the use of story-telling as a survival strategy or resistance against patriarchal and colonial dominance, the exploration of the triadic relationship among mother, motherland, and mother country, as epitomized in varying manifestations of the immigrant mother-daughter relationship, and the colonization and decolonization of the mother as the racial other. The delineations of the mother-daughter relationship, as compounded by the different racial, cultural, and social registers of diasporas, have problematized the theoretical premise of feminist psychoanalysis. But on the other hand, Benjamin's later formulation of her intersubjective theory, that of the intervention of the other, has reverberations with these diasporic women writers' portrayals of the otherness in their representations of the maternal figure. Further, the different ways these women writers of diasporas construct or fictionalize matrilineal narratives have also suggested their different interpretations of matrilinealism. For instance, Budnitz's "negative, matrophobic" construction of matrilineal narrative,[9] *If I Told You Once*, eschew almost all the thematic recurrences as illustrated in the other four diasporic women's texts and also reverse a recurrent narrative pattern of matrilineal romances discussed in part 2. Although Budnitz's text is a failed example, seen from a feminist attempt to reclaim the mother and matrilineage in a positive way, it can be perceived as a converse approach to feminist matrilinealism. This possibility as created by Budnitz's text should *not* be viewed as a backlash against feminism but as a way of rethinking and reformulating feminist matrilinealism.

What I have gleaned from my study of contemporary matrilineal narratives is that a clear majority of them assert a feminist celebratory mode. Although the antifeminist perceptions as exhibited in certain texts written by women flout my feminist reading of them, they have also added dimensions to the overall topos of my book. By investigating in this book the textual practices of a variety of contemporary women's writing, a continuum of theorizing and fiction emerges that can both accommodate and engender texts, both theoretical and literary, with other provenances, other agendas. This poetics of matrilineal narratives suggests its heterogeneity and inconclusiveness, which will be broadened and enriched by encompassing more of different narratives and discourses such as lesbian mothering, alternative women-women genealogies (e.g., aunt-niece relationships), and male identity in relation to matrilineal narratives, which are worth pursuing from the perspective of feminist maternal scholarship. The burgeoning development of women's writing of matrilineal narratives since the 1970s has also continued into the twenty-first century. All these make the subject of matrilinealism an exciting, stimulating, and ongoing feminist project.

Notes

1. Jo Malin, *The Voice of the Mother: Embedded Maternal Narratives in Twentieth-Century Women's Autobiographies* (Carbondale and Edwardsville: Southern Illinois University Press, 2000), 1–2.
2. Margaret Whitford, "Rereading Irigaray," in *Between Feminism and Psychoanalysis*, ed. Teresa Brennan (London and New York: Routledge, 1989), 108–13.
3. Nancy Chodorow and Susan Contratto, "The Fantasy of the Perfect Mother," in *Feminism and Psychoanalytic Theory*, ed. Nancy Chodorow (Oxford: Basil Blackwell, 1989), 79–96.
4. Whitford, *Luce Irigaray: Philosophy in the Feminine* (London and New York: Routledge, 1991), 77–8.
5. Jessica Benjamin, *The Bonds of Love: Psychoanalysis, Feminism, and the Problem of Domination* (New York: Pantheon Books, 1988), 11–50.
6. Benjamin, *Like Subjects, Love Objects: Essays on Recognition and Sexual Difference* (New Haven and London: Yale University Press, 1995), 47.
7. Benjamin, *Shadow of the Other: Intersubjectivity and Gender in Psychoanalysis* (New York and London: Routledge, 1998), 96–105.
8. Janet L. Surrey, "Relationship and Empowerment," in *Women's Growth in Connection: Writings from the Stone Center*, ed. Judith V. Jordan et al. (New York and London: Guilford Press, 1997), 164–5, emphasis original.
9. Tess Cosslett, "Feminism, Matrilinealism, and the 'House of Women' in Contemporary Women's Writing," *Journal of Gender Studies* 5, no. 1 (1996): 8.

Bibliography

Primary Sources

Budnitz, Judy. *If I Told You Once*. 1999. London: Flamingo, 2001.
Chang, Jung. *Wild Swans: Three Daughters of China*. 1991. New York: Anchor Books, 1992.
Drabble, Margaret. *The Peppered Moth*. London and New York: Viking, 2000.
Forster, Margaret. *Hidden Lives: A Family Memoir*. 1995. London: Penguin, 1996.
Fredriksson, Marianne. *Hanna's Daughters*. 1994. Joan Tate trans. London: Orion, 1998.
Kincaid, Jamaica. *Annie John*. 1983. London: Vintage, 1997.
Kingston, Maxine Hong. *The Woman Warrior: Memoirs of A Girlhood Among Ghosts*. 1976. London: Picador, 1981.
Kogawa, Joy. *Obasan*. 1981. New York: Anchor, 1994.
Lorde, Audre. *Zami: A New Spelling of My Name*. 1982. London: Sheba, 1990.
Morrison, Toni. *Beloved*. 1987. London: Picador, 1988.
Tan, Amy. *The Joy Luck Club*. 1989. London: Mineva, 1990.

Secondary Sources

Alexander, Simone A. James. *Mother Imagery in the Novels of Afro-Caribbean Women*. Columbia and London: University of Missouri Press, 2001.
Anderson, Linda. "The Re-Imagining of History in Contemporary Women's Fiction." In *Plotting Change: Contemporary Women's Fiction*. Edited by Linda Anderson. London: Edward Arnold, 1990. 129–41.
Armstrong, Isobel. *New Feminist Discourses: Critical Essays on Theories and Texts*. London and New York: Routledge, 1992.
Ashcroft, Bill, Gareth Griffiths, and Helen Tiffin, eds. *The Post-Colonial Studies Reader*. London and New York: Routledge, 1995.
——. *Key Concepts in Post-Colonial Studies*. London and New York: Routledge, 1998.
Bassin, Donna, Margaret Honey, and Meryle Mahrer Kaplan, eds. *Representations of Motherhood*. London: Yale University Press, 1994.
Bell-Scott, Patricia, et al., eds. *Double Stitch: Black Women Write About Mothers and Daughters*. 1991. New York: Harper Perennial, 1993.
Benjamin, Jessica. *The Bonds of Love: Psychoanalysis, Feminism and the Problem of Domination*. New York: Pantheon, 1988.
——. *Like Subjects, Love Objects: Essays on Recognition and Sexual Difference*. New Haven and London: Yale University Press, 1995.
——. *Shadow of the Other: Intersubjectivity and Gender in Psychoanalysis*. New York and London: Routledge, 1998.
Benson, Kristin M. and Cayce Hagseth. "Jamaica Kincaid." In *Voices from the Gaps:*

Women Writers of Color, 23 May 2001. <http://www.voices.cla.umn.edu/newsite/authors/TANamy.htm> (26 May 2004).
Bethke, Laura, et al. "Joy Kogawa." In *Voices from the Gaps: Women Writers of Color*, 11 June 1998, <http://www.voices.cla.umn.edu/newsite/authors/TANamy.htm> (26 May 2004).
Bhabha, Homi K., *The Location of Culture*. London: Routledge, 1994.
Birch, Eva Lennox. "Toni Morrison: The Power of the Ancestors." In *Black American Women's Writing: A Quilt of Many Colors*. Edited by Eva Lennox Birch. New York and London: Harvester Wheatsheaf, 1994. 149–94.
Bowlby, Rachel. *Virginia Woolf: Feminist Destinations*. Oxford and New York: Basil Blackwell, 1988.
Brennan, Teresa. *Between Feminism and Psychoanalysis*. London and New York: Routledge, 1989.
Brown-Guillory, Elizabeth. "Disrupted Motherlines: Mothers and Daughters in a Genderized, Sexualized, and Racialized World." In *Women of Color: Mother-Daughter Relationships in Twentieth-Century Literature*. Edited by Elizabeth Brown-Guillory. Texas: University of Texas Press, 1996. 188–207
Campbell, Janet. "The Mother as Subject Within the Writings of Psychoanalysis and Women's Literature." Ph.D. diss., University of Sussex, 1994.
Chamberlain, Mary. "The Global Self: Narratives of Caribbean Migrant Women." In *Feminism and Autobiography: Texts, Theories, Methods*. Edited by Tess Cosslett, Celia Lury, and Penny Summerfield. London and New York: Routledge, 2000. 154–66.
Chamberlain, Mary, ed. *Caribbean Migration: Globalised Identities*. London and New York: Routledge, 1998.
Cheung, King-kok. *Articulate Silences: Hisaye Yamamoto, Maxine Hong Kingston, Joy Kogawa*. Ithaca: Cornell University Press, 1993.
Chodorow, Nancy. *The Reproduction of Mothering: Psychoanalysis and the Sociology of Gender*. London: University of California Press, 1978.
———. *Femininities, Masculinities, Sexualities: Freud and Beyond*. London: Free Association Books, 1994.
Chodorow, Nancy, and Susan Contratto. "The Fantasy of the Perfect Mother." In *Feminism and Psychoanalytic Theory*. Edited by Nancy Chodorow. Cambridge and Oxford: Polity Press, 1989. 79–96
Cohen, Robin. *Global Diasporas: An Introduction*. 1997. London: University College of London Press, 1999.
Collins, Patricia Hill. *Black Feminist Thought: Knowledge, Consciousness, and the Politics of Empowerment*. 1990. New York and London: Routledge, 1991. 115–37.
Cosslett, Tess. "Matrilineal Narratives." Paper presented at the WINGS conference on Autobiography and Gender at Nijmegen Catholic University, The Netherlands, 1993.
———. "Feminism, Matrilinealism, and the 'House of Women' in Contemporary Women's Fiction." *Journal of Gender Studies* 5, no. 1 (1996): 7–17.
———. "Fairytales: Revisiting the Tradition." In *Women, Power and Resistance: An Introduction to Women's Studies*. Edited by Tess Cosslett, Alison Easton, and Penny Summerfield. Buckingham and Philadelphia: Oxford University Press, 1996. 81–90.
———. "Matrilineal Narratives Revisited.' In *Feminism and Autobiography: Texts, Theories, Methods*. Edited by Tess Cosslett, Celia Lury and Penny Summerfield. London and New York: Routledge, 2000. 141–53.
Cudjoe, Selwyn R. "Jamaica Kincaid and the Modernist Project: An Interview." In

Caribbean Women Writers: Essays from the First International Conference. Edited by Selwyn R. Cudjoe. Massachusetts: Calaloux, 1990. 215–31.

Daly, Brenda O., and Maureen T. Reddy, eds. *Narrating Mothers: Theorizing Maternal Subjectivity.* Knoxville: University of Tennessee Press, 1991.

Davidson, Cathy, and E. M. Broner, eds. *The Lost Tradition: Mothers and Daughters in Literature.* New York: Ungar, 1980.

Davies, Carol Boyce. "Mothering and Healing in Recent Black Women's Fiction." *Sage* 2 (1985): 41–3.

———. "Mother Right/Write Revisited: *Beloved* and *Dessa Rose* and the Construction of Motherhood in Black Women's Fiction." In *Narrating Mothers: Theorizing Maternal Subjectivity.* Edited by Brenda O. Daly and Maureen T. Reddy. Knoxville: University of Tennessee Press, 1991. 46–50.

de Abruna, Laura Niesen. "Twentieth-Century Women Writers from the English-Speaking Caribbean." *Caribbean Women Writers: Essays from the First International Conference.* Edited by Selwyn R. Cudjoe. Massachusetts: Calaloux, 1990. 86–97.

———. "Family Connections: Mother and Mother Country in the Fiction of Jean Rhys and Jamaica Kincaid." In *Motherlands: Black Women's Writing from Africa, the Caribbean and South Asia.* Edited by Susheila Nasta. New Jersey: Rutgers University Press, 1992. 257–289.

de Lauretis, Teresa, ed. *Feminist Studies/Critical Studies.* 1986. London: Macmillan, 1988.

Dinnerstein, Dorothy. *The Mermaid and the Minotaur: Sexual Arrangements and Human Malaise.* New York: Harper & Row, 1976.

DiQuinzio, Patrice. *The Impossibility of Motherhood: Feminism, Individualism and the Problem of Mothering.* London and New York: Routledge, 1999.

Doane, Janice, and Devon Hodges. *From Klein to Kristeva: Psychoanalytic Feminism and the Search for the 'Good Enough' Mother.* Michigan: University of Michigan Press, 1992.

Dutton, Wendy. "Merge & Separate: Jamaica Kincaid's Fiction." *World Literature Today* 63 (Summer 1989): 396–411.

Dyer, Rachel Louise. "Reading and Writing in Collaboration: Dialogues with Scottish and Canadian Women Writers." Ph.D. diss., Lancaster University, 2000.

Eagleton, Mary. *Working with Feminist Criticism.* Oxford: Blackwell, 1996.

Edelman, Hope. *Mother of My Mother: The Intricate Bond Between Generations.* New York: Dial Press, 1999.

Eisenstein, Hester. *Contemporary Feminist Thought.* London: George Allen & Unwin, 1984.

Eisenstein, Hester, and Alice Jardine, eds. *The Future of Difference.* 1980. New Jersey: Rutgers University Press, 1994.

Fisher, Jerilyn, and Ellen S. Silber, eds. *Analyzing the Different Voice: Feminist Psychological Theory and Literary Texts.* New York and Oxford: Rowman & Littlefield, 1998.

Flax, Jane. "The Conflict between Nurturance and Autonomy in Mother-Daughter Relationships and within Feminism." *Feminist Studies* 4, no. 2 (June 1978): 171–91.

Foster, M. Marie Booth. "Voice, Mind, Self: Mother-Daughter Relationships in Amy Tan's *The Joy Luck Club* and *The Kitchen God's Wife.*" In *Women of Color: Mother-Daughter Relationships in Twentieth-Century Literature.* Edited by Elizabeth Brown-Guillory. Austin: University of Texas Press, 1996. 208–27.

Freud, Sigmund. "Family Romances." In *The Standard Edition of the Complete Works of Sigmund Freud.* Edited by J. Strachey. London: Hogarth Press and the Institute of Psychoanalysis, 1953. 235–41.

Friedman, Susan Stanford. "Creativity and the Childbirth Metaphor: Gender Difference in Literary Discourse." *Feminist Studies* 13, no. 1 (1987): 49–82.
Fultz, Lucille P. "To Make Herself: Mother-Daughter Conflicts in Toni Morrison's *Sula* and *Tar Baby*." In *Women of Color: Mother-Daughter Relationships in 20th-Century Literature*. Edited by Elizabeth Brown-Guillory. Austin: University of Texas Press, 1996. 228–43.
Fujita, Gayle K. "'To Attend the Sound of Stone': The Sensibility of Silence in *Obasan*." *Melus: Journal of the Society for the Study of the Multi-Ethnic Literature of the United States* 12, no. 3 (Fall 1985): 33–42.
Gallop, Jane. *Feminism and Psychoanalysis: The Daughter's Seduction*. 1982. London: Macmillan, 1983.
———. "Reading the Mother Tongues: Psychoanalytic Feminist Criticism." *Critical Inquiry* 13 (1987): 314–29.
———. *Around 1981: Academic Feminist Literary Theory*. New York and London: Routledge, 1992.
Garner, Shirley Nelson, Claire Kahane, and Madelon Sprengnether, eds. *The (M)other Tongue: Essays in Feminist Psychoanalytic Interpretation*. Ithaca: Cornell University Press, 1985.
Gates Jr., Henry Louis, and K. A. Appiah, eds. *Toni Morrison: Critical Perspectives Past and Present*. New York: Amistad, 1993.
Gilbert, Sandra M., and Susan Gubar. *The Madwoman in the Attic: the Woman Writer and the Nineteenth-Century Literary Imagination*. New Haven and London: Yale University Press, 1979.
———. *No Man's Land: the Place of the Woman Writer in the Twentieth Century*, vol. 2. New Haven: Yale University Press, 1988.
Glenn, Evelyn Nakano, Grace Chang, and Linda Rennie Forcey, eds. *Mothering: Ideology, Experience and Agency*. London: University of California Press, 1997.
Goellnicht, Donald C. "Father Land and/or Mother Tongue: the Divided Female Subject in Kogawa's *Obasan* and Hong Kingston's *The Woman Warrior*." In *Redefining Autobiography in Twentieth-Century Women's Fiction: An Essay Collection*. Edited by Janice Morgan, Colette T. Hall, and Carol L. Snyder. New York: Garland, 1991. 119–34.
Gottlieb, Erika. "The Riddle of Concentric Worlds in *Obasan*." *Canadian Literature* 109 (Summer 1986): 34–53.
Grice, Helena. "Reading the Nonverbal: The Indices of Space, Time, Tactility and Taciturnity in Joy Kogawa's *Obasan*." *Melus: Journal of the Society for the Study of the Multi-Ethnic Literature of the United States* 24, no. 4 (Winter 1999): 93–105.
Grimshaw, Jean. *Feminist Philosophers: Women's Perspectives on Philosophical Traditions*. Brighton, Sussex: Wheatsheaf, 1986.
Hansen, Elaine Tuttle. *Mother without Child: Contemporary Fiction and the Crisis of Motherhood*. London: University of California Press, 1997.
Harris, Mason. "Broken Generations in *Obasan*: Inner Conflicts and the Destruction of Community." *Canadian Literature* 127 (Winter 1990): 41–57.
Heung, Marina. "Daughter-Text/ Mother-Text: Matrilineage in Amy Tan's *Joy Luck Club*." *Feminist Studies* 19, no. 3 (Fall 1993): 597–613.
Hirsch, Marianne. "Review Essays: Mothers and Daughters." *Signs: Journal of Women in Culture and Society* 7, no. 1 (1981): 200–22.
———. *The Mother/Daughter Plot: Narrative, Psychoanalysis, Feminism*. Bloomington and Indianapolis: Indiana University Press, 1989.
———. "Feminism at the Maternal Divide: A Diary." In *The Politics of Motherhood: Activist*

Voices from Left to Right. Edited by Annelise Orleck, Diana Taylor, and Alexis Jetter. Hanover: University of New England Press, 1996. 352–81.
Hirsch, Marianne, and Evelyn Keller, eds. *Conflicts in Feminism.* London: Routledge, 1990.
Ho, Wendy. *In Her Mother's House: The Politics of Asian American Mother-Daughter Writing.* Oxford: Altamira Press, 1999.
Howe, Karen G. "Daughters Discover Their Mothers through Biographies and Genograms: Educational and Clinical Parallels." In *Motherhood: A Feminist Perspective.* Edited by Jane Rice Knowles and Ellen Cole. New York: Haworth Press, 1990. 31–40
Humm, Maggie. *The Dictionary of Feminist Theory.* 2nd ed. Brighton: Harvester, 1995.
Huntley, E. D. *Amy Tan: A Critical Companion.* London: Greenwood Press, 1998.
Irigaray, Luce. "And the One Doesn't Stir without the Other." Trans. by Helene Vivienne Wenzel. *Signs: Journal of Women in Culture and Society* 7, no. 1 (1981): 60–7.
———. *This Sex Which Is Not One.* 1977. Trans. by Catherine Porter with Carolyn Burke. Ithaca: Cornell University Press, 1985.
———. "The Bodily Encounter with the Mother." Trans. by David Macey. In *The Irigaray Reader.* Edited by Margaret Whitford. Oxford and Massachusetts: Basil Blackwell, 1991. 34–46.
———. "Body Against Body: In Relation to the Mother." Trans. by Gillian C. Gill. In *Sexes and Genealogies.* 1987. New York: Columbia University Press, 1993. 9–21.
Jardine, Alice. "Notes for an Analysis." In *Between Feminism and Psychoanalysis.* Edited by Teresa Brennan. London and New York: Routledge, 1989. 73–86.
Jenkins, Nina Lyon. "Black Women and the Meaning of Motherhood." In *Redefining Motherhood: Changing Identities and Patterns.* Edited by Sharon Abbey and Andrea O'Reilly. Toronto: Second Story Press, 1998. 201–13.
Joannou, Maroula. "Motherhood." In *Contemporary Women's Writing: From the Golden Notebook to the Color Purple.* Manchester and New York: Manchester University Press, 2000. 42–62.
Jones, Ann R. "Writing the Body: Towards an Understanding of *L'ecriture Feminine.*" *Feminist Studies* (1981): 247–61.
Jordan, Judith V. "Empathy and the Mother-Daughter Relationship." In *Women's Growth in Connection: Writings from the Stone Center.* Edited by Judith V. Jordan et al. New York and London: Guilford Press, 1991. 28–34.
———. "The Meaning of Mutuality." In *Women's Growth in Connection: Writings from the Stone Center.* Edited by Judith V. Jordan et al. New York and London: Guilford Press, 1991. 81–96
———. "A Relational Perspective for Understanding Women's Development." In *Women's Growth in Diversity: More Writings from the Stone Center.* Edited by Judith V. Jordan et al. New York: Guilford Press, 1997. 9–24.
———. "Clarity in Connection: Empathic Knowing, Desire, and Sexuality." In *Women's Growth in Diversity: More Writings from the Stone Center.* Edited by Judith V. Jordan et al. New York: Guilford Press, 1997. 50–73.
Kahane, Claire. "Questioning the Maternal Voice." *Genders* 3 (1988): 82–91.
Kaplan, Alexandra G. "Empathic Communication in the Psychotherapy Relationship." In *Women's Growth in Connection: Writings from the Stone Center.* Edited by Judith V. Jordan et al. New York: Guilford Press, 1991. 44–50
Kaplan, E. Ann. *Motherhood and Representation: The Mother in Popular Culture.* New York: Routledge, 1992.
Keller, Evelyn Fox, and Helene Moglen. "Competition and Feminism: Conflicts for

Academic Women." *Signs: Journal of Women in Culture and Society* 12, no. 3 (1987): 493–511.

Kim, Elaine H. *Asian American Literature: An Introduction to the Writings and Their Social Context*. Philadelphia: Temple University Press, 1982.

Klein, Melanie, and Joan Riviere. *Love, Guilt and Reparation*. New York: Norton, 1967.

Knowles, Jane Price, and Ellen Cole, eds. *Motherhood: A Feminist Perspective*. New York: Haworth, 1990.

Koh, Karlyn. "The Heart-of-the-Matter Question." In *The Other Woman: Women of Colour in Contemporary Canadian Literature*. Toronto: Sister Vision Press, 1994. 18–41.

Kristeva, Julia. *Desire in Language: A Semiotic Approach to Literature and Art*. Trans. by Thomas Gora, Alice Jardine, and Leo S. Roudiez. Edited by Leo S. Roudiez. Oxford: Basil Blackwell, 1980.

———. *Power of Horror: An Essay on Abjection*. Trans. by L. S. Roudiez. New York: Columbia University Press, 1982.

———. "Stabat Mater." In *The Kristeva Reader*. 1986. Edited by Toril Moi Oxford: Basil Blackwell, 1990. 160–86.

———. "About Chinese Women." In *The Kristeva Reader*. 1986. Edited by Toril Moi. Oxford: Basil Blackwell, 1990. 138–59.

Kuykendall, Eleanor H. "Toward an Ethic of Nurturance: Luce Irigaray on Mothering and Power." In *Mothering: Essays in Feminist Theory*. Edited by Joyce Trebilcot. Maryland: Rowman & Littlefield, 1983. 263-74.

Lawler, Steph. "Mothering the Self: A Study of the Mother-Daughter Relationship." Ph. D. diss., Lancaster University, 1995.

———. "'I never felt as though I fitted': Family Romances and the Mother-Daughter Relationship." In *Romance Revisited*. Edited by Lynne Pearce and Jackie Stacey. London: Lawrence & Wishart, 1995. 265–78.

———. *Mothering the Self: Mothers, Daughters, Subjects*. London: Routledge, 2000.

Lawson, Erica. "Black Women's Mothering in a Historical and Contemporary Perspective: Understanding the Past, Forging the Future." *Journal of the Association for Research on Mothering* 2, no. 2 (Fall/Winter 2000): 21–30.

Lim, Shirley Geok-Lin. "Japanese American Women's Life Stories: Maternality in Monica Sone's *Nisei Daughter* and Joy Kogawa's *Obasan*." *Feminist Studies* 16, no. 2 (Summer 1990): 289–312.

Lowinsky, Naomi Ruth. *Stories from the Motherline: Reclaiming the Mother-Daughter Bond, Finding Our Female Souls*. Los Angeles: Jeremy P. Tarcher, 1992.

———. "Mother of Mothers, Daughter of Daughters: Reflections on the Motherline." In *Mothers and Daughters: Connection, Empowerment, and Transformation*. Edited by Andrea O'Reilly and Sharon Abbey. New York and Oxford: Rowman & Littlefield, 2000. 227–35

Mackenzie, Suzie. "Mothers and Daughters." *Guardian Weekend*, December 16, 2000, 39–43.

Mackey, Allison. "Return to the [M]other to Heal the Self: Identity, Selfhood and Community in Toni Morrison's *Beloved*." *Journal of the Association for Research on Mothering* 2, no. 2 (Fall/Winter 2000): 42–51.

Maglin, Nan Bauer. "Don't Never Forget the Bridge That You Crossed Over On: the Literature of Matrilineage." In *The Lost Tradition: Mothers and Daughters in Literature*. Edited by Cathy N. Davidson and E. M. Broner. New York: Frederick Ungar, 1980. 257–67.

Magnusson, A. Lynne. "Language and Longing in Joy Kogawa's *Obasan*." *Canadian Literature* 116 (Spring 1988): 58–66.

Malin, Jo. *The Voice of the Mother: Embedded Maternal Narratives in Twentieth-Century Women's Autobiographies*. Carbondale and Edwardsville: Southern Illinois University Press, 2000.

Mathieson, Barbara Offutt. "Memory and Mother Love: Toni Morrison's Dyad." In *Narrating Mothers: Theorizing Maternal Subjectivity*. Edited by Brenda O. Daly and Maureen T. Reddy. Knoxville: University of Tennessee Press, 1991. 212–32.

Meaney, Gerardine, *(Un)like Subjects: Women, Theory, Fiction*. London and New York: Routledge, 1993.

Mens-Verhulst, Janneke, Karlein Schreurs, and Liesbeth Woertman, eds. *Daughtering and Mothering: Female Subjectivity Reanalysed*. London: Routledge, 1993.

Miller, Jean Baker. *Toward a New Psychology of Women*. Boston and Mass: Beacon Press, 1976.

Miller, Jean Baker, et al. "Some Misconceptions and Reconceptions of a Relational Approach." In *Women Growth in Diversity: More Writings from the Stone Center*. Edited by Judith V. Jordan et al. New York and London: Guilford Press, 1997. 25–49.

Miller, Nancy K., ed. *The Poetics of Gender*. New York: Columbia University Press, 1986.

Minh-ha, Trinh T. *Women, Native, Other: Writing Postcoloniality and Feminism*. Bloomington and Indianapolis: Indiana University Press, 1989.

Mistron, Deborah. *Understanding Jamaica Kincaid's Annie John: A Student Casebook to Issues, Sources, and Historical Documents*. London and Connecticut: Greenwood Press, 1999.

Morris, Ann R., and Margaret M. Dunn. "'The Bloodstream of Our Inheritance': Female Identity and the Caribbean Mothers'-Land." In *Motherlands: Black Women's Writing from Africa, the Caribbean and South Asia*. Edited by Sushelia Nasta. New Jersey: Rutgers University Press, 1992. 219–37.

Murdoch, H. Adlai. "Severing the (M)other Connection: The Representation of Cultural Identity in Jamaica Kincaid's *Annie John*." *Callaloo* 13.2 (1990): 325–40.

Nasta, Susheila. *Motherlands: Black Women's Writing from Africa, the Caribbean and South Asia*. New Jersey: Rutgers University Press, 1992.

Nice, Vivien E. *Mothers and Daughters: the Distortion of a Relationship*. New York: St. Martin's Press, 1992.

Nicholson, Linda, ed. *Feminism/Postmodernism*. London: Routledge, 1990.

O'Brian, David, and Stephen S. Fugita. *The Japanese American Experience*. Bloomington: Indiana University Press, 1991.

Ockerbloom, Mary Mark, ed. *A Celebration of Women Writers*, 1994-2004. <http://www.digital.library.upenn.edu/women/> (26 May 2004).

O'Reilly, Andrea, "Mothers, Daughters, and Feminism Today: Empowerment, Agency, Narrative, and Motherline." *Canadian Woman Studies/les cahiers de la femme* 18, no. 2 & 3 (Summer/Fall 1998): 16–21.

———. "Maternal Redemption and Resistance in Toni Morrison's *Paradise*." *Journal of the Association for Research on Mothering* 1, no. 1 (1999 Spring/Summer): 187–95.

———. "In Black and White: Anglo-American and African-American Perspectives on Mothers and Sons." In *Mothers and Sons: Feminism, Masculinity, and the Struggle to Raise Our Sons*. Edited by Andrea O'Reilly. New York and London: Routledge, 2000. 91–118.

———. "'I come from a long line of Uppity Irate Black Women': African-American Feminist Thought on Motherhood, the Motherline, and the Mother-Daughter Relationship." In *Mothers and Daughters: Connection, Empowerment, and Transformation*. Edited by

Andrea O'Reilly and Sharon Abbey. New York and Oxford: Rowman & Littlefield, 2000. 143–59.

———. "Maternal Conceptions in Toni Morrison's *The Bluest Eyes* and *Tar Baby*: 'A Woman Has To Be a Daughter Before She Can Be Any Kind of Woman.'" In *This Giving Birth: Pregnancy and Childbirth in American Women's Writing*. Edited by Julie Tharp and Susan MacCallum-Whitcomb. Bowling Green, OH: Bowling Green State University Press, 2000. 83–102.

O'Reilly, Andrea, and Sharon Abbey, eds. *Redefining Motherhood: Changing Identities and Patterns*. Toronto: Second Story Press, 1998.

———. *Mothers and Daughters: Connection, Empowerment, and Transformation*. New York and Oxford: Rowman & Littlefield, 2000.

Pearce, Lynne, and Jackie Stacey, eds. *Romance Revisited*. London: Lawrence & Wishart, 1995.

Pearlman, Mickey, ed. *American Women Writing Fiction*. Lexington: University of Kentucky Press, 1989.

———. *Mother Puzzles: Daughters and Mothers in Contemporary American Literature*. Westport, Conn: Greenwood, 1989.

Pearlman, Mickey, and Katherine Usher Henderson, eds. *A Voice of One's Own: Conversations with America's Writing Women*. London and New York: the University Press of Kentucky, 1990.

Perry, Donna. "Initiation in Jamaica Kincaid's *Annie John*." In *Caribbean Women Writers: Essays from the First International Conference*. Edited by Selwyn R. Cudjoe. Massachusetts: Calaloux, 1990. 245–53.

Phillips, Shelley. *Beyond the Myths: Mother-Daughter Relationships in Psychology, History, Literature and Everyday Life*. London: Penguin, 1996.

Phoenix, Ann, Anne Wollett, and Eva Lloyd, eds. *Motherhood: Meanings, Practices, Ideologies*. London: Sage, 1991.

Piyali, Nath Dalal. "Toni Morrison." In *Voices from the Gaps: Women Writers of Color*, 12 June 1996, <http://www.voices.cla.umn.edu/newsite/authors/TANamy.htm> (26 May 2004).

Powell, Betty Jane. "'Will the Parts Hold?': The Journey Toward a Coherent Self in *Beloved*." *Colby Quarterly* 31, no. 2 (1995): 105–13.

Reddy, Maureen T. "Motherhood, Knowledge and Power." *Journal of Gender Studies* 1, no. 1: 1–5

———. "Maternal Reading: Lazarre and Walker." In *Narrating Mothers: Theorizing Maternal Subjectivity*. Edited by Brenda O. Daly and Maureen T. Reddy. Knoxville: University of Tennessee Press, 1991. 222–38.

Reddy, Maureen, Martha Roth, and Amy Sheldon, eds. *Mother Journeys: Feminists Write About Mothering*. Minneapolis: Spinsters Ink, 1994.

Rich, Adrienne. *Of Woman Born: Motherhood as Experience and Institution*. 1976. London: Virago, 1992.

Rody, Caroline. "Toni Morrison's *Beloved*: History, 'Rememory,' and a 'Clamor for a Kiss.'" *American Literary History* 7, no. 1 (1995): 92–119.

Roman, Camille, Suzanne Juhasz, and Christanne Miller, eds. *The Woman and Language Debate: A Sourcebook*. New Jersey: Rutgers University Press, 1994.

Ross, Ellen. "New Thoughts on 'the Oldest Vocation': Mothers and Motherhood in Recent Feminist Scholarship." *Signs: Journal of Women in Culture and Society* 20, no. 2 (Winter 1995): 397–413.

Ruddick, Sara. "Maternal Thinking." In *Mothering: Essays in Feminist Theory*. Edited by Joyce Trebilcot. Maryland: Rowman & Littlefield, 1983. 213–30.

———. "Preservative Love and Military Destruction: Some Reflections on Mothering and Peace." In *Mothering: Essays in Feminist Theory*. Edited by Joyce Trebilcot. Maryland: Rowman & Littlefield, 1983. 231-62.
———. *Maternal Thinking: Towards a Politics of Peace*. Boston: Beacon Press, 1989.
———. "Thinking Mothers/Conceiving Birth." In *Representations of Motherhood*. Edited by Donna Bassin, Margaret Honey, and Meryle Mahrer Kaplan. New Haven and London: Yale University Press, 1994.
———. "Making Connections Between Parenting and Peace." *Journal of the Association for Research on Mothering* 3, no. 2 (Fall/Winter 2001): 7-20.
Sasaki, Betty. "Reading Silence in Joy Kogawa's *Obasan*." In *Analyzing the Different Voice: Feminist Psychological Theory and Literary Texts*. Edited by Jerilyn Fisher and Ellen S. Silber. New York and Oxford: Rowman & Littlefield, 1998. 117-39.
Schapiro, Barbara Ann. "The Bonds of Love and the Boundaries of Self in Toni Morrison's *Beloved*." *Contemporary Literature* 32, no. 2 (1991): 191-210.
———. *Literature and the Relational Self*. New York: New York University Press, 1994.
Sellers, Susan. *Language and Sexual Difference: Feminist Writing in France*. London: Macmillan, 1991.
Sizoo, Edith, ed. *Women's Lifeworlds: Women's Narratives on Shaping Their Realities*. London and New York: Routledge, 1997.
Shear, Walter. "Generational Differences and the Diaspora in *The Joy Luck Club*." *Critique* 34, no. 3 (Spring 1993): 193-99.
Shen, Gloria. "Born of a Stranger: Mother-Daughter Relationships and Storytelling in Amy Tan's *The Joy Luck Club*." In *International Women's Writing: New Landscapes of Identity*. Edited by Anne E. Brown and Marjanne E. Gooze. Connecticut and London: Greenwood Press, 1995. 233-44.
Smith, Barbara. "Toward a Black Feminist Criticism." In *But Some of Us Are Brave*. Edited by Gloria Hull et al. New York: Feminist Press, 1982.
Smith, Sidonie, and Julia Watson, eds. *Women, Autobiography, Theory: A Reader*. Wisconsin: University of Wisconsin Press, 1998.
Snitow, Ann. "Feminism and Motherhood: An American Reading." *Feminist Review* 40 (1992): 32-51.
Sonquist, Ted J. "Amy Tan." In *Voices from the Gaps: Women Writers of Color*, 6 December, 1996. <http://www.voices.cla.umn.edu/newsite/authors/TANamy.htm> (26 May 2004).
Spelman, Elizabeth. *Inessential Woman: Problems of Exclusion in Feminist Thought*. London: Women's Press, 1990.
Stanton, Domna C. "Difference on Trial: A Critique of the Maternal Metaphor in Cixous, Irigaray, and Kristeva." In *The Poetics of Gender*. Edited by Nancy K. Miller. New York: Columbia University Press, 1986. 157-82.
Suleiman, Susan Rubin. "Writing and Motherhood." In *The (M)other Tongue: Essays in Feminist Psychoanalytic Interpretation*. Edited by Shirley Nelson Garner, Claire Kahane, and Madelon Sprengnether. Ithaca: Cornell University Press, 1985. 352-77.
———. "On Maternal Splitting." *Signs: Journal of Women in Culture and Society* 14 (1988): 25-41.
Suleiman, Susan Rubin, ed. *The Female Body in Western Culture*. London: Harvard University Press, 1986.
Surrey, Janet L. "The 'Self-in-Relation': A Theory of Women's Development." In *Women's Growth in Connection: Writings from the Stone Center*. Edited by Judith V. Jordan et al. New York and London: Guilford Press, 1991. 51-66.

———. "Relationship and Empowerment." In *Women's Growth in Connection: Writings from the Stone Center*. Edited by Judith V. Jordan et al. New York and London: Guilford Press, 1991. 162–80.

Tatar, Maria. *The Hard Facts of the Grimms' Fairy Tales*. New Jersey: Princeton University Press, 1987.

Thorne, Barrie, and Marilyn Yalom, eds. *Rethinking the Family: Some Feminist Questions*. Boston: Northeastern University Press, 1992.

Timothy, Helen Pyne. "Adolescent Rebellion and Gender Relations in *At the Bottom of the River* and *Annie John*." In *Caribbean Women Writers: Essays from the First International Conference*. Edited by Selwyn R. Cudjoe. Massachusetts: Calaloux, 1990. 233–42.

Tong, Rosemarie. *Feminist Thought: A Comprehensive Introduction*. London: Routledge, 1989.

Trebilcot, Joyce. *Mothering: Essays in Feminist Theory*. Maryland: Rowman & Littlefield, 1983.

Troester, Rosalie Riegle. "Turbulence and Tenderness: Mothers, Daughters, and 'Othermothers' in Paule Marshall's *Brown Girl, Brownstones*." In *Double Stitch: Black Women Write About Mothers and Daughters*. Edited by Patricia Bell-Scott et al. New York: Harper Perennial, 1993. 163–72.

Ty, Eleanor. "Struggling with the Powerful (M)other: Identity and Sexuality in Kogawa's *Obasan* and Kincaid's *Lucy*." *International Fiction Review* 20, no. 2 (1993): 120–26.

von Hassell, Malve. "*Issei* Women: Silences and Fields of Power." *Feminist Studies* 19, no. 3 (Fall 1993): 549–69.

Voth Harman, Karin. "Speak It Mama!: The Voice of the Mothers in Contemporary British and North American Fiction and Poetry." Ph.D. diss., University of Sussex, 1998.

Walker, Alice. *In Search of Our Mothers' Gardens*. 1983. London: Women's Press, 1984.

Walters, Suzanna Danuta. *Lives Together, World Apart: Mothers and Daughters in Popular Culture*. Berkeley: University of California Press, 1992.

Whitford, Margaret. *Luce Irigaray: Philosophy in the Feminine*. London and New York: Routledge, 1991.

Whitford, Margaret, ed. *The Irigaray Reader*. Oxford and Massachusetts: Basil Blackwell, 1991.

Williams, Linda R. "Happy Families? Feminist Reproduction and Matrilineal Thought." In *New Feminist Discourses: Critical Essays on Theories and Texts*. Edited by Isobel Armstrong. London and New York: Routledge, 1992. 48–64.

Williamson, Janice. "Joy Kogawa: 'In writing I keep breathing, I keep living.'" In *Sounding Differences: Conversations with Seventeen Canadian Women Writers*. Toronto and London: University of Toronto Press, 1993. 148–59.

Wong, Sau-Ling Cynthia. "'Sugar Sisterhood': Situating the Amy Tan Phenomenon." In *The Ethnic Canon: Histories, Institutions, and Interventions*. Edited by David Palumbo-Liu. Minneapolis: University of Minnesota Press, 1995. 174–210.

Woolf, Virginia. *A Room of One's Own*. London: Granada, 1929.

Wright, Elizabeth et al, eds. *Feminism and Psychoanalysis: A Critical Dictionary*. Oxford and Massachusetts: Basil Blackwell, 1992.

Xu, Ben. "Memory and the Ethnic Self: Reading Amy Tan's *The Joy Luck Club*." In *Memory, Narrative, and Identity: New Essays in Ethnic American Literatures*. Edited by Amritjit Singh, Joseph T. Skerrett, Jr., and Robert E. Hogan. Boston: Northeastern University Press, 1994. 261–77.

Yu, I-Lin. "M/other Lines: the Mother-Daughter Relationship in Feminist Theory and Three Women's Texts." M.A. diss., University of York, 1993.

Index

Abbey, Sharon, 10n6, 11n6, 75n5, 76n15, 149n3
African American, 10n6, 19, 75n5, 135, 137–9, 149n3, 206
Afro-Caribbeans
  in *Annie John*, 152
Afrocentric (trism), 137–8, 145, 147–8, 206
  See also motherhood, Afrocentric viewpoint of
Alexander, Simone, 161 n2–3, n12, n18, 129–32, 134n11, n13, 178
ambivalence, 9, 17, 23, 25–7, 37, 39, 46, 67, 69, 71–2, 113–6, 122, 152–3, 157–8, 202–3, 209, 213–5
  in *Hanna's Daughters* (Fredriksson), 81, 84
  in *Hidden Lives* (Forster), 98
  matrilineal, 90
  mother-daughter, 64, 81
  in *The Peppered Moth* (Drabble), 103, 107, 108n5
  in *Wild Swans* (Chang), 90–1

Amy Denver (*Beloved*), 143–4
Amy Tan phenomenon, 180, 191n6
Angelou, Maya, 1
An-Mei Hsu (*The Joy Luck Club*), 184, 186, 189
Anna (*Hanna's Daughters*), 9, 75, 77–84n1, 111–5, 118–9
Annie John (characters, mother and daughter) (*Annie John*), 151–159n1, 160n2–3, n6–7, n9, 161n12, n14–5, n17, n19, n22–3
Annie John (novel by Kincaid)
  matrilineal syncretism in, 152–3
  obeah woman in, 153–4, 158, 161n15
  psychoanalytic readings in, 151, 153
  storytelling in, 154–7, 161n15

Annie John, characters in. *See* Annie John; Ma Chess; Pa Chess
antiromance, 107
Ari (*If I Told You Once*), 194–5
Ashcroft, Bill, Gareth Griffiths, and Helen Tiffin, 128, 133–134n4, n8, 161n21
Asian American (literature), 180, 191n6, n8, 192n9, n18
assimilation, 128, 131, 154, 166–7, 173, 203
  in *Annie John* (Kincaid), 154
  and resistance, 128, 203
Aunt Alice, 95, 112
Aunt Emily (*Obasan*), 163, 168, 172–3, 175, 209
Aunt Nan, 98
auto/biography, 1–2, 32, 73–5, 130, 182
  See also mother biography

Baby Suggs (*Beloved*), 139–40, 144–5
Bailey, Eleanor, 127
Barrons, the (*The Peppered Moth*), 101
Bawtrys, the (*The Peppered Moth*), 101, 104
Bell-Scott, Patricia, 148n3
Beloved (character) (*Beloved*), 10, 132, 135–7, 139–43, 145–149n6, n8–9, n12, 160n8, 205–6, 208
Beloved (novel by Morrison)
  childbirth in, 144
  maternal milk in, 142
  mother-daughter symbiosis in, 143
  motherline in, 135–6, 139, 140–3, 145, 147–8
  othermother in, 142, 144–5, 147
Beloved, characters in. *See* Amy Denver; Baby Suggs; Beloved; Denver; Mrs. Jones; Paul D; Sethe; Stamp Paid
Benjamin, Jessica, 7, 9, 34–5, 48–54, 57n5,

59n54, 69–70, 122, 136, 141, 143, 147–149n20, 150n21, 159, 162n24, 176, 178n40, 181, 183, 189–90, 192n19, n25–6, 209–211n1, 213–7, 217n5–7
Bessie (*The Peppered Moth*), 103–7, 121
Birch, Eva Lennox, 220
Bhabha, Homi K., 157, 161, 220
bloodmother, 146–7
bond, 3, 11n22, 46, 67, 70–1, 76n15–6, 92, 94n3, 100n2, 109n12, 135, 142, 151–2, 154, 161, 176, 180, 188, 191, 194, 204n12, 214
    mother-child, 65
    mother-daughter, 4, 38, 45, 47, 63, 92, 142, 151–2, 154, 161n15, 214
Bowlby, Rachel, 28n16
Brennan, Teresa, 217n2
brothers Grimm, the, 193
Brown-Guillory, Elizabeth, 148n1
Budnitz, Judy, 2, 7, 10, 45, 130, 133, 193–4, 201–203n3, 205, 207–211, 216–7

Carter, Angela, 193
Chamberlain, Mary, 129, 134n9, 152–3, 160n2–4
Chang, Jung, 2, 9, 75, 87, 88–94n1, 99, 111–5, 119, 122, 215
Chang's father, 91
Chang's grandmother, 87–92
Chang's mother, 92–3
Cheung, King-kok, 168, 172, 174–5, 177n19, 178n30–1, n33, n36
childbirth
    in *Beloved* (Morrison), 144
childrearing, 206
Chin, Frank, 144, 180, 188, 197
Chinese American (literature), 179–80, 182, 190, 191n6, 197
Chloe (*If I Told You Once*), 199
Chodorow, Nancy, 5, 9, 34–8, 40, 45–7, 204n6, 213–4, 217n3
    and Susan Contratto, 18, 28n11, 45–6, 58n48, 204n6, 217n3
Chrissie (*The Peppered Moth*), 103, 105, 107, 121
co-ethnic, 128
    in *Obasan* (Kogawa), 163, 177n9
co-feeling, 50
    See Kundera, Milan

Cohen, Robin, 129, 134n3, n6, 160n3, 161n13
Colette, 1
Collins, Patricia Hill, 137–8, 140, 148n3, 149n4
    See also motherhood, Afrocentric viewpoint of
colonialism, 127–8, 131, 205
colonization, 127–8, 216
    in *Annie John* (Kincaid), 156
colonizer/colonized, 128, 131
    in *Annie John* (Kincaid), 156–8, 161n12
communism
    in *Wild Swans* (Chang), 87, 89–90
co-mother
    in *If I Told You Once* (Budnitz), 199
complicity (and resistance)
    in *Annie John* (Kincaid), 156–8
connection/separation, 46
Cosslett, Tess, 2–10n5, 11n15, n20, 21, 25–28n22, 29n39, 31, 34, 69–71, 75n3, 89, 94n2, 96, 100n3, 108n7, 117, 123, 134, 160, 164, 177n5, 191, 203n1, 211n5
Cotterhall Man (*The Peppered Moth*), 101, 105–6
creole culture, 129
creolization, 127, 129
Cudjoe, Selwyn R., 160n3, 161n9, n15
Cultural Revolution
    in *Wild Swans*, 87, 89
Cutworths, the (*The Peppered Moth*), 101

Daly, Brenda O., and Maureen T. Reddy, 148n1, 149n12, 178n37
daughterly subjectivities, (motherly and), 47
    in *The Joy Luck Club* (Tan), 191
Davidson, Cathy, and E. M. Broner, 29n38, 57n9, 85n5, 191n3
Davies, Carole Boyce, 149
de Abruna, Laura Niesen, 160n9
deathbed, 92
de Beauvoir, Simone, 1
decolonization, 128, 216
Denver (*Beloved*), 139, 143–6, 149n17
descendant, 106, 207
diachronic, vertical axis, 21, 27, 34, 99, 118, 122, 199–200
    See also matrilinealism, feminist;

Cosslett, Tess
diaspora, 10, 127–9, 131–2, 154, 159, 193, 195–6, 202, 205, 208
  African, 133, 135
  Asian, 133
Dinnerstein, Dorothy, 35
discourse, maternal/matrilineal, 5, 15, 42, 44, 100, 127–8, 131, 157, 180, 183, 189
Doane, Janice, and Devon Hodges, 57n22
Dora Bawtry (Aunt Dora) (*The Peppered Moth*), 101
double voice, 21, 179, 181, 189–90
Dr. Robert Hawthorn (*The Peppered Moth*), 101, 121
Drabble, Margaret, 166, 195
dreamland, 42
drive energies, 154, 160n2, 161n10
Dunn, Margaret M., 6, 8, 38, 108, 122, 130, 146, 148, 149n14, 216
dyad, 6, 8, 108, 122, 130, 216
  Beloved-Sethe, 146
  mother-child, 6, 38
  mother-daughter, 122

Eagleton, Mary, 28n20, n23, n32–3, 29n37
Edelman, Hope, 71–3, 76n16, n21, 92, 94n3, 109n12, 161n22
Eisenstein, Hester, 15, 27n1
Eli (*If I Told You Once*), 194, 196

fairy tale (rewrites), 83, 133, 194
  in *If I Told You Once* (Budnitz), 193, 196, 202
family romances, 9, 61, 63–7, 75, 75n6, 85n4, 97, 99–100, 100n6, 108, 111, 113–4, 116, 118, 122–3, 153, 157, 196, 202, 215–6
See also Freud, Sigmund; romances
fantasy of the perfect mother, 17–8, 28n11, 45–6, 65, 196, 204n6, 214, 217n3
  See also Chodorow, Nancy, and Susan Contratto
Faro (*The Peppered Moth*), 101–3, 105–7, 112, 121, 202
fatherline, 71, 102

female family romances, 65, 108, 114, 202
  in *Hanna's Daughters* (Fredriksson), 81, 84
  in *The Hidden Lives* (Forster), 97–100
  in *The Peppered Moth*, 108
  See also Lawler, Steph; romances
female fusion and merger, 143
female genealogy, 5, 63, 73, 82, 160
  See also motherline
female rivalry 9, 22
feminism, 3–4, 9–10, 10n5–6, 11n15, n20, 16–7, 26, 28n11, n22, n24, n30, 29n39, 31, 36, 38, 58n48, 75n2–3, n5, 76n13, 94n2, 97, 100n3, n5, n9, 108n7, 109n16, 123n1, n4–5, n11, 134n9, 160n4, 164, 177n5, 180, 191n1, n4, 192n19, 203n2, 204n6–7, n13, n15, 211n5, 217, 217n2–3, n5, 218n9
  cultural, 16
  and matrilinealism, 3–4, 15
  and motherhood, 8
  psychoanalytic, 5–6, 35
feminist progress, 27, 34, 164
  See also matrilinealism, feminist
First, Elsa, 52
Fisher, Jerilyn, and Ellen S. Silber, 178n23
Flax, Jane, 9, 34, 36–8, 45–7, 97–8, 123n4, 214
  See also nurturance and autonomy
Forster, Margaret, 2, 7, 95–9, 100n1, 102, 111–3, 115, 120, 122, 215
Foster, M. Marie Booth, 147, 192n15
Fredriksson, Marianne, 2, 7, 77–8, 82, 84n1, 112–3, 122, 215
Freud, Sigmund, 45, 64, 67, 75n6
Freudian Oedipal conflict, 22
Fugita, Stephen S., 178n26
Fujita, Gayle K., 168, 177n21

Gallop, Jane, 9, 23–4, 28n32, 38, 42
General Xue, 89
General Xue's wife, 89
genogram, 68, 73–5, 88, 95, 102, 115, 119
  in *Hanna's Daughters* (Fredriksson), 81–2, 84
  in *Hidden Lives* (Forster), 95
  See also mother biography

Gilbert, Sandra, and Susan Gubar, 9, 22–3, 28n26
giving birth, 91, 144, 171, 194
(grand)daughter, 7, 73, 78, 84, 95–7, 103, 111–2, 114, 121, 203
Grand Inquisitor, the (*Obasan*), 173–4
Grandma Kato (*Obasan*), 168, 174
(grand)mother, 7, 78, 82, 111, 203, 207
Great Mothers, 21
Grice, Helena, 177n22, 178n23
Griffiths, Helen, 128, 133n1, 134n4, n8, 161n21
Grimshaw, Jean, 18, 28n12

Hanna (*Hanna's Daughters*), 77–82, 111, 118–9
Hanna's Daughters (Fredriksson), 9, 75, 77–9, 84, 84n1, 111–5, 118
  ambivalence in, 81, 84
  female family romances in, 81, 84
  matrilineage in, 79, 80–1, 83–4
  motherline in, 83
  mother's subjectivity in, 79, 82
Hanna's Daughters, characters in. *See* Anna; Hanna; Johanna; Ragnar; Rickard
Hansen, Elaine Tuttle, 4–6, 11n8, n11, n21, 15, 76n23
Harris, Mason, 177n14, n20, 178n29
Hegel, G. W. F., 50
Henderson, Katherine Usher, 191n5, 192n21
Heung, Marina, 192n13, n23
Hidden Lives (Forster), 9, 75, 89, 95–6, 98–100, 100n1, 102, 111–5, 120
  ambivalence in, 98
  class in, 95, 97–9, 100
  female family romances in, 97, 99–100
  genogram in, 95
  mother's subjectivity in, 96
  recovery and progress in, 99
Hidden Lives, characters in. *See* Aunt Alice; Aunt Nan; Lilian; Margaret; Margaret Ann
Hirsch, Marianne, 7, 45–6, 65, 67, 75n2, 76n11, 179, 189, 192n24
  See also maternal voice
Ho, Wendy, 134n17, 192n18, n22
Howe, Karen G., 73, 76n17, 85n6

Huntley, E. D., 182, 192n8, n14, n16–7
hybridity, 127, 129, 160n3

identification, 3, 17, 23–4, 31, 43, 45, 47, 49, 70, 72, 83, 90–1, 99, 107, 114–5, 151, 168, 186, 193, 203, 214
  and belonging, 185, 209
  mother-daughter, 141, 190, 194
  pre-Oedipal, 46
  primary, 36
  and recognition, 140–1
  through mirroring, 190
identification/differentiation, 23, 46
If I Told You Once (Budnitz), 10, 133, 193, 202, 203n2, 205, 207–8, 211, 216
  antifeminist family romance in, 193
  fairy tales rewrites in, 193
If I Told You Once, characters in. *See* Ari; Chloe; Eli; Ilana; Ilana's mother; Jonathan; Mara; Nomie; Sashie; Wolf;
Ilana (*If I Told You Once*), 193, 207–9
Ilana's mother (*If I Told You Once*), 193, 207
imperialist/subaltern, 182, 189, 206
independence/dependence, 39, 143, 153, 196
Indo-Caribbeans
  in *Annie John* (Kincaid), 152
industrial revolution 196
internalization theory, 23
intersubjective empathy or attunement, 74
intersubjective space, 159, 176
intersubjectivity, 33, 35, 47, 49, 54, 69, 122, 140, 162n24, 178n40, 181, 189–192n26, 210–211n1, 217n7
  maternal subjectivity as, 7, 9, 32, 213, 215
  and relationality, 136, 216
intrapsychic theory, 48
Irigaray, Luce, 9, 34, 75n1, 217n4
irrecoverability, the mother's, 112
  in *Obasan* (Kogawa), 164, 176
issei, 163, 166–7, 170, 176n1, 178n25, n27
  in *Obasan* (Kogawa), 171

Japanese American, 166, 176n1, 177n9–10, n15, n17–8, 178n35
Jenkins, Nina Lyon, 149

Jing-mei Woo (*The Joy Luck Club*), 184
Joe Barron (*The Peppered Moth*), 104
Johanna (*Hanna's Daughters*), 77–9, 81–3, 111–2, 118–9
Jonathan (*If I Told You Once*), 194, 199
Jordan, Judith V., 11, 14, 19n42, 33, 57, 218n8
Joy Luck Aunts (*The Joy Luck Club*), 186, 206

Keller, Evelyn Fox, and Helen Moglen, 9, 22–3, 28n30
Kim, Elaine H., 177n10, n15
Kincaid, Jamaica, 2, 130, 161n14
Kingston, Maxine Hong, 1, 177n19, 180
Kogawa, Joy, 2, 45, 130, 163, 176n2, 177n3, n19, 216
Koppelman, Susan, 1, 2, 10n1
Kristeva, Julia, 9, 34
Kundera, Milan, 50
    See also co-feeling
Kuykendall, Eleanor H., 44

Lawler, Steph, 75n6, 81, 85n4, 97, 100n6
    See also female family romances; romances
Lena St. Clair (*The Joy Luck Club*), 184
lifeline, 3, 68
Lilian, 120
Lim, Shirley Geok-Lin, 167, 177n17
Lindo Jong (*The Joy Luck Club*), 184, 187–9
looping, (mother-daughter), 68–70, 74, 96, 99
    See also Lowinsky, Naomi Ruth
Lorde, Audre, 63, 75n3, 123n7
Lowinsky, Naomi Ruth, 8, 11n22, 55, 68, 76n15, 100n2, 204n12

Ma Chess, 153, 158, 160n6
Mackenzie, Suzie, 101, 108n2, 113, 123n3
Mackey, Allison, 160
Maglin, Nan Bauer, 9, 29n38, 81, 85n5, 191n3
    See also matrilineal literature
Mahler, Margaret, 36
Malin, Jo, 7, 10n4, 217n1
Mara (*If I Told You Once*), 193, 196–201, 203
Margaret Ann, 120

maternal love, 17, 135
maternal mirroring, 24, 190
    See also mother-daughter mirroring
maternal narratives, 2–3, 10n4, 63, 217n1
maternal subjectivity, 7, 9, 27, 51, 74, 82, 148n1, 149n12, 177n4, 178n37, 191, 191n2, 213, 215
    retrieving, 84, 122, 164, 179
maternal thinking, 9, 16–9, 27n4, 28n6, n10, 69, 175
    See also Ruddick, Sara
maternal voice, 43–7, 83, 95, 97–8, 122, 215
    See also Hirsch, Marianne
maternity, 4, 44, 65, 136, 139, 189, 191, 214
matrilineage, 9, 21–2, 25–7, 29n38, 34, 65, 73–4, 79–81, 83–85n5, 89, 93, 96, 99, 102–3, 105–6, 108, 111–2, 114–6, 119, 121, 131, 135, 143, 147, 152, 159, 172, 179–181, 189, 191n3, n6, 192n13, 193, 195–6, 201–3, 206–7, 209, 213, 216
    black, 136, 139–40, 208
    feminist thought on, 8, 15, 19
    Japanese, 171
    maternal thinking and, 16
    patrilineage and, 87
    reclaiming, 20
    syncretism and, 151, 153
matrilinealism, 2–5, 9, 10n3, 11n15, n20, 15, 25, 28n22, 29n39, 35, 76n13, 100n9, 109n16, 123, 123n5, n11, 151, 153, 191n4, 199, 203n2, 204n7, n13, n15, 211n5, 218n9
    feminist, 4, 8, 34, 66, 69–71, 117–8, 164, 170, 175–6, 181, 189, 200, 207, 216–7
matrilineal literature, 26, 34, 81, 135, 179–80, 191n6
matrilineal narratives, 23, 6–10, 10n5, 15, 21, 25–7, 31, 34, 47, 63–7, 73–5, 75n3–4, 76n20, 77, 79, 82, 84, 94n2, 95, 98–9, 100n3, n7, n10, 101, 103, 108n7, 111–2, 115–6, 122, 123n1, 164–5, 176, 177n5, 178n39, 179, 181, 197, 202, 213, 215, 217
    black, 136
    diasporic, 127, 171–3, 206–11, 216
matrix, 123

mother-daughter, 2, 113, 189
motherhood and, 8
matrophobia, 64, 103, 108, 164, 188, 197
Miller, Jean Baker, 33
Minh-ha, Trinh T., 20, 28n20, n23, 161n16
Mistron, Deborah, 159n1
Mitchell, Stephen, 31
mitochondrial DNA, 202
  in *The Peppered Moth* (Drabble), 101–2, 106–8
Moglen, Helene, 9, 22, 28n30
Morris, Ann R., 154
Morrison, Toni, 1–2, 7, 130, 149n8
mother(s)
  African American, 135, 138
  black, 138, 147
  immigrant, 180, 182, 190, 197–8, 205–6, 209
  slave, 136, 140
  substitute, 132, 142, 186
  surrogate, 92, 169, 216
  who leave their children, 8
  as writing subjects, 7
(m)other, 9, 11n18, 38–9, 48–9, 115, 148, 159, 175–177n4, 191, 210
mother-blaming, 7, 214
mother country, 130, 132, 158–9, 203, 208–9, 216
mothercultures, 129
motherhood, 1–2, 7, 9–10n2, 11n8, n10, n18, 16, 18, 24, 27, 27n2, 28n13, 42–4, 64–6, 74, 76n17, n23, 77, 84n2, 85n6, 127, 129–31, 140–2, 148n2, 149n3–4, n12, 164, 177n4, 191n2, 214, 216
  adoptive, 8
  Afrocentric ideology of, 138
  See also Collins, Patricia Hill
  biological, 8
  black, 136–8, 148n3
  collective, 71
  essential, 6, 70
  Eurocentric ideology of, 137–8
  as experience and institution, 15
  See also Rich, Adrienne
  feminism and, 8
  Japanese, 169
  and maternal subjectivity, 191n1, 213
  and mother-daughter relationships, 4
  and mothering, 3–6, 8
  nonbiological, 5, 8
  recuperative, 4, 15
  relational, 5, 8
  single, 8
  surrogate, 180
mothering, 15–6, 18, 27, 27n4, 28n5, 36–7, 40, 47, 64, 66, 72, 83, 137–8, 145, 148, 148n2, 149n10, 160n8, 206, 213–4
  collective, 199
  feminist, 5, 35
  genocentric, 63
  intersubjective, 7
  lesbian, 217
  motherhood and, 2–6, 8
motherland/mother('s)land, 81, 87, 93, 129–30, 132–3, 152, 154–5, 158–9, 181, 190, 195–6, 201, 203, 208–9, 216
motherline, 3, 8, 21, 63, 67–71, 83, 87, 95–6, 99, 114, 121, 135, 139–41, 143, 148, 170–1, 175, 186, 201–3, 206–8, 210, 216
  black, 136, 142, 145, 147
  See also female genealogy
motherline web, 71
mothertongues, 129
Mr. Rory (*The Joy Luck Club*), 187–8
Mrs. Jones (*Beloved*), 145
Murdoch, H. Adlai, 16, 159n1, 225
mutuality, 33, 44–5, 183
mutual recognition, 26, 49, 136, 140–2, 147–8, 183, 189–90, 210, 215

Nakayama-sensei (*Obasan*), 174
Naomi (*Obasan*), 8, 11n22, 59n56, 67, 76n15, 133, 135, 163–5, 168–76, 201, 204n12, 207, 209
Naomi's mother (*Obasan*), 164, 167–9, 174
Nasta, Susheila, 28n25, 134n10, 160n2
nativism, 128, 131
neocolonialism, 131, 159, 205
neo-slave narrative, 132, 136
new world, 197, 203
nisei, 163, 166–7, 170, 176n1, 177n17
  in *Obsan* (Kogawa), 171
Nisei Daughters (Monica Sone), 167
Nomie (*If I Told You Once*), 193, 197, 199–202
nonmother (ing), 6
nurturance, 5, 17, 44–5, 123n4, 141–2,

159, 208
  and autonomy, 36–8, 46, 97–8, 115
  See also Flax, Jane

Obasan (character) (*Obasan*), 135
Obasan (Kogawa), 10, 113, 163–76, 177n3, n22, 178n23–4, n26, n28, n32
  binary opposition between silence and speech in, 163
  mother's absence in, 180, 205–7, 209
Obasan, characters in. *See* Aunt Emily; the Grand Inquisitor; Grandma Kato; Nakayama-sensei; Naomi; Naomi's mother; Obasan (Aunt Aya); Stephen
obeah woman, 153–4, 158, 161n15
object relations, 9, 34–8, 40, 46–7, 49, 52, 65, 213
O'Brian, David, 178n26
old world, 203
omnipotence/recognition, 2, 7, 16, 25–6, 37, 46, 49, 67, 70–1, 74, 81, 84, 99, 108, 113–5, 136–7, 140–2, 147–149n20, 157, 179, 183, 189–90, 202–3, 210, 215, 217n6
O'Reilly, Andrea, 3–4, 10n6, 11n6, 75n5, 76n15, 149n3
othermother, 6, 132, 142, 147
  community, 144–5
  See also Beloved (Morrison); Collins, Patricia Hill

Pa Chess, 153, 156
pacifism, 5, 17
Paul D (*Beloved*), 139, 145–7
peacemaking, 17
Pearce, Lynne, and Jackie Stacey, 76n6, 85n4, 100n6
Pearlman, Mickey, and Katherine Usher Henderson, 191n5, 192n21
Perry, Donna, 155, 161n15, n17, n19, n23
Phillips, Shelley, 76n17
Plath, Sylvia, 1, 22
post-Lacanian theory, the, 35
post-slavery, 133
Powell, Betty Jane, 149n9
pre-Oedipal phase, the, 17, 35, 45
preverbal/language, 43
psychoanalysis, 1, 6, 9, 24, 35, 38, 40, 45–6, 75n2, 160n8, 162n24, 178n40,

191n1, 192n19, n26, 211n1, 213, 217n2, n5, n7, 219, 220–3
  feminist, 47, 216

racism, 19, 131, 136, 138, 144, 147, 159, 166–7, 188, 205–6
Ragnar (*Hanna's Daughters*), 82
rapprochement, 50
recognition/assertion, 2, 7, 16, 25–6, 37, 46, 49, 67, 70–1, 74, 81, 84, 99, 108, 113–5, 137–8, 140–2, 147–149n20, 157, 179, 183, 189–90, 202–3, 210, 215, 217n6
recovery (and progress), 3, 51, 96, 99, 103, 107–8, 112–5, 118–9, 122, 128, 142, 148, 167, 175, 179, 202–3, 206, 209
recuperation (and repudiation), 4, 5, 8, 15, 52, 65–6, 175, 201, 206
Reddy, Maureen T., 7, 148n1, 149n12, 178n37
relationality, 4–6, 8–9, 27, 31, 34, 122, 136, 179, 213, 215–6
relational model, 34
rememory, 139
resistance, 18, 94, 128, 131, 137, 149n10, 154, 157–8, 164, 203, 203n1, 207, 216
  assimilation and, 128, 154, 203
resonance and difference, 49, 70, 143, 176, 179, 190, 193, 197, 200
Rich, Adrienne, 1, 10, 10n2, 15, 27n2, 38, 64, 77, 84n2, 127
  See also motherhood, as experience and institution
Rickard (*Hanna's Daughters*), 82
Rivera, Margo, 53
Rody, Caroline, 149n6
romances
  family, 9, 63–7, 75n6, 85n4, 97, 99–100, 100n6, 108, 113–4, 116, 122, 153, 157, 196, 215
  female family, 202
  feminist family, 75, 114, 116, 215
  matrilineal, 67, 113, 216
  new feminist family, 111, 118, 122–3, 216
Rose Hsu Jordan (*The Joy Luck Club*), 184
Ross, Ellen, 4, 11n10
Ruddick, Sara, 7, 16, 27n4
  See also maternal thinking

Sasaki, Betty, 170, 178n23
Sashie (*If I Told You Once*), 193, 196–201, 203, 209
Schapiro, Barbara Ann, 47, 147, 149n9
Sebastian (*The Peppered Moth*), 106
Second-Wave feminist movement, the, 5, 15, 63
Second World War, the, 133, 163, 167, 172, 177n9
Sellers, Susan, 55n34, n42
semi-auto/biographical novel
  in *The Peppered Moth* (Drabble), 102
semiotic/the maternal, 42–3, 45–6, 214
semiotic/the symbolic, 43, 214
separation/connection, 23, 36, 39, 43, 45–6, 48, 65, 67, 70, 92–3, 97–8, 113, 116, 140, 151–2, 155, 159, 160n2, 175, 180, 190, 203, 205, 211, 214
separation/differentiation, 151
separation-individuation theory, 48
Sethe, 135, 139–48, 206
sexism, 19, 131, 136, 147, 159, 205
sickbed
  in *Hanna's Daughters*, 79, 82
Sledge, Linda Ching, 182, 192n16
space-time continuum, 122
Stamp Paid (*Beloved*), 145
Stanton, Domna C., 41
Stephen (*Obasan*), 31, 171–2, 178n26
Steve Nieman (*The Peppered Moth*), 101, 106, 202
storytelling, 21, 68, 80, 111, 135, 140, 207–8, 210
  in *Annie John*, 154–7, 161n15
  in *The Joy Luck Club*, 179, 181–4, 186, 190–1
  in *If I Told You Once*, 195, 198, 201–2
subject/object, 1–2, 4–5, 7, 9, 31, 33, 41, 43, 47, 49, 53, 64, 89, 101, 108, 127, 132–134n17, 136
  in *The Joy Luck Club*, 140–1, 143, 147, 153, 156, 160n2, 164, 189, 205–6, 213–4, 217
subject relations, 9, 33, 47, 141
subjugated, the, 128, 131, 205
Suleiman, Susan Rubin, 7, 11n18, 44, 177n4
Surrey, Janet L., 11n14, 29n42, 104, 107, 217n8
Suyuan Woo (*The Joy Luck Club*), 184

symbiosis, 36, 153
  mother-daughter, 143
  pre-Oedipal mother-child, 151
synchronic, horizontal plane, 21, 27, 34, 67, 99, 118, 122, 199–200
syncretism, 129, 151, 160n3
  matrilineal, 152–3

tables, 10, 111, 122
talk story, 208, 210
  in *The Joy Luck Club*, 181–4
Tan, Amy, 2, 7, 130, 179–80, 191n6, 192n8, n14, n16–7, n20
Tatar, Maria, 203n4
The Joy Luck Club (Tan), 10, 26, 132–3, 135, 179, 181, 183–5, 189–90, 192n15, n20, 197
  intersubjectivity in, 181, 189, 190–1
  mother-daughter conflicts in, 179–80, 184
  mother-daughter mirroring in, 181, 188
  mother-daughter voices in, 179, 190
  resolution and recognition of matrilineage in, 179
  storytelling in, 179, 181–4, 186, 190–1
The Joy Luck Club, characters in. See An-Mei Hsu; Jing-mei Woo; Joy Luck Aunts; Lena St. Clair; Lindo Jong; Mr. Rory; Rose Hsu Jordan; Suyuan Woo; Waverly Jong; Ying-ying St. Clair
The Peppered Moth (Drabble), 9, 75, 101–3, 108, 108n1, 112–5, 121, 193, 202, 204n14
  ambivalence in, 103, 107, 108n5
  female family romance in, 108
  matrilineal romance in, 102, 107–8
  matrophobia in, 103, 108
  mother's subjectivity in, 108
  recovery and progress in, 103
  retrieving matrilineage in, 103
The Peppered Moth, characters in. See Bessie; Chrissie; Cotterhall Man; Dora Bawtry (Aunt Dora); Dr. Robert Hawthorn; Faro; Joe Barron; Sebastian; Steve Nieman; the Barrons; the Bawtrys; the Cutworths
The Woman Warrior (Kingston), 3, 180, 191n6

Third World, 25
Timothy, Helen Pyne, 160n3, 161n22
transculturation, 129
triad, 6, 65, 78, 90, 92, 97, 103, 118–9, 122, 130, 216
  grandmother-mother-daughter, 2, 6, 63, 66–8, 73, 75, 107, 111, 116–7, 122, 134n17, 207
  mother-motherland-mother country, 2, 6, 63, 65–8, 73, 75, 92, 97, 107, 111, 116–9
trichotomy, 82, 130, 209
two time-frames (of feminist matrilinealism), 117
  See also diachronic, vertical axis; synchronic, horizontal plane

von Hassell, Malve, 170, 178n25

Walker, Alice, 9, 19, 28n18
Waverly Jong (*The Joy Luck Club*), 184, 187–8, 190
West/East, 20, 89, 90, 115, 137, 156, 161n15, 167
  in *The Joy Luck Club*, 189

Whitford, Margaret, 40, 75n1, 217n2
Wild Swans (Chang), 9, 75, 87–91, 93, 94n1, 95, 99, 111–5, 119
  ambivalence in, 90–1
  genogram in, 88
  mother-daughter identification in, 91
  progress in, 89–90
  subjectivity in, 89
Wild Swans, characters in. *See* Chang, Chang's father, Chang's grandmother, Chang's mother, General Xue, General Xue's wife
Williams, Linda R., 9, 24, 28n33
Williamson, Janice, 176n2
Winnicott, D. W., 51
Wolf (*If I Told You Once*), 194, 196
woman centeredness, 5, 44
womanculture, 5
Wong, Sau-Ling Cynthia, 180, 191n6
Woolf, Virginia, 1, 9, 19, 28n16, 84n3
Wright, Elizabeth, 55n22, 47.

Year of the Dragon (Chin), 180
Ying-ying St. Clair (*The Joy Luck Club*), 184

ADVANCE PRAISE FOR

Mother, She Wrote

"Yi-Lin Yu's deployment of powerful psychoanalytic ideas of subject-relation theorists is complex and persuasive, her wide choice of literary texts challenges oversimple formulations of matrilineal narratives, and her attention to narrative structure demonstrates her attention to textual detail and structure. In addition, the exposition is beautifully lucid and the scholarship well grounded."

Alison Easton, Senior Lecturer in English Literature,
Lancaster University, United Kingdom

"Yi-Lin Yu's exciting and innovative work on matrilineal family romances is an admirable study of theories and texts in the most recent phase of feminist maternal scholarship. Her feminist readings of matrilineal narratives extend into new areas, such as the diasporic narrative, bringing the complex insights afforded by literary texts into a new synthesis of theory and literary practice."

Tess Cosslett, Author of Women Writing Childbirth:
Modern Discourses of Motherhood

www.ingramcontent.com/pod-product-compliance
Lightning Source LLC
Chambersburg PA
CBHW050629300426
44112CB00012B/1727